EDUCATION POLICY, NEOLIBERALISM, AND LEADERSHIP PRACTICE

D0165292

Education Policy, Neoliberalism, and Leadership Practice is a foundational book describing all aspects of neoliberalism and its broad scale impact in education. Drawing on research and canvassing policy developments across a range of contexts, this book critically analyzes neoliberal education policies, the practices and outcomes they spawn, and the purposes they serve. It interrogates how education leaders perceive and interpret neoliberal influences and the dilemmas and opportunities they create, while unpacking questions of why neoliberalism is the basis for education policy, how neoliberalism impacts on education, and what this means for the future.

Karen Starr is Professor and Inaugural Chair of School Development and Leadership at Deakin University, Australia.

EDUCATIONAL LEADERSHIP AND POLICY DECISION-MAKING IN NEOLIBERAL TIMES

Series Editors: Stephanie Chitpin, John P. Portelli, and Colin W. Evers

Confronting Educational Policy in Neoliberal Times
International Perspectives
Edited by Stephanie Chitpin and John P. Portelli

Education Policy, Neoliberalism, and Leadership Practice
A Critical Analysis
Karen Starr

For more information about this series, please visit:
https://www.routledge.com/Educational-Leadership-and-Policy-Decision-Making-in-Neoliberal-Times/book-series/ELPDM

EDUCATION POLICY, NEOLIBERALISM, AND LEADERSHIP PRACTICE

A Critical Analysis

Karen Starr

Routledge
Taylor & Francis Group

NEW YORK AND LONDON

First published 2019
by Routledge
52 Vanderbilt Avenue, New York, NY 10017

and by Routledge
2 Park Square, Milton Park, Abingdon, Oxon OX14 4RN

Routledge is an imprint of the Taylor & Francis Group, an informa business

© 2019 Taylor & Francis

The right of Karen Starr to be identified as author of this work has been asserted by her in accordance with sections 77 and 78 of the Copyright, Designs and Patents Act 1988.

All rights reserved. No part of this book may be reprinted or reproduced or utilised in any form or by any electronic, mechanical, or other means, now known or hereafter invented, including photocopying and recording, or in any information storage or retrieval system, without permission in writing from the publishers.

Trademark notice: Product or corporate names may be trademarks or registered trademarks, and are used only for identification and explanation without intent to infringe.

Library of Congress Cataloging-in-Publication Data
Names: Starr, Karen (Karen Elizabeth), author.
Title: Education policy, neoliberalism, and leadership practice : a critical analysis / by Karen Starr.
Description: New York : Routledge, 2019. | Series: Educational leadership and policy decision-making in neoliberal times | Includes bibliographical references.
Identifiers: LCCN 2018056877| ISBN 9781138721036 (hardback) | ISBN 9781138721043 (pbk.) | ISBN 9781315194745 (ebook)
Subjects: LCSH: Education and state. | Educational leadership. | Neoliberalism.
Classification: LCC LC71 .S785 2019 | DDC 379--dc23
LC record available at https://lccn.loc.gov/2018056877

ISBN: 978-1-138-72103-6 (hbk)
ISBN: 978-1-138-72104-3 (pbk)
ISBN: 978-1-315-19474-5 (ebk)

Typeset in Bembo
by Taylor & Francis Books

This book is dedicated to the people leading and managing education institutions who informed the research on which it is based.

CONTENTS

SERIES INTRODUCTION

The series "Educational Leadership and Policy Decision-Making in Neoliberal Times" is based on the belief that those in educational leadership and policy-constructing roles have a moral obligation to educate for a critically and democratically robust citizenry, so that educators can contribute to an open and fair society while steering the leadership and policy discourse and practices away from the neoliberal orthodoxy, which works contrary to the aims of critical democracy.

The scope and vision of the series advances theoretical and empirical discussions on educational leadership and policy by incorporating different perspectives and paradigms that encourage educators to act meaningfully and fairly in diverse settings. In an attempt to assert a progressive, multidimensional leadership and policy agenda, renowned scholars in the field of education are invited to contribute thought-provoking and insightful work that challenges the dominant mainstream neoliberal leadership and policy discourses. The transformative rationale lying at the heart of this series is the disruption of the neoliberal narrative and the problematization of contradictory leadership and policy practices prevalent in educational spheres. In other words, the series aims to publish work that challenges and offers alternatives to the excessive individualism, reductionism, standardization, deficit, and narrowly pragmatic neoliberal agenda that has increased marginalization and disengagement in education.

The series is built on a critical-democratic perspective that honors agonism (rather than antagonism), the symbiotic relationship between theory and practice (rather than the absolute dominance of either), all voices including traditionally marginalized voices (rather than dominant western voices), and a pedagogy of hope (rather than a pedagogy of deficit and fatalism), in an effort to foster a more inclusive, diverse, and anti-colonial environment that deals with leadership and policy as problem-solving and decision-making processes.

ACKNOWLEDGMENTS

Although writing is a usual and ongoing academic task and expectation, it is much easier when one has the time. Hence, I am very grateful to Deakin University for awarding me a period of Academic Study Leave to commence this work and to my colleagues in the School of Education for stepping in and taking up my supervision and teaching responsibilities during my absence. Particular thanks go to Professor Christine Ure, Head of the School of Education, Faculty of Arts and Education; to Dr. Cheryl Ryan who took over as Director of the Education Business Leadership program; to Associate Professor Damian Blake, Dr. Trace Ollis, and Dr. Cheryl Ryan who assumed supervision responsibilities for some of my PhD students; and to the Education Business Leadership team who got on with developments in this emerging and rapidly growing field while I was away – Mark Donehue, Glenn Brown, Kim Neilson, Jo Hendrickson, and Matthew McDonough.

This book is based on several previous research projects over the past three decades. It documents an increasingly neoliberal policy environment and chronicles the experiences and perspectives of education leaders – research respondents – who generously gave their time to be involved. To these people I am sincerely indebted and thankful. However, the contents of this book cannot be isolated or disconnected from my own experiences in education leadership. My reflections as a practitioner in different contexts have immersed me in the policies and activities of which I write, so, from first-hand experience, I can empathize with research respondents and understand the opportunities, joys, and dilemmas – personal and professional – that keep them motivated and excited, and awake at night.

Thank you to the series editor, Professor Colin Evers at the University of New South Wales, Australia, and to Heather Jarrow and Katharine Atherton at Routledge and Katie Finnegan, our copyeditor, whose communications were always helpful and appreciated. It has been a pleasure to work with all of you on this project.

Last (and always left until last), but by no means least – my warmest acknowl-edgment is to Ian McDonald who has 'put up' with me writing yet another book requiring my absence, physically and metaphorically. Here, however, I must express extra special gratitude for Ian's support. While on study leave a severe leg and knee injury necessitated months of medical interventions and home care, interrupting normal life and usual working routines immensely. I appreciated having a book to write to occupy some of my attention during this frustrating period of lost inde-pendence, but an extra toll was exacted on Ian, whose care was brilliant and whose patience with the whole situation far exceeded my own. Suffice to say, my love and gratitude goes beyond expression.

PART I

A Rising Tide Lifts All Boats

'*A rising tide lifts all boats*' – a neoliberal aphorism – sums up Part I of this book, which discusses neoliberalism in education. The chapters in this section explain the origins of neoliberalism, its major principles or axioms, and describes and critiques how these ideas play out in education policy and leadership practice.

Chapter 1 sets the scene for the discussion in the rest of the book. It summarizes the impetus for the book, the research underpinning it, and explains the conception of 'policy' as the term is used throughout the book.

Chapter 2 is foundational to all subsequent chapters – it discusses the intersecting influences of globalization, free market economics, and attendant neoliberal discourses as the dominant organizing framework for education policy. Chapter 2 explores how these forces function and perform recursively and influence each other. It discusses the history, evolution, and current manifestations of global free market neoliberalism, explains how and why education policy is caught up in neoliberal pursuits, and the interests so served. This is an important backdrop and essential information for the arguments pursued through the remainder of the book.

Neoliberalism's fundamental tenets are inextricably linked and mutually reinforcing. However, to provide a thorough explanation, each axiom is discussed in turn to form the focus of an individual chapter. Chapters 3 through 11 analyze the sentiments behind each neoliberal precept, the education policies and practices so inspired, and the impact, implications, and consequences for leadership practice. As a set these chapters describe the powerful coalition of ideas that form 'neoliberalism', but each chapter is also designed to stand alone. They focus on:

- Individualism, including institutional autonomy
- Privatization
- Choice
- Competition
- Improvement, innovation, and entrepreneurialism
- Efficiency
- Productivity
- Performativity
- Accountability.

1

INTRODUCTION

The Misguided Impatience of Education Policy

What is education for? What is its purpose? These are simple yet important, foundational questions for any education system or institution anywhere. The answers to these questions – even if implicit and unspoken – have profound effects on all aspects of life. This statement may sound far-fetched, yet our beliefs about education's purposes reveal our hopes for the society we want to live in, now and in the future. Of course, there can be many answers to these questions, and the purposes of education are contested. However, one might hope that there would be some broad agreement about education's fundamental objectives and functions.

We may assume, for example, that the major purpose of education in developed democracies is to prepare students for family and community life, productive work, engaged democratic citizenship, and lifelong learning.[1] Behind such a purpose is a vision of the kind of society we wish to develop: a peaceful, democratic, and just society of educated, informed citizens, cohesive and functional communities and families, and effective representative governments, where everyone can make a fulfilling contribution through employment and recreation. Our collective hopes, therefore, would be for individuals to be respected, supported to make wise decisions that benefit themselves and others, while contributing to the common weal through their social, cultural, economic, and political engagement.

Underpinning this vision, we may further assume that people matter and that we bear some collective responsibility to take care of everyone as we strive to develop and maintain a good life. Infused in a vision of a 'good' society are notions of freedom, inclusion, democracy, peace, sustainability, justice, and equity. These are perhaps best summarized as "life, liberty and the pursuit of happiness" mentioned in the United States Declaration of Independence and in its Constitution, which speaks to justice, tranquility, common defense, general welfare, liberty, and national posterity. In other words, we collectively want these things for ourselves, others and future generations and we are willing to defend these ideals. If we think about it, who could disagree? Is there anyone wishing for an unhappy, unfortunate life for themselves or their children?

In a society wishing to pursue such ideals as these, education is pivotal. It is so important, in fact, that during the years of primary and secondary schooling it is compulsory and free. Every young person, irrespective of background, is compelled to be educated, so as to enable this vision and pursuit of a 'good' society.

Perhaps these contentions sound like 'the bleeding obvious' yet one would be hard pushed to find any clear statements like these or other explicit purposes on the websites of major education systems and authorities anywhere. But we should ponder what functions we want education to perform on behalf of all of us. Because at the current time many educators are concerned about policy direction and have serious doubts about where education and their work are heading. There is a general sense that things are off course – that the democratic, just and socially cohesive societies we imagine to be at the heart of the education vision are being undermined, even corrupted – and this disquiet is palpable and wide-spread. Discussions with education leaders leave one with the strong and sad sense that all is not right in education and it's getting worse.

Powerful politicians and policymakers (most of whom have never worked as teachers or with students) are viewed as arrogantly pronouncing that education is failing and in crisis, undertaking to ramp up its efforts, squeezing educators and learners for more productivity, demanding 'efficiencies' to save rising costs in the belief that education returns little value for money, while instigating high-stakes measurement and compliance schemes to whip the whole 'enterprise' into shape. This entrenched and inimical state of play stretches left and right of politics while an obliging media uncritically applauds and drums up legitimacy for even tougher 'reforms.'

But to what end? What's gone wrong? Why is education perceived and pro-nounced in such deficit terms? Why are educators so widely disrespected and denounced? Why is the bleak mood amongst educators so broad-sweeping – what do they fear and why are they cynical and pessimistic? And, of critical importance to this book, what does this mean for education leadership practice and education policy futures?

What's wrong and what's causing widespread anxiety lies at the heart of this book. What's wrong concerns a widening gulf between the views of educators – who thought they were pursuing the kind of purposes described above – and a new wave of politics and economics that have been embraced across developed democracies as the organizing framework for society, including education and all other social services. We can no longer assume we know what education is for – we now have to question who and what education is serving, why, and to what ends. This is the prime focus of this book.

Although there is a long list of tensions, struggles, and grievances mentioned in the following chapters, they mostly stem from the same roots: globalization and the pervasive infiltration of neoliberal market principles in education policy and practice. This book is about the macro international events and circumstances that impact national governments and local education systems and their policymakers, with concomitant effects in individual education institutions where their leaders are responsible for policy enactment.

Governments of varying political hues have instigated ongoing structural reforms to align national education agendas with the demands of intensified global economic competition. As a result, education policies throughout the westernized world have subsumed increasingly economistic imperatives to achieve these national objectives.

Current education policy is heavily influenced by the needs, values, and underlying philosophy of neoliberal market agendas which frustrate and undermine, rather than enhance and support, traditional education aims. As a *laissez-faire* economic and neoliberal policy hegemony is constantly reinvigorated and fortified, so education policies, operations, and leadership behaviors are regulated to adapt and adjust to align with market imperatives. In so doing, education's role in national and international economic fortunes has assumed primacy over its individual, civic, or social benefits.

The way we envisage, experience, and conduct learning, teaching, and education leadership is rapidly changing, as are the ways in which we speak and think about education. Public assumptions once steeped in the common weal appear to have been sullied and weakened as faith in the neoliberal free market continues to triumph and intensify. These are turbulent times for educators and education leaders who must come to grips with the incongruities that neoliberal policy produces, but which always demand change – from minor adjustments to radical transformations. The new remit of education leadership rests on the aims, expectations, and decisions embodied in neoliberal policy ambitions and pursuits.

Education Policy, Neoliberalism, and Leadership Practice critically analyses education policies, processes, and assumptions, their rationale/s and the purposes they serve. It bases this analysis on the perceptions and sentiments of those who lead and manage education institutions. This book traces the origins of leaders' experiences and concerns back to their neoliberal roots, and analyzes influences on education, education policy and practice, education outcomes, and the professional lives of education leaders. It interrogates how education leaders perceive, comprehend, and rationalize policy decisions, the factors that influence their reactions and actions, and documents emerging concerns and ideas for redress. The book responds to the following questions:

- Why are neoliberal policies influencing education and education policy?
- How is education influenced by neoliberal policy agendas? How are neoliberal policy agendas enacted?
- What are the effects?

- Whose interests are served?
- How do education leaders explain and respond to neoliberal policy agendas in practice?

While reporting on a very disheartening state of affairs, the book looks to opportunities within neoliberal policy regimes. It chronicles how education leaders perceive, interpret, and try to use policy discourses for education pursuits of a very different kind – a kind that speaks to what Biesta (2013) calls "the beautiful risk of education," highlighting how its 'weakness' – in neoliberal terms – is its strength, and how its strength lies in the minds of thinking, agential, free-willed human beings who can shape rather than react to policy futures.

Policy

'Policy' is generally understood to refer to "a course or principle of action, adopted or proposed by a government, party, business or individual" (Oxford English Dictionary, 2013). Policy is part of the schemata of government, government agencies, organizations, and institutions (see for example, The University of Sydney, 2011; John Hopkins University, 2013). Policy concerns direction, a stance, a platform, corporate goals, or a position that informs a set of actions towards institutionalizing definitive goals. In this sense, policy refers to an intention to institutionalize certain values and actions, usually developed, controlled, and regulated in hierarchical and authoritarian ways. However, this is quite a conservative definitional stance.

Policies are not simply material artifacts or statements of formal goals and intentions. Policymaking is necessarily a political process. Many ideologies, philosophies, agendas, discourses, and activities comprise policy. In terms of education, policy activities are imbued with the political positions, demands, and expectations of numerous stakeholders,[2] such that policy statements are an amalgam of compromises that will never suit everybody, making it *ad hoc* and messy. Dealing with many stakeholders and interest groups makes policymaking convoluted and complex, so what emerges often embraces many paradoxes and contradictions (Starr, 2015), which makes education leadership all the trickier.

Formal education policy decisions made by governments carry weight and affect numerous people. It is unrealistic, however, to view the people affected by policy as impartial players in a value-neutral exercise. Education institutions cannot be relied upon to accommodate policy intentions with the unerring fidelity that policymakers intend.

Education leaders charged with policy 'implementation' make varying interpretations, have unpredictable levels of commitment or endorsement, undertake and experience numerous other activities and events, have untold demands on their time, and differing methods of undertaking change, some of which will be more 'successful' than others. Policy mandates may thus be subverted, altered, resisted, or ignored as leaders so decide. If policy is unpopular it can be distorted or disguised to fit real or perceived needs, or leaders may report that policy has been implemented, knowing that nothing is going to change.

Adding to 'implementation' problems is the fact that education policies often come and go so quickly, with one policy announced only to be replaced with a new policy issuing revised aims and intentions. Incoming governments focusing on short-term political agendas change the education policies of their predecessors, often appealing to popular concerns legitimated through negative political and media commentary. A consequence is that education policy changes constantly, making full 'implementation' impossible and policy effects inestimable while ensuring that educational institutions are constantly responding in some way to externally imposed change.

Uncertainty, complexity and policy fluidity are exacerbated by short-term governments and frequently changing business models. Constant major change is the new norm, which makes leadership, management, and governance more challenging, demanding, and inherently riskier. Further, policy can have unimaginable and unintended consequences and can inadvertently introduce 'wicked problems' (Kets de Vries, 2001; Rittel & Webber, 1973). Hence, policy cannot be viewed as a tangible phenomenon in its definition, formulation, or 'implementation.'

Policies, therefore, are processes and outcomes (Ball, 1994), with policy processes embodying a gamut of political influences from formulation through to practice. Policy discourses 'move' and morph as they circulate, with further mutation in enactment, with 'whom?,' 'with what intent?,' and 'to what extent?' or 'if at all?' being key. Hence, Ball argues that 'policy' refers to processes and outcomes that are "always in a state of 'becoming,' of 'was' and 'never was' and 'not quite'" (1994, p. 16). In reality, "everything is (at best) incremental or (at worst) a mess" (Raab, 1994, p. 8). A tidy, efficient, and methodical achievement of policy aims without political contestation would be improbable. As a 'bottom line', policy attempts to legitimate certain values, which immediately begs the question – whose values and towards what ends?

Policy contexts – historical, geographical, political, economic, cultural, and technological – are important aspects of any analysis of education policy. However, globalizing policy discourses have created similarities in education policy 'reforms' around the westernized world, even though there are remnants of traditional conventions and discourses circulating which are useful in quelling major opposition.

The Research

This book canvasses policy developments and education leaders' views across a range of contexts in Australia, the USA, the UK, Canada, and New Zealand, and draws on research in education leadership and policy conducted for over three decades. Many previous publications chronicle the research quantum that informs this text. This book attempts to consolidate this volume of past research to present an overall picture and sense of what has happened and is happening on a broad scale in education, while getting to the substance of why, how, and what this means for the future. Past research with leaders provides a longitudinal record which was great grist for this book.

These past research projects with education leaders were exercises in grounded theory building (Glaser & Strauss, 1967), through which theory emerges inductively through data as they are gathered. Emerging research themes and unexpected ideas are analyzed and continually tested, producing further evidence and/or new theoretical insights (Corbin & Strauss, 2008). Data are validated when common themes recur such that no new insights emerge: data are 'saturated', with subsequent interviews validating information from previous respondents.

Grounded theory building demonstrates how large-scale social structures affect tangible realities in complex, contextualized, historical practice. Privileged are individual standpoints and perspectives in context, with analyses exploring the inextricable links between the macro, meso, and micro. Real-life experience is the starting point connecting individual agents corporeally and emotionally to the structural – political and economic, and social realities.

Besides personal research with education leaders (see personal citations in each chapter), this critical analysis also draws on public education policy discourses, media coverage, official press statements, and extant research literature.

Those working in education will identify with the discussion in the following chapters. Given the global hegemony of neoliberalism, educators will recognize similarities between the policy examples described and the local education policies and practices with which they are familiar. They will understand the everyday assumptions, explanations, worries, and uneasiness of education leaders. The hope is that this discussion may spark political debate towards change that is rooted in very different policy motivations.

Before discussing leaders' responses to neoliberal policy agendas in Part II of this book, it is necessary and important to explore and describe 'neoliberalism' in a globalized, free market context. The following chapters examine and critique the roots of political and economic objectives and the social visions underpinning neoliberal education policy, their consequences for education, and effects on leadership practice.

Notes

1 'Lifelong learning' has become a neoliberal notion in and of itself (with individuals bearing responsibility for enhancing their learning currency – keeping their knowledge and skill development up-to-date – to ensure their employability and productivity throughout life).
2 'Stakeholder' is also a neoliberal notion (Biesta, 2017). It resonates with neoliberal emphases on the individual, the 'customer,' as well as consumer empowerment at the local level (for example, parents as 'stakeholders' in local school governance).

References

Ball, S. (1994). *Education reform: A critical and post-structural approach.* Buckingham, England: Open University Press.

Biesta, G. J. J. (2013). *The beautiful risk of education.* New York, NY: Routledge.

Biesta, G. J. J. (2017). *The rediscovery of teaching.* New York, NY: Routledge.

Corbin, J., & Strauss, A. (2008) *Basics of qualitative research* (3rd ed.). Thousand Oaks, CA: SAGE.

Glaser, B., & Strauss, A. L. (1967). *The discovery of grounded theory: Strategies for qualitative research.* New Brunswick, NJ: Aldine Transaction.

John Hopkins University (2013). *John Hopkins Institute of Policy Studies website.* Accessed: 29 July 2013. Available at: http://ips.jhu.edu/index.cfm

Kets de Vries, M. (2001). *The leadership mystique: A user's manual for the human enterprise.* Upper Saddle River, NJ: FT Press.

Oxford University Press (2013). *Oxford English Dictionary.* Oxford, UK: Oxford University Press. Available at: www.oed.com/

Raab, C. (1994). Theorising the governance of education. *British Journal of Educational Studies,* 42(1), 6–22.

Rittel, H. W. J., & Webber, M. M. (1973). Dilemmas in a general theory of planning. *Policy Sciences,* 4, 155–169.

Starr, K. (2015). *Education game changers: Leadership and the consequence of policy paradox.* Lanham, MD: Rowman & Littlefield.

The University of Sydney (2011). *Policies development and review, rule 2011.* Retrieved March 1, 2017 from http://sydney.edu.au/legal/policy/what/index.shtml

2

GLOBALIZATION, THE FREE MARKET, AND NEOLIBERALISM

To set the scene and context of this book it is important to discuss the prime provocations behind education policy texts and leadership practice. This chapter discusses the potency of globalization, the free market, and neoliberalism, and their influences on education – its purposes, policies, and practices across post-industrial nations – while their inextricable links form the meta-theoretical lens for this critical policy analysis.

Over the past four decades, education and its administration has changed irrevocably through economic reform at global, national, and local levels. Restructuring has transformed the purposes, nature, and scope of government departments and agencies, and reformed government policy and procedure in line with free market and neoliberal axioms (Apple, 2006). The term 'structural reform' is used to refer to fundamental reconfigurations of dominant discourses and the philosophical, organizational, and economic bases of the public sector and its agencies along market lines.

Education has not escaped the impacts of structural reforms which are a response to globalization, motivated primarily by concerns for nations' international competitiveness in trade, workforce capability, innovation, and education outcomes. The triumvirate of globalization, the free market, and neoliberalism are studied below. And, as there are no agreed definitions about these subjects, the understandings and positions that inform this book are also discussed.

Globalization

Globalization is the defining feature of our time in history. Globalization is a complex phenomenon that is constantly changing and evolving, but it is not new. Marx and Engels wrote about the effects of globalization on local industries and trade in *The Communist Manifesto* (1848), and Keynes described the effects of globalization on the everyday life of the London citizen in *The Economic Consequences of Peace* (1919).

Globalization is a concept that has no clearly defined beginning and no foreseeable endpoint. It is a fluid, unfinished project that morphs and adapts to world events, recalibrations of power, and shifting circumstances, making complexity, change, and uncertainty the new normal.

Definitions of globalization are many and contested. In their analysis of various definitions of globalization, Al-Rodhan and Stoudmann arrive at their own, preferred definition, thus:

> Globalization is a process that encompasses the causes, course, and consequences of transnational and transcultural integration of human and non-human activities.
>
> *(Al-Rodhan & Stoudmann, 2006, p. 2)*

From this definition, globalization is both cause and effect, and it is ubiquitous. And Giddens' explanation from the last decade of the last century retains resonance:

> Globalization is not only... an economic phenomenon;... it... does not only concern the creation of large-scale systems, but also the transformation of the local, and even personal, contexts of social experience.... Globalization is not a single process but a complex mixture of processes, which often act in contra-dictory ways, producing conflicts, dis-junctures and new forms of stratification.
>
> *(Giddens, 1994, pp. 4–5)*

Globalization's main features concern greater global interdependence and the breakdown of regional, national, and cultural boundaries alongside the transition from national 'protected' economies towards global 'free' trade and markets (discussed further below). Globalization has stimulated an exponential rise in global flows of capital, people, goods, services, information, and culture, with English as the international lingua franca. These are aided by enhanced interconnections through globalized infrastructure: ubiquitous technologies, transport and banking systems, enabling the rapid diffusion of knowledge, information, ideas, and innovations through the compression of time and space across the planet.

Globalization has encouraged the expansion of transnational corporations, a diminution of post-war welfarism and social democratic political agendas, and, importantly for the topic of this book, the incorporation of market values in public policy.

Globalization challenges the foundations of nation states as it unsettles the taken-for-granted modernist assumptions that formed the basis of life for most of the last century. It accelerates the astonishing disruption and exponential progress unfolding through technology that is taxing the responsiveness of governments, organizations, and individuals, as the world becomes smarter, faster, and smaller. Rapid change is defying prevailing customs, antagonizing long-established thinking, long-held traditions and assumptions, and fundamentally altering the way we live, work, produce, consume, and behave.

Recent shifts in globalization demonstrate its adaptability – it shapes and is shaped by time and context. Currently, we are witnessing the breakdown of a traditional hegemonic western focus. Capital, people, trade, and communications extend east and west, and financial markets are tipping towards regions rapidly breaking out of protectionist and isolationist and/or colonialist pasts.

But globalization does not suit everybody. Recent events that have shaken the world suggest a backlash against globalization – the rise of religious and cultural fundamentalisms; anti-establishment movements like the anti-World Trade Organization protests across the world; Britain's exit from the European Union ('Brexit'); the rise of populist forms of nationalism in the USA and Europe; and widespread reactions against profit-driven practices of transnational corporations and their ability to evade taxation, including demands for ethical standards and boycotts of goods for highly developed economies manufactured by the world's poorest peoples.

A host of recent changes such as these stem from a range of factors – political upsets, changing demographics and geography, new demands from emerging markets and rising power bases, conflicts and terrorism, environmental degradation and species extinction – all are unsettling. These sorts of events create difficulties for governance of any kind, with political standpoints and nationalist interests becoming more polarizing and divisive. Coming to a global consensus on urgent issues that affect the entire planet seemingly cannot get past parochial nationalistic self-interests.

Globalization's complex forces and processes incorporate many dimensions – perhaps too neatly summed up in the term 'globalization' – but the combined effects profoundly influence power relations between and within countries and amongst peoples. Effects are positive and negative; there are winners and losers, but no one is unaffected. Globalization fundamentally influences the ways the world currently works. It challenges traditional notions and the behaviors of nation states, governments, corporations, institutions, communities, families, and individuals. In sum, without us even being aware of it, globalization profoundly influences everything and everyone.

Globalized Education

Education is seen to play a major role in enhancing national competitiveness and productivity in a global marketplace by increasing knowledge yield and ensuring a well-educated, effective, hard-working, and productive workforce and citizenry (see Productivity Commission, 2013). Hence, education policy discourses have increasingly subsumed economistic imperatives to achieve national objectives. While creating both new problems and new opportunities, globalization is changing the nature and focus of education policy, teaching, learning, education leadership, education business, governance, and institutional relationships with the state.

Globalization has created greater cultural, linguistic, religious, and age diversity in education institutions; student and educator populations are mobile across the world; policy pursuits in one region are soon adopted in others; and, governments everywhere seek increased productivity and a greater return on their investment so are becoming more interventionist in education policy, practice, and leadership via an increasing range of accountabilities.

Free Market Economics

Current-day global economic structures are based on ideas emanating from liberal theorists from the 17th to the 20th centuries – for example, John Locke, Thomas Hobbes, Adam Smith, Alfred Marshall, Ludwig von Mises, Milton Friedman, and Friedrich Hayek – whose theories have been revised or fortified to produce the free market economy we experience today.

At the basis of economic theories are assumptions about human nature and human emotions. Adam Smith's works (*The Wealth of Nations*, 1776 and *The Theory of Moral Sentiments*, 1759) provide the clearest examples of this and have been revisited in today's neoliberal free market context. Smith suggests that economic theory is underpinned by two essential human motivations: 'self-interest' and 'fellow feeling.' Self-interest concerns individuals' motivations to meet their own needs and desires. Fellow feeling concerns regard for other individuals, which includes community connections and the social 'good.'

Free market economic theory contends that individuals pursuing their self-interests spur production, consumption, and competition for goods and services. The market is a place of exchange, and it is assumed that individuals will rationally weigh up all options in making transactions that meet their needs and interests. This is the notion of 'Rational Economic Man' (REM) indicating the market's contingency on individual rational agency in buying and selling. Individuals seeking to meet their personal needs and wants heighten demand for quality and incentivize innovation and invention amongst suppliers. The market rewards successful entrepreneurs if their innovation satisfies consumer needs and demand. The market, therefore, creates incentives for entrepreneurialism, which in turn encourages 'progress' through continual improvements and, as other market players emulate good ideas, through competition via cheaper consumer prices.

Competition is a natural outcome as the market enables individuals to choose the best quality for the best price, whether this be the choice of workers, phone companies, or schools. The same applies to employment – individuals 'sell' their skills, knowledge, and capabilities in the market of exchange. The best employees raise overall quality because they will be sought after and they also raise consumer expectations about the quality of goods or services provided.

Through these processes, consumer demand signals the need for market supply in order to meet the demand – production increases or decreases as the market caters for changing consumer needs and expectations. The market adjusts automatically to establish an equilibrium of supply and demand which arises out of the millions of individual actions in pursuit of self-interests through which everyone ultimately benefits. However, the market cannot be criticized if particular aims are not achieved because it is not based on pre-established goals. The market is purported to be value-neutral and unbiased, hence the outcomes of market competition are the responsibilities of individuals. The market naturally serves and organizes all competing claims in an unplanned, unbiased way – this is what Adam Smith referred to as 'the invisible hand of the market.'[1]

Self-interest is the prime motivating human factor that also serves fellow feeling. The assumption is that individuals pursuing their own self-interests and needs concurrently serve their fellow citizens. Individuals provide goods and services to each other for mutual benefit. On a larger scale, in the free market, communities and nations behave in the same way. In other words, the process of individuals pursuing their self-interests brings economic advantages to one and all. The belief is that the market raises the living standards of everybody. To Adam Smith, the survival of the individual and achievement of an individual's optimal potential is reached through fellow feeling and the collective good of the populace. This idea is often referred to in current times as the 'trickle-down' effect.

These ideas lead to the main tenet of the free market: that the economic social order or any facet of social life is not the result of extensive human planning or design but is the result of unplanned market machinations between individuals. Everyday citizens buying and selling, producing and consuming, without any grand plan is the 'spontaneous order' of the 'free market' – also referred to as 'extemporization.' The social order is thus unplanned and unpredictable, but produces its own natural liberty resulting in better outcomes for everyone.

Free market proponents suggest that interference or interventions from the state (governments and government agencies) are disruptive to the market's naturally occurring spontaneous order because they interrupt the prices and trends that serve as indicators of demands for, and availability of, goods and services.

Hence, human nature is the integral component – the free will of individuals creates free market operations for the common good, whereas market incursions disturb its natural rhythms by creating disincentives to individual effort, competition, inventiveness, and efficiency while muddying market indicators of demand and supply. Without obstruction to the natural market order, everyone will benefit, although some will gain more than others. As Hutton explains in his best-selling book, *The State We're In*:

The stated objective has been to improve efficiency, raise economic growth and so advance the welfare of all. Those at the top of the pile may do especially well, but the argument is that their enhanced efforts will improve the lot of those at the bottom of the income scale – who will do better under this system than any other.

(Hutton, 1995, p. 169)

This thinking underpins the free market mantra: 'a rising tide lifts all boats.'

Over the past few decades it is the economic views of Friedrich Hayek that have been privileged by most post-industrial capitalist economies. Hayek was a Nobel prize-winning economist who considered the market in terms of a game – a game of life requiring skill and luck for wealth creation. He named this the game of 'catallaxy' (Hayek, 1978, pp. 108–109). The term catallaxy was purportedly first used by Ludwig von Mises, but Hayek popularized the word, defining it as "the order brought about by the mutual adjustment of many individual economies in a market."[2] As Butler (1983) explains:

…how is it that the market seems to be able to satisfy millions of individual purposes and to reconcile the diverse aims and activities of people without requiring any concise planning or control? Hayek suggests… the market system is… like a 'game' of exchange…

What goals will be achieved first, and to what degree each player will benefit from the game of wealth-creation is… unknown at the beginning. As in a competitive sport, it is only a measure of doubt about the outcome which makes the activity interesting and worthwhile, stimulating people to take risks and make efforts which, in the market system, benefit others as well. It would be pointless to play a game where we knew the results in advance; the most we can do is set the rules fairly so that there is an equal chance for everyone to benefit and to make such efforts as they deem worthwhile. As in any game, the rules governing the market exchange must not aim at improving the chances of any individual or aim at any overall pattern of results, but should treat everyone equally…

(Butler, 1983, p. 45)

The Role of the State

In the post-industrial countries in focus in this book, the state (the national political community or government and its agencies) has bedrock needs deriving essentially from the needs of capital. State representatives including politicians support capital accumulation and economic growth, which requires its promotion of legitimate capitalist modes of production and consumption – especially through state policymaking.

The role of government from a free market perspective concerns the protection of individual freedoms through law and order and national defense, for example.

Taxation should be low and less progressive – meaning government spending on social welfare should be a 'safety net' only, limited and targeted more at those who are unable to provide for themselves. With reduced spending, governments are expected to produce balanced budgets and budget surpluses to reduce further taxation imposts.

Being against an interventionist state, free market proponents encourage private ownership of property and private ownership of the means of production – these being issues of sovereign freedom and individual enterprise. A 'free' market, therefore, hopes for a 'rolled-back' state (meaning a cut-back public sector concerning itself with essential services only) – also referred to as 'small government' – a lean, efficient, public sector that enables and supports both free market operations and the sovereignty of individuals. As mentioned above, 'small' government or the 'minimal' state is proposed so that government interference does not disrupt the natural 'spontaneous market order.' The state itself becomes 'anti-state.'

Businesses, industries, and corporations have to compete to sell their goods or services to maximize profits and compete for customers wanting the highest quality for the lowest price. In line with free market thinking, national governments are seen to interfere or get in the way – they best serve the market by reducing 'red tape' (regulation) and anti-competitive policies and behaviors to ensure trading and workforce practices are as flexible and agile as possible so as to meet changing market needs (points explained further below). And, in line with market assumptions about self-interest and competition, businesses may lower their costs of production by transferring capital, resources, and infrastructure anywhere across the world to attract lower wage and production costs and taxes. Some have become more 'efficient' by eliminating the need for a traditional workplace altogether by conducting virtual businesses.

This creates a vicious circle. National governments aim to be economically competitive in the international marketplace and want local industries and businesses to survive and thrive. Tax incentives and public bailouts for failing industries may keep jobs and stop industries closing up or moving off-shore, but in doing so, governments 'interfere.'

The state interferes because reducing levels of taxation from business and industry 'efficiencies' (cost savings) affect government budgets and the subsequent quantum available for spending on public services and infrastructure – including essential services like education. As a consequence, many if not most governments not only 'interfere' with the market to some extent but also carry some level of public debt to cover their costs.

As they vie for economic competitiveness, governments are into the efficiency game themselves – instigating various structural reforms such as reducing the public sector workforce, cutting funding levels to public institutions, services, and social benefits, emphasizing efficiency, productivity, getting service 'users' to contribute to their costs (user-pays principles), selling public assets, outsourcing public work, or developing public-private partnerships to build and manage public infrastructure. In this way, key strategic alliances, trade agreements, and foreign policy projects are formed to secure advantages for the state (see for example, Litz, 2011).

Population increases pressure governmental focus on job creation, and the development of housing and infrastructure, while keeping a leash on the social wage (social 'welfare' payments). With aging populations there are emphases for all people to work and work to older ages. The state may also encourage skilled immigration or increased birth rates to expand younger sectors of the population to ensure sufficient revenue from taxation – through employment (income tax) and consumption (goods and services [sales] taxes). To support economic 'growth' the state wants to ramp up production and consumption, increase exports, reduce imports, and expand GDP (gross domestic product). The state wants economic 'growth.'

Despite their efforts and in light of their own support for 'free' unfettered markets, many western governments are experiencing budget deficits. Being such a large item of public expenditure, education funding is a major focus for funding reforms and governments everywhere seek cost savings, 'efficiencies,' and greater returns on investment (ROI). This is occurring at the same time that many countries are experiencing massive population growth, requiring many new schools and other education institutions to be built to keep up. The pressure is for the state to get out of the market's way, but since the state deems education to be compulsory and wants to ensure quality, it guarantees (mandates) and oversees education and its operations. The state produces policy to meet its aims and national objectives (albeit amidst competing interests).

Policy discourses portray education as a major means of producing a stable, well-qualified workforce, thereby raising national productivity essential for the nation's international economic competitiveness. Being an area of social spending, free marketeers would prefer the state to disentangle from expensive education provisioning by leaving this to the private sector or requiring individuals to meet costs (or some proportion of the costs) themselves.

For the free market to operate optimally, including in education, it requires the state to develop and pursue a sympathetic and enabling policy philosophy and stance. It is to this requirement that the discussion now turns.

Neoliberalism

Hayek's views supported what we now refer to as neoliberalism – his form of free market capitalism took classical liberal ideas in a new direction, primarily underpinned with tenets of small government and the rolled-back state and sovereign individualism, as described earlier.

Neoliberalism is assimilated with globalization – it is the foot servant of a globalized free market economy. It provides the ideological policy climate promoting market practices to aid consumption, production, improvement, innovation, and investment. The Hayekian version of free market neoliberalism is upheld by governments and powerful global corporations and financial organizations such as the World Bank and the International Monetary Fund.

Neoliberalism means 'new liberalism.' But, it isn't easy to define – there isn't one neat and true meaning that can be ascribed to the word 'neoliberalism.' Neoliberalism is an assemblage of complex and interlinked political, economic, and social philosophies underpinned epistemically by the fundamental belief in the free market as the most efficient and effective means of organizing all aspects of life (Birch, Tyfield, & Chiappetta, 2018).

Neoliberalism encapsulates a strident resurgence of classical laissez-faire economic policy, a doctrine of individualism and human choice and human capital theories, a circumvention of state interventionism, an incentive for investors, developers, and entrepreneurs. Neoliberalism infiltrates economic coordination, social distribution, and personal motivation (Sparke, 2013). In this context the government's role is to protect individual freedoms while holding individuals accountable for new obligations. (Discussion of how these fundamental neoliberal tenets play out in education are the basis of the following chapters.)

While often described as an ideology, neoliberalism is also referred to as an 'experiment' with real-life laboratories, a technocratic exercise, a "radical rupture in theory and practice" (Venugopal, 2015, p. 8; see also Kipnis, 2008; Peck, 2008, 2010). It is subject to a 'typology' of critiques (Venugopal, 2015).

Venugopal describes neoliberalism's evolution but still finds definition evasive:

> There are three related summary points that emerge. Firstly, in the course of its conceptual evolution from market deregulation policies to political agendas of class rule, and beyond, to technologies of the self, the term neoliberalism has come to describe a very broad assortment of real-life phenomena. A generous and sympathetic assessment of this multiplicity would hold that these new theoretical frameworks have helped to illuminate different elements of what has turned out to be an extraordinarily vast, complex, nuanced, networked, and contradictory creature. There are also grounds for a different and less generous reading: that conceptual proliferation has instead led to the over-identification of different sets of otherwise unconnected phenomena under a single, and thus increasingly unstable and ambiguous label.
>
> *(Venugopal, 2015, p. 5)*

Hence, at this point it is also worth mentioning that people referred to as 'neoliberals' rarely if ever use the term to describe themselves and the same applies to their policies – it appears to be a term that "dares not speak its own name" (Venugopal, 2015, p. 13). As Venugopal explains:

> There is no contemporary body of knowledge that calls itself neoliberalism, no self-described neoliberal theorists that elaborate it, nor policy-makers or

practitioners that implement it. There are no primers or advanced textbooks on the subject matter, no pedagogues, courses, or students of neoliberalism, no policies or election manifestoes that promise to implement it (although there are many that promise to dismantle it).

(Ibid.)

Consequently:

> ... neoliberalism is defined, conceptualized, and deployed exclusively by those who stand in evident opposition to it, such that the act of using the word has the two-fold effect of identifying oneself as non-neoliberal, and of passing negative moral judgment over it. Consequently, neoliberalism often features, even in sober academic tracts, in the rhetorical toolkit of caricature and dismissal, rather than of analysis and deliberation.

(Ibid.)

Neoliberalism is a term thus described variously as 'elusive,' 'fluid,' 'polymorphic,' 'contradictory,' 'impossible to define,' 'an ill-defined signifier.' There are numerous criticisms about the usage within the social sciences where definitions are often not provided, are inconsistent and contradictory, incoherent, weak, loose, nebulous, scant, 'conceptually stretched,' populist, misguided, dysfunc- tional, lacking precision, and morally laden (Boas & Gans-Morse, 2009, Mudge, 2008; Roberts, 1995; Sartori, 1970; Stiglitz, 2012; Venugopal, 2015). While often described as an ideology, it is also referred to as an 'experiment' with real-life laboratories, a technocratic exercise, a "radical rupture in theory and practice" (Venugopal, 2015, p. 8; see also Kipnis, 2008; Peck, 2008, 2010). Neoliberal critics are in turn criticized as being economically illiterate so as to produce inadequate explanations (Chang, 2003).

Despite these shortcomings and definitional difficulties, neoliberalism has been and is used to suit differing needs in different contexts over time. But at its base, neoliberalism is "a broad indicator of the historical turn in macro-political economy" (Venugopal, 2015, p. 15).

Origins

The origins of neoliberalism entail different schools of thought emanating at dif- ferent times from various parts of the world, but there is a lack of agreement about neoliberalism's exact origins or the timing of its re-emergence in more recent history. Birch (2017), for example, cites neoliberalism's origins in an article by R. A. Armstrong in *The Modern Review* in 1884, which defined neoliberalism as a new form of liberalism promoting the benefits of economic interventions by the state – the opposite conception to its current iteration. Birch also cites early mention of neoliberalism by Charles Gide in *The Economic Journal* in 1898, which describes the work of Italian economist Maffeo Pantaleoni promoting free competition as the best means of producing maximum pleasure and indulgence for the greatest number of people – a view not dissimilar to the meanings of today which are articulated later in this section.

Waddock (2016) argues that neoliberalism has been a major influence in western democracies for around 70 years. She suggests that modern neoliberalism commenced at a meeting of economists at Mont Pelerin in Switzerland in 1947, which included famous names in recent neoliberal history such as Milton Friedman, Friedrick Hayek, Karl Popper, and George Stigler. The Mont Pelerin meeting was called to discuss concerns about government expansions impinging on individual freedoms and hindering free enterprise at the time.

The meeting's reports described neoliberalism as we mostly know it now. Each participant took these views back to their domiciling countries to promote neoliberal ideas of individual freedom, private rights, and a free market. (However, Hayek, and eventually Freidman, rejected 'neoliberalism' as a term that described their economic position. Hence, Boas and Gans-Morse (2009) argue that current negative connotations and meanings ascribed to 'neoliberalism,' and assumptions that Hayek, Mises, and Friedman were 'neoliberal' proponents are historically incorrect.)

Historians and analysts also mention the German Freiberg School as being influential in modern neoliberal history. Boas and Gans-Morse (2009) suggest that the word 'neoliberalism' entered scholarly usage in the twentieth century in Europe between the two world wars through the German Freiberg School, who also referred to neoliberalism as 'ordoliberalism' (from the Latin 'ordo' meaning 'order'). At that time, the word embodied completely different understandings to its current popular usage and meaning. German Freiberg neoliberals argued that classical liberalism was outdated and needed to be tempered with government intervention (legislation, regulation, redistributory, or 'ordered' policies) to counter its worst effects. German Freiberg neoliberals saw this form of neoliberalism or ordoliberalism as a necessary measure to reduce the negative impacts such as unfettered and powerful commercial monopolies creating threats to fair market competition. They also believed that social egalitarian values should not be subsumed by economic ones.

The original Freiberg School neoliberals opposed unfettered free market proponents such as Mises, Friedman, and Hayek (referring to them as 'paleo-liberals'), and instead supported humanism and social justice – concepts at odds with Hayek and Mises. In other words, the German Freiberg form of neoliberalism did not support market fundamentalism, but quite the opposite, such that it corresponded more closely to what we now refer to as 'liberal progressivism' (defense of social justice, equality, and inclusion while also supporting liberty and justice).

In the 1970s and 1980s the word neoliberalism began to be used by Latin American scholars during Pinochet's coup in Chile. The meaning and usage of the word neoliberalism hence underwent a 180-degree transformation from that ascribed by the German Freiberg School which denoted moderation – the Chilean usage connoted fundamentalist market liberalism (Boas & Gans-Morse, 2009).

By the 1980s, neoliberalism became widely used and referenced and took on the characteristics to which this book refers – heralding market deregulation, privatization, and the contraction of the state and state welfarism.

Neoliberalism's influence became global when Friedman's work (from the Mont Pelerin meeting) received support and endorsement in the 1980s by President Ronald Reagan in the USA (see Friedman, 1962). Reagan supported small government, lower tax rates, the rolling back of regulation and red tape, and support for free trade, saying "In this present [economic] crisis, government is not the solution to our problem, government is the problem" (1981, p. 2), and "Government's first duty is to protect the people, not run their lives" (1982). He summed up his criticisms of the social democratic, welfare state sarcastically: "Government's view of the economy could be summed up in a few short phrases: if it moves, tax it. If it keeps moving, regulate it. And if it stops moving, subsidize it" (1986). With support and agreement from Prime Minister Margaret Thatcher in the UK, neoliberalism took root.

Thatcher believed a sense of welfare entitlement had taken root in UK, and that the purpose of government was not to assume responsibility for people's lives. In free market fashion, she believed people should be encouraged to take responsibility for their own lives without depending on government. She returned to Hayek's views that had been ignored for many years. Thatcher's most famous quote (underlined in the citation below) expressing her support for a neoliberal policy stance came from an interview in 1987 with *Women's Own*, a British women's magazine:

> I think we've been through a period where too many people have been given to understand that if they have a problem, it's the government's job to cope with it. 'I have a problem, I'll get a grant.' 'I'm homeless, the government must house me.' They're casting their problem on society. And, you know, <u>there is no such thing as society</u>. There are individual men and women, and there are families. And no government can do anything except through people, and people must look to themselves first. It's our duty to look after ourselves and then, also to look after our neighbour. People have got the entitlements too much in mind, without the obligations. There's no such thing as entitlement, unless someone has first met an obligation.

These sentiments are imbued with notions of 'self-interest' flowing on to 'fellow feeling' and from that time on, neoliberalism has proliferated through to the current age.

Neoliberalism was advantaged through rapid economic restructuring and social reforms that freed capital from parochial policy strictures. In line with notions of 'small government' it hastened the disengagement of government control, dismantling protection and subsidies, and reducing entitlements and dependency, to advance benefits derived from the sovereign freedoms of individuals and private institutions. Capitalism began to move away from its social obligations and

Keynesian goals of full employment (discussed further below) which were criticized for involving and accommodating too many vested interests. To neoliberals, full employment involved acceptance of all, irrespective of quality or need, such that 'bad,' 'inefficient,' or low-quality workers/providers could still remain in business. The more pragmatic neoliberalism would aid market distribution to meet consumer demand, while dis-endorsing businesses that were under-performing, and not meeting customer expectations, or needs. It was a rebalancing act between capital and labor in favor of the former, arguments of which went back to World War 2 (Kalecki, 1943; Hayek, 1973; Gamble & Payne, 1996).

Neoliberalism dismantled government interference in market-distorting matters such as wage and price controls and introduced corporate governance strictures over the economy. The rationale was that old-fashioned Keynesianism restricted capital, corporate economic outcomes, and the entrepreneurial spirit. It was past its 'use-by' date. The inflexibilities of trade unionism and the welfare state were the enemies of capitalism and growth, but neoliberalism's inbuilt remedies of individualism, including the individualization of risk and responsibility, enabled responsibility to be shifted from the state to individuals. The social contract was changed. Increasingly growing market protections and subsidies were anathema to the new globalized neoliberal economic consensus.

Sang Ben and Van der Horst (1992) argue that neoliberalism describes the distinct characteristics of modern capitalism, including the monolithic nature of the free market into all areas of life, without serious attention being paid to alternatives. New forms of globalized neoliberalism ensure nothing is secure from disruption. What makes current capitalism different from past classical forms of liberalism is ubiquitous globalization: the boundless nature of trade, services, communications, corporations, and knowledge which undermine and challenge traditional, classical liberal tenets. For example, knowledge, discovery, and the democratization of ideas and opinions through new technologies all represent new forms of property that challenge traditional property rights and the legal frameworks built around them. Given the vast difference between classical liberalism and neoliberalism, Sang Ben and Van der Horst (1992) go so far as to say that a better descriptor for current times would be 'anti-liberalism'.

However, for staunch neoliberals, the failure of states to totally dismantle the welfare state, social democratic ideals, and tax imposts is a huge disappointment. Social welfare payments are a trade-off for policies that protect and promote capitalism and ensnare all citizens within its clasp irrespective of their circumstances (Dragsbaek Schmidt & Hersh, 2006; Gamble, 2001).

While generally considered to promote conservative standpoints, neoliberalism has been accepted and expanded by governments of all political persuasions. In this regard, Waddock (2016) emphasizes the role and influence of neoliberal 'nemes' developed at the Mont Pelerin meeting which have aided neoliberalism's infiltration across what might otherwise be broad divides. Nemes are the ideas, phrases, symbols, and images that replicate and resonate from person to person so as to become established as universal beliefs and understandings about how the world works. Neoliberal nemes now pervade thoughts, everyday narratives, actions, and plans – they are hegemonic.

Steeped in nemes associated with individual sovereignty, neoliberalism advocates for political, economic, and social freedoms – the freedom to own property, to sell one's labor power, to own private property and businesses, for example, and attendant individual rights such as freedom of religion, speech/expression, media, and association. Individualism encourages entrepreneurship which is purported to benefit everyone, and competitive individualism encourages the pursuit of excellence, innovation, and continual improvement – for the benefit of individuals and society. Neoliberalism also endorses individual responsibilities – individuals should accept risks associated with personal decisions and take personal responsibility for their lifelong needs (education, health, employment, retirement).

Neoliberalism enables the state's capital accumulation and growth processes to move from cumbersome, heavily regulated mass consumption and provisioning towards flexible, deregulated, and differentiated forms of production, consumption, and investment.

Neoliberalism valorizes supply-side economics (production, hence the interests of producers/suppliers/corporations) over the demand-side (consumption, hence the interests of consumers – the general public). Supply-side economics is sometimes referred to as Reagonomics (referring to President Reagan's support for macroeconomic theory). Briefly, the theory is that economic growth occurs through capital investment and removing barriers to the production of goods or services – lowered taxation rates, fewer regulations, and less state bureaucratic red tape (small government), and the non-interference of governments in determining the amount of money in circulation (monetary policy).

The contrast is the previous Keynesian economics (prior to the Reagan and Thatcher eras) espousing government intervention in fiscal and monetary stimulus to avoid recession if market demand weakens, emphasizing the economic 'demand-side' (see Keynes, 1936). In this way, neoliberalism aligns with the fundamental tenets of trade liberalization and the free market economics which are believed to operate best when individuals are free to make personal choices about goods and services. In other words, supply-side economists believe that producers drive the economy whereas in Keynesian economics consumption and demand are considered the prime economic drivers.[3]

Keynesianism and social welfarism are viewed as mollycoddling individuals by way of the 'nanny state,' raising expectations about rights, social entitlements, and ever-increasing labor costs – in much the same way as Margaret Thatcher explained (quoted above). Strong state oversight and intervention incurs responsibility for day-to-day living, continual expansions, and rising expenditures in the social wage and the subsequent requirement of high taxation levels to fund redistributive welfare policies. This disincentivizes individual efforts, innovation, development, and the creation of profits (surplus value). In short, Keynesian-inspired state interventions are seen to distort market functioning – they are anathema to, and the enemy of, the free market.

For example, world economists, such as Christine Lagarde of the IMF, argue that the current rise in protectionism (implicit in things like President Trump's "let's make America great again" and sentiments on tariffs, Britain's decision to exit the European Union, political uncertainty, and the rise in anti-immigration sentiments around the developed world) is a threat to investment, productivity, innovation, and growth. According to Lagarde, trade growth is the solution to economic problems and as such, markets cannot be restricted or distorted but must be open, fair, and inclusive to facilitate opportunity (see for example, Donnan, Tett, & Fleming, 2016).

Neoliberals encourage an entrepreneurial spirit amongst the populace, but government is viewed as a typically bad entrepreneur because the conditions under which it operates are radically different from those facing private players. Market-driven economies are dynamic; they have to be to survive, whereas state-driven economies, or what Nobel laureate economist Edmund Phelps calls 'social economies,' are considered to be "fatally lacking in dynamism" (2013, p. 127).

The effect is a striking change in the role of governments and their relationships with citizens, official public policy discourses and provisioning, and, in education, a major change in intersubjective relationships between education institutions and their 'clients.'

In collusion with these dominant discourses are those supporting new public administration systems based on corporate (private-sector-styled) management and control – or corporate managerialism. The rise of neoliberalism reforms suggest that the market is the most propitious way to deliver education, hence valorized are individualism – including institutional autonomy, competition through differentiation to enable greater consumer choices, and empowered local governing bodies. Meanwhile, centralized policy expectations call for compliance and accountability, and an emphasis on quality assurance, continuous improvement, and higher performativity and 'outputs' gauged through performance indicators, standards, capability statements, and benchmarks (Ball, 2006; Duignan, 2006). Along with all aspects of life, neoliberalism transforms individual subjectivities, with policy encouraging this.

Different names have been used to describe the phenomenon of free market neoliberalism: 'laissez-faire capitalism' (the non-interference of governments in a 'free' market); 'economic rationalism' in reference to the supposition that markets operate through human rationality; the self-adjusting, efficient market; and many neoliberal beliefs are also embodied in the term 'neo-conservatism' (although neoliberalism is associated with governments of many political hues).

Neoliberalizing Education

Policy devised to benefit economic growth and capital accumulation are rarely effective in the public sector and in education in particular. Exercising small government usually means a reduction in public spending with legitimation for education reforms and heightening of centralized controls usually justified in terms of the need for harsh fiscal restraint over concern about the sector's lack of responsiveness to improvement and competition. Adding impetus to cost-cutting trends, critics argue that education's outcomes represent a low return on investment (ROI) and poor value for money (VFM). Government ministers and media commentators regularly roll out reproaches and a long list of education's 'failures':

- ideological bias and provider capture
- a lack of rigor and accountability
- resistance to change
- a lack of incentive for improvement
- dropping standards and rising costs
- under-achievement and falling standards in learning and teaching
- unresponsiveness to public expectations and therefore to market impetus
- students being ill-prepared for the workforce
- a lack of parental involvement or influence
- out-of-touch and obstructive teacher unions.

So, despite the notion of small government and non-interference, and calls for deregulation and the reduction of red tape by neoliberal advocates, education is fertile ground for government intervention, regulation, and oversight. Governments have increased control over education through stringent accountabilities, including policies sponsoring continual high-stakes performance measurement, as they wrestle with the sector to 'implement' neoliberal agendas.

Governments are more interventionist in education and its leadership in an effort to ensure policy compliance. They have subscribed to an increasingly unidimensional policy purpose which submits educational practice to forms of governmentality to unite education with political and economic objectives. To achieve this, decisions about education policy and accountability mechanisms have been effectively restricted to bureaucratic and government levels. Policymaking is separated from the realm of education practice.

In education, neoliberal structural reforms have generally taken two distinct forms. First, there are those which have swept across entire public infrastructures: corporatization, privatization, outsourcing, re-engineering (replacing people with technology), and organizational 'downsizing' (headcount reductions – through redundancies, 'no new hire' policies and the casualization of previously permanent jobs which are contract based and offer none of the employment conditions enjoyed by tenured staff). This has involved the sale, closure, or mothballing of public institutions, the suspension or slowdown of public works, the cessation of many ancillary education services, and drastic budget cutbacks.

The second type of reforms concern delivering increased autonomy to service sites, through policies referring to 'local management,' 'devolved authority,' or 'deregulated' or 'default' autonomy. These reforms complement the first type –

for example, as education bureaucracies 'downsize,' it makes sense to divert the work previously conducted centrally to be managed by education leaders within individual institutions. Similarly falling under this second form of public sector restructuring is the promotion of greater consumer rights in terms of choice and decision-making influence in education institutions, thereby assuming oversight and some responsibility (Starr, 1999). Both forms of restructuring are in line with notions of small government and the rolled-back state.

The combination of these two forms of restructuring has created what were once referred to as quasi-markets in education (see for example, Ball, 1994), but which, over time, have become more stridently aligned with free market neoliberalism.

Concomitantly, education policy discourse and nomenclature has changed. Business terms have been transported and are now in regular use in education, with the aim being to align education with neoliberalism and the market.

However, for centuries, scholars have expressed discomfort about a totally unfettered free market operating in education. Adam Smith's *The Wealth of Nations* (1776) warned of the market's potentially destructive capacity without the construction of social institutions that would enhance the wealth, potential, and social harmony of a nation. In education Smith saw inequities emanating simply from birthright and argued for education provision for those whose life circumstances offered limited opportunities for personal advancement:

> The education of the common people requires, perhaps, in a civilized and commercial society, the attention of the public, more than that of people of some rank and fortune.
>
> *(Smith, 1776, p. 328)*

Smith's foresights into the possibilities for the market to exacerbate inequities is further pursued in *The Theory of Moral Sentiments* (1759), although his warnings have been conveniently forgotten by those who quote him to support neoclassical economic revivalism.

Neoliberalism Critiques

The globalized neoliberal free market is inevitably inextricably linked to politics. Like every area of social life, understandings and meanings are contested and neoliberalism has its detractors even though its supporters are currently in the ascendency. Theory is one thing, but laissez-faire neoliberal practice is quite another.

From early on, researchers and commentators warned of neoliberalism's effects. Marginson (1993), for example, pointed out the pervasive nature of market theory in all spheres of life, including non-economic spheres such as education, dominating its discourses and dismantling traditional practices. Referring to Hayekian free market theory as 'economic rationalism,' he argued:

One of the most striking features of economic rationalism is its *universalising* aspect, whereby market economics 'colonises' non-economic areas of public policy and in so doing crowds out other knowledges and practices.

(Marginson, 1993, pp. 63–64)

There are criticisms about the assumptions underpinning free market liberalism. Each agent in a market for assets, goods, or services possesses incomplete knowledge about factors that affect prices or quality in that market. For example, no agent has full information and in busy lives, it is practically impossible to be 'rational' in one's decision-making. No one has all the facts or can foresee all the consequences or effects of decisions. Individuals rely on trends and reputations, but they are not all-knowing when it comes to exercising choices. Stiglitz (2008, p. 43) explains that "...markets by themselves do not produce efficient outcomes when information is imperfect and markets are incomplete."

Hence, free market theory ignores behavioral realism. Humans cannot be relied upon to be rational. Emotions influence decisions and actions, while fear and greed affect supply and demand. Individuals have feelings – they cannot make rational decisions when they panic, for example, and can be more impulsive and act instinctively in the short term but more logical over the long term (Lo, 2017). The matter of feelings and emotions is inconvenient, making markets less efficient than supply-side economic theory suggests. Both rationality and irrationality exist concurrently but rarely are economic forecasts or reforms predicated on this reality (see Thaler & Sunstein, 2008).

There are criticisms about the neoliberal emphases on economic growth and its measuring instrument, GDP. GDP is supposed to measure output, but this does not include unpaid work such as care work and housework or volunteering efforts, for example. (This is also a criticism of gender scholars who see this aspect of GDP eliding much of the world's essential work undertaken primarily by women [see for example, Starr, 1999].)

Claims that the market is unbiased, value-free, and apolitical is a political stance in and of itself. In the game of catallaxy, some market players have clear advantages over others. There is no 'level playing field' in the market, as Adam Smith (1759, 1776) and many others have pointed out. The endowments of birth and personal talents and abilities make for clear differences from the start. Further, market theory ignores the effects of unequal power and authority – the power differentials in market transactions for example, between employers as owners of the means of production and employees who are selling their labor power.

Further, important influencers such as economic status and inherent discrimination such as racism or sexism also come into play. And, while neoliberalism endorses market forces as the organizer of social and economic life, this stance embeds a social Darwinist 'survival of the fittest' influence as self-interests preside over broader social needs. The end results are power shifts from the majority to the influential minority, including renewed imperialism and neocolonialism amongst nations. Hence, Gamble (2001) argues that neoliberalism generates social conflict and disrupts local, national, and international relations. Neoliberalism is accused of 'debasing' democracy' as the interests of powerful elites rise in influence and effect.

'Fellow feeling' is never lauded or pursued as rigorously as self-interest. For example, globalization has aided the rise of multinational, global organizations that can evade the taxes of their domiciled countries by shifting profits to low-taxing jurisdictions (with some reportedly paying no tax at all [see for example, Hutchens, 2017]). Multinationals want to be located in countries with stable governments, an educated workforce, and adequate infrastructure – but by shifting their profits off-shore, they are evading responsibility for contributing to the common good (fellow feeling) and the benefits everyone thus receives. Similarly, individuals may evade their civic responsibilities, for example, through operating in the cash economy to avoid paying tax. And governments – making decisions on behalf of the populace of whole states or countries – also 'bend the rules' to gain competitive advantage, by reneging on election promises, refusing to meet obligations under international agreements, or by hiding deals struck with private companies through 'commercial-in-confidence' contracts, for example.

With global economic competition on the rise and neoliberalism firmly entrenched, governments want greater productivity, more jobs, and economic growth – for their own good (the chance to be re-elected) as much as for the good of the citizenry – and neoliberalism may sway logic. A good example is divisive debate about climate change, with some wanting to impose a carbon tax to change consumer behaviors to meet global emission reduction targets, while others want to scrap these policies to aid and enable industries such as manufacturing, power production, or mining. In all these ways, free market theory breaks down. Even pro-free market governments behave in ways that contradict market mantras, disturbing and distorting market competition to satisfy diverse stakeholders and to garner support and legitimacy (see for example, Kelly, 2014). Self-interest can outmaneuver fellow feeling at all levels, and it usually does.

Neoliberalism has not demonstrated delivery of the trickle-down effect. Unemployment, underemployment, and work casualization are rife, labor unions are diminished, manufacturing and other industries have closed, CEOs can earn up to 2000 times the wage of their workforce, the social wage is insufficient, while the middle classes carry the can through their taxes amidst wage stagnation. Reich (2012, p. xvi) calls this "the decline of almost everything... the public relies on." Further, in opposition to Thatcher's views quoted above, Reich (2018) argues that without the common good, there is no society.

There is a rightful place for regulation in the interests of the common good, and there are vivid examples over recent times of cases where an ounce of regulation at international, national, and regional levels would have prevented catastrophic events and enormous public outrage – banking and finance, environmental and occupational health and safety regulations – to name only a few, would have been beneficial and essential in hindsight. These too are issues of globalization.

Rewards have been funneled to the top, while the poor and middle classes have borne the costs and the risks (while their taxes have also funded corporate bailouts). Social welfare safety net measures have been reduced, while corporate welfare and tax incentives have increased alongside regulation decreases. Some of the severest consequences – perhaps unintended but foreseeable nevertheless – concern major environmental and climatic challenges, and concerns about the overall welfare and wellbeing of human beings and other species, and the communities and ecosystems in which they live.

As competing demands on the public purse multiply, and as cultural diversity and inclusion disrupts local traditions and customs, globalization is causing many to feel they have been forgotten, are being left out, are losing out or missing out. However, even the most marginalized can bite back and create change of their own making when it comes to voting power, as recent major elections have shown. The backlash of the marginalized against globalization concerns calls for a re-slicing of the pie, a return to times past, and a focus on nationalistic interests. Yet short-term political cycles elide long-term consequences and ensure change doesn't happen quickly if it does at all. The common people are feeling they are subject to government rather than government being subject to the people, by the people, for the people. Chomsky (1999, p. 11) cynically sums up the neoliberal free market thus:

> Instead of citizens, it produces consumers. Instead of communities, it produces shopping malls. The net result is an atomized society of disengaged individuals who feel demoralized and socially powerless.

Few would support the anarchic view that governments are not needed but widespread cynicism suggests that governments govern for some more than others. An *Animal Farm* scenario has emerged where all animals are equal but some are more equal than others (Orwell, 1945). Effectively within a free market the state equates to the administrative division of the market – there to do the market's bidding. The effects are clear: policies supporting continual growth and supply-side economics have degraded the conditions of production, reduced the standard of living for too many, and eroded the environment and the long-term health of a finite planet.

Warnings about the market's shortcomings have been longstanding. Adam Smith believed that market forces would eventually lead to a 'stationary' or 'steady-state' economy, and John Stuart Mill (1863) saw the impossibility of continual growth, viewing a 'stationary state' as desirable, inevitable, and necessary. Keynes also foresaw problems with never-ending growth, predicting that capital accumulation would eventually reach saturation and bring about a quasi-stationary community.

So where to from here? Some suggest we are nearing the end of decades of neoliberal hegemony (Denniss, 2018) while others foresee the end of democracy (see for example, Hertz, 2001), and the end of history (Fukuyama, 2006). Others argue that the forces of the common good will rise to see neoliberalism tempered with social concerns (see Stiglitz, 2012, 2015), while others see the end game could be a return to protectionism and antagonistic regional blocs (Gamble, 2001; Gamble & Payne, 1996). The latest developments reveal many tendencies. Hence, Gamble warns:

> What has to be avoided… is a tendency to reify neo-liberalism and to treat it as a phenomenon which manifests everywhere and in everything. This kind of reductionism is not very useful, and it is also politically paralyzing. Far better to deconstruct neo-liberalism into the different doctrines and ideas which compose it and relate them to particular practices and political projects.
>
> *(Gamble, 2001, p. 134)*

This is exactly the role of the following chapters in this section. They de-construct neoliberalism into its component doctrines and axioms and demonstrate how they have been enacted in education towards specific political and economic ends.

Notes

1 The 'invisible hand' – a term conceived by Adam Smith (1759, 1776) – speaks to the ways in which the pursuit of self-interests has the unanticipated effect of producing social benefits for others.
2 Catallaxy derives from the Greek word *katalatto*, primarily referring to the process of exchange.
3 Theory is one thing and practice is another. During the global financial crisis of 2008, governments intervened in major ways, bailing out banks because they were 'too big to fail' with public money, instigating new practices such as quantitative easing to encourage banks to pump money into the economy – to raise stock prices, lower interest rates, and boost investment – because the usual method of making adjustments to interest rates had failed. In this crisis, governments did not trust the market to remedy problems created through bad market behaviors and poor regulation.

References

Al-Rodhan, N. A. F., & Stoudmann, G. (2006). *Definitions of globalization: A comprehensive overview and a proposed definition*. Geneva, Switzerland: Geneva Centre for Security Policy.

Apple, M. (2006). Producing inequalities: Neo-liberalism, neo-conservatism, and the politics of educational reform. In H. Lauder, P. Brown, J. Dillabough, & A. H. Halsey (Eds.), *Education, globalization & social change* (pp. 468–489). Oxford, England: Oxford University Press.

Ball, S. (1994). *Education reform: A critical and post-structural approach*. Buckingham, England: Open University Press.

Ball, S. (2006). *Education policy and social class: The selected works of Stephen J. Ball*. London, England: Routledge.

Birch, K. (2017). What exactly is neoliberalism? *The Conversation*, November 3, 2017. Retrieved April 4, 2017 from http://theconversation.com/what-exactly-is-neoliberalism-84755

Birch, K., Tyfield, D., & Chiappetta, M. (2018). From neoliberalizing research to researching neoliberalisms: STS, rentiership and the emergence of Commons 2.0. In D. Cahill, M.Cooper, M.Konings, & D. Primrose (Eds.), *The SAGE handbook of neoliberalism* (pp. 596–608). London, England: SAGE.

Boas, T. C., & Gans-Morse, J. (2009). Neoliberalism: From new liberal philosophy to anti-liberal slogan. *Studies in Comparative International Development*, 44(2), 137–161.

Butler, E. (1983). *Hayek: His contribution to the political and economic thought of our time.* London, England: Temple Smith.

Chang, H-J. (2003). The market, the state and institutions in economic development. In Chang, H-J. (Ed.), *Rethinking development economics* (pp. 41–60). London, England: Anthem Press.

Chomsky, N. (1999). *Profit over people: Neoliberalism and the global order.* New York, NY: Seven Stories Press.

Denniss, R. (2018). Dead right: How neoliberalism ate itself and what comes next. *Quarterly Essay*, Issue 70, 1–79.

Donnan, S., Tett, G., & Fleming, S. (2016). Lagarde warns Trump-style protectionism would hit world economy. *Financial Times*, July 7, 2016. Retrieved April 4, 2017 from www.ft.com/content/134aac12-4403-11e6-9b66-0712b3873ae1

Dragsbaek Schmidt, J., & Hersh, J. (2006). Neoliberal globalization: Workfare without welfare. *Globalizations*, 3(1), 69–89.

Duignan, P. (2006). *Educational leadership: Key challenges and ethical tensions.* New York, NY: Cambridge University Press.

Friedman, M. (1962). *Capitalism and freedom.* Chicago, IL: University of Chicago Press.

Fukuyama, F. (2006). *The end of history and the last man.* New York, NY: Free Press.

Gamble, A., & Payne, A. (1996). Introduction: The political economy of regionalism and world order. In A. Gamble & A. Payne (Eds.), *Regionalism and world order* (pp. 1–20). London, England: Red Globe Press.

Gamble, A. (2001). Neoliberalism. *Capital & Class*, 25, 127–134.

Giddens, A. (1994). *Beyond left and right: The future of radical politics.* Cambridge, England: Polity Press.

Hayek, F. A. (1973). *Law, legislation, and liberty: A new statement of the liberal principles of justice and political economy. Volume 2: The mirage of social justice.* Chicago, IL: The University of Chicago Press.

Hertz, N. (2001). *The silent takeover: Global capitalism and the death of democracy.* New York, NY: Free Press.

Hutchens, G. (2017). Australian tax office says 36% of big firms and multinationals paid no tax. *The Guardian*, December 7, 2017. Retrieved December 10, 2017 from www.theguardian.com/australia-news/2017/dec/07/australian-tax-office-says-36-of-big-firms-and-multinationals-paid-no-tax

Hutton, W. (1995). *The state we're in.* London, England: Jonathan Cape.

Kalecki, M. (1943). Political aspects of full employment. *Political Quarterly*, 14, 322–331.

Kelly, P. (2014). *Triumph & decline.* Melbourne, VIC: Melbourne University Press.

Keynes, J. M. (1919). *The economic consequences of peace.* London, England: Macmillan & Co.

Keynes, J. M. (1936). *General theory of employment, interest and money.* London, England: Palgrave Macmillan.

Kipnis, A. (2008). Audit cultures: Neoliberal governmentality, socialist legacy, or technologies of governing? *American Ethnologist*, 35(2), 275–289.

Litz, D. (2011). Globalization and the changing face of educational leadership: Current trends and emerging dilemmas. *International Education Studies*, 4(3), 47–61. Retrieved April 4, 2017 from www.ccsenet.org/journal/index.php/ies/article/view/9921/8114

Lo, A. K. (2017). *Adaptive markets: Financial evolution and the speed of thought*. Princeton, NJ: Princeton University Press.

Marginson, S. (1993). *Education and public policy in Australia*. Cambridge, England: Cambridge University Press. Marx, K., & Engels, F. (1848). *The communist manifesto*. London, England: Workers' Educational Association.

Mill, J. S. (1863). *Utilitarianism*. London, England: Parker, Son & Bourn.

Mudge, S. (2008). What is neo-liberalism? *Socio-Economic Review*, 6(4), 703–731.

Orwell, G. (1945). *Animal farm*. London, England: Secker & Warburg.

Peck, J. (2008). Remaking laissez-faire. *Progress in Human Geography*, 32(1), 3–43.

Peck, J. (2010). *Constructions of neoliberal reason*. Oxford, England: Oxford University Press.

Phelps, E. (2013). *Mass flourishing: How grassroots innovation created jobs, challenge, and change*. Princeton, NJ: Princeton University Press.

Productivity Commission (2013). *Productivity update, May 2013*. Canberra, ACT: Productivity Commission, Australian Government.

Reagan, R. (1981). Inaugural address. Washington, DC, January 20, 1981.

Reagan, R. (1982). Remarks to the National Conference of the Building and Construction Trades Department, AFL-CIO, March 30, 1982.

Reagan, R. (1986). Remarks to the White House Conference on Small Business, August 15, 1986.

Reich, R. B. (2012). *Beyond outrage: What has gone wrong with our economy and our democracy and how to fix it*. New York, NY: Alfred Knopf.

Reich, R. B. (2018). *The common good*. New York, NY: Alfred Knopf.

Roberts, K. (1995). Neoliberalism and the transformation of populism in Latin America: The Peruvian case. *World Politics*, 48(1), 82–116.

Sang Ben, M., & Van Der Horst, A. (1992). Ideales de antaño, necesidades presentes: El liberalismo dominicano como filosofía emergente. In B. B. Levine (Ed.), *El desafío neoliberal: El fin del tercermundismo en América Latina* (pp. 339–357). Bogotá, Colombia: Editorial Norma.

Sartori, G. (1970). Concept misformation in contemporary politics. *American Political Science Review*, 64(4), 1033–1053.

Smith, A. (1759). *The theory of moral sentiments*. Edinburgh, Scotland: Alexander Kincaid & J. Bell.

Smith, A. (1776). *The wealth of nations*. London, England: W. Strahan & T. Cadell.

Sparke, M. (2013). *Introducing globalization: Ties, tension and uneven integration*. Maldon, MA: Wiley-Blackwell.

Starr, K. (1999). *That roar which lies on the other side of silence: An analysis of women principals' responses to structural reform in South Australian education* (Doctoral dissertation, University of South Australia). Retrieved from http://search.ror.unisa.edu.au/media/researcharchive/open/9915955288701831/53111935600001831

Stiglitz, J. (2008). Is there a Post-Washington consensus? In N. Serra & J. Stiglitz (Eds.), *The Washington consensus reconsidered: Towards a new global governance* (pp. 41–56). New York, NY: Oxford University Press.

Stiglitz, J. (2012). *The price of inequality: How today's divided society endangers our future*. New York, NY: WW Norton & Company.

Stiglitz, J. E. (2015). *The great divide: Unequal societies and what we can do about them*. New York, NY: W.W. Norton & Company.

Thaler, R. H., & Sunstein, C. R. (2008). *Nudge: Improving decisions about health, wealth, and happiness*. Newhaven, CT: Yale University Press.

Thatcher, M. (1987). Interview with Douglas Keay for *Women's Own*, September 23, 1987, No. 10 Downing Street, London.

Venugopal, R. (2015). Neoliberalism as concept. *Economy and Society*, 44(2), 165–187. Retrieved April 2, 2018 from http://personal.lse.ac.uk/venugopr/venugopal2014a ugneoliberalism.pdf

Waddock, S. (2016). Neoliberalism's failure means we need a new narrative to guide the global economy. *The Conversation*, December 6, 2016. Retrieved April 19, 2018 from https://theconversation.com/neoliberalisms-failure-means-we-need-a-new-na rrative-to-guide-global-economy-69096

3

INDIVIDUALISM AND AUTONOMY

Sovereign Rationality in Market Exchange

Individualism is the fundamental axiom and central principle underpinning free market neoliberal thinking. Individualism conjures up many meanings: the singular and indivisible, separateness, uniqueness, selfhood and self-determination, independence and autonomy. In neoliberal terms, individualism means all these things – it denotes sovereignty, liberty, and freedom, which form the foundation of free market 'self-interest.' Negative connotations of individualism include selfishness, hedonism, egotism, and greed (see Rand, 1964).

In 1532, Machiavelli conceded the importance of individualism as the essential force in human nature designed to protect one's own rights, comforts, actions, behaviors, and associations (Machiavelli, 2009; see also Spencer, 2012).

The expression of individualism rests on freedoms, including the right to choose and make decisions, personal freedoms of speech, religion, and association, as well as rights to independent thought, opinion, preferences, and tastes, and to privately own property.

Individual freedom conveys the primacy of the private sphere in neoliberal thought. The United States Declaration of Independence captures individualism in terms of 'life, liberty and the pursuit of happiness' within 'the land of the free.' Individual rights are extended to all as basic human rights. Hence, implicitly, individual freedom also implies tolerance for diversity and difference and the right of free individuals to pursue their self-interests, personal goals, and their vision of a good life. From a neoliberal perspective, society is simply an amalgam of individuals, as indicated in the quotes of Mises and Campbell:

> All rational action is in the first place individual action. Only the individual thinks. Only the individual reasons. Only the individual acts.
>
> — *(Ludwig von Mises)*

The function of the society is to cultivate the individual. It is not the function of the individual to support society.

— *(Joseph Campbell)*

Individualism is inextricably bound with neoliberal principles of choice and competition. It goes hand-in-glove with personal choice – individuals must be free to choose goods and services to exercise sovereignty, express particularized preferences and interests, and enact personal pursuits. Free market liberalism assumes that individual, rational economic agents make rational decisions and choices based on market indicators such as availability (supply and demand), amidst considerations of price, quality, reputation, value, accessibility, and personal needs. Individual choices spur competition as providers compete to be chosen above others, and competition encourages creativity and original thought, bringing about improvement, inventiveness, and entrepreneurship for custom and favor. (These are topics canvassed in the following chapters, but they are mentioned here to demonstrate the inextricable interconnectedness of neoliberal principles, with all enforcing the primacy of individualism.)

The concept of individualism applies not only to people, but to individual companies and institutions that also operate according to their self-interests, based on competition, productivity, efficiency, profit, and growth (see section on institutional autonomy below).

Inherent in neoliberal individualism is the belief that the exercise of personal interests and pursuits should be as free and unfettered as possible, with freedom of choice and expression facilitating the optimum operation of the free market. Governments, therefore, constituted as a body of representatives elected by individuals, are expected to protect individual rights, freedoms, and security. Incorporated is the notion that individuals should encounter as little interference as possible from the state – in line with endorsement for 'small government' and low-taxing regimes. Individualism is upheld by civil liberty, civic rights, societal law, order, and national defense. Hence, from a market-liberal perspective, the role of the government should be limited to ensuring the adequacy of laws and instrumentalities to protect the individual and national rights and freedoms, and to provide safety net welfare provisions (targeted at individuals experiencing severe hardship). The quotes by Camus and Fromm encapsulate these beliefs:

More and more, when faced with the world of men, the only reaction is one of individualism. Man alone is an end unto himself. Everything one tries to do for the common good ends in failure.

(Camus, 1940, as cited in de Gramont, 1991, p. 12)

We are not on the way to greater individualism but are becoming an increasingly manipulated mass civilization.

(Fromm, 2011, p. 36)

Activities outside the 'core business' of government should be outsourced to, or bought in from, the private sector. This thinking over the past 40 years has led many governments to sell off and privatize previously publicly owned assets such as public transport, utilities (including water companies), banks, and airlines, and to allow private companies to create and operate public infrastructure for profit. Governments also cooperate with private enterprise to build social infrastructure and services through public-private partnerships (PPPs) and use private consultants to provide policy research, reviews, and advice.

However, individualism and sovereignty come with strings attached. Individuals are expected to take responsibility for themselves and their dependents, and not be reliant on the state for aid and assistance except in dire circumstances. Individualism entails taking care of one's life, with inherent responsibilities to be self-reliant, self-directed, and resourceful to achieve optimal life benefits. This means taking responsibility for costs and risks associated with one's life: managing one's ongoing learning, employment, and income, household affairs, health, family welfare, and making provisions for retirement. It also entails bearing responsibility for the consequences of one's decisions and actions. Private endeavors and insurance protection is encouraged to avoid reliance on welfare safety nets.

In this sense, a prime purpose of education is to produce self-sufficient individuals who will compete and fend for themselves and assume responsibility for their own risks and life outcomes, as rational economic subjects in the marketplace. The educated citizen going about his/her business in rational exchange thereby assists and aids fellow market players. This is the neoliberal notion of Rational Economic Man [sic] or REM. Following on from assumed rationality, REM infers a separate, self-interested, and instrumental approach to others (Hewitson, 2001).

Individualism in Education

In education, individual students or their parents/guardians exercise choice over their enrolling education institution. As individuals progress through their years of education, they exercise personal choice in the subjects they study or specialisms they wish to pursue based on individual preferences and interests. They make decisions about the length of time they will spend in formal education, including the qualifications they will attain.

Neoliberal policies suggest that education should run in parallel with economic and business needs and operate as such by being open to market competition (e.g. Productivity Commission, 2016). The current emphasis on 'consumer' choice and competition amongst 'providers' positions education as a commodity or service, with students and their parents or guardians positioned as customers or clients, vying for their individual interests and needs to be served and satisfied.

Individualism incurs individuals taking personal responsibility, including paying for the goods and services they use and from which they gain personal advantages, including in education. 'User-pays' principles apply, but under the safety net of consumer rights and protections. (Payments for education include tuition costs and costs of materials or activities, but in the compulsory years of education, most of the actual costs of education are borne by taxpayers – a point of contention for many neoliberal thinkers.)

Further, individuals are also expected to become self-regulating in terms of their personal productivity and performativity, taking responsibility for their own ongoing training and education, employability, and productivity in the workplace and society generally.

Individuation

The neoliberal principle of individualism positions education as a service that can and should be adapted and customized to meet bespoke, individual 'client' or 'customer' needs. Individualism has infiltrated stakeholder expectations such that failure for any student is no longer accepted (although this is not to say this doesn't happen). Every student is expected to learn successfully and educators are expected to tailor their programming to ensure all students' learning needs are met – referred to in policy as 'individuation.' Curriculum content, pedagogical methods, or forms of 'instruction,'[1] the speed of progression, decisions about remediation or extension – are all part of individuated learning.

Students learn at different rates (both overall and in particular learning areas), and have different strengths and interests, so there will be many methods employed to capture diverse needs. Contemporary learning spaces, especially in early learning centers and schools, are designed to cater for individual learning preferences and differences. Students can work in large or small groups or can work alone. Some students will require individual attention, others may work in small or larger groups, with activities coordinated, but not constantly controlled and directed by teachers. Students can learn from each other. With every individual being different in every way, such a learning environment is designed to be inclusive and to cater for all, while breaking down power barriers and making schooling more enjoyable, less threatening, and establishing learning as a more natural pursuit. Teachers are required to know students very well based on their everyday interactions, reflections, and assessments.

Teachers are held to account for student learning achievement and outcomes via a range of measurement schemes. Suffice to say here, stakeholders such as governments and parents want to see what students have learnt and want to know how individual student performance compares with peers of the same age via standardized testing. These stakeholders also want to see proof of progression over short periods of time (see for example, Gonski, 2018). In this way teachers and education leaders – rather than the students – often bear the blame for negative learning outcomes (based on standards, benchmarks, and comparative data).

Individuals (including parents/guardians) also expect flexibility in provisioning to suit their expectations and life circumstances. New forms of education have developed to coach and/or provide an advanced 'edge' for individuals in a competitive education system. An example is the growing trend in Pre-K education designed for pre-kindergarten-aged children (including the option of full-day courses, designed to give individuals a head start in mathematics and reading and learning to work with others to improve future school performance). In addition, education as a service focused on 'client' needs commonly offers extended hours or out-of-hours care to meet the needs of working parents/guardians.

Such is the emphasis on student success that education institutions may provide extra learning support through a range of learning support services, peer mentoring, academic study skills advisors, language assistance, student counsellors, and welfare officers. There is also a huge (unregulated) private tutoring industry providing out-of-hours tuition for those wishing to purchase extra learning support beyond regular tuition. Flexible, individualized, competency-based learning programs aim to create improved learning outcomes, including greater employment prospects and 'job readiness.'

Institutional Autonomy

Individual education institutions are expected to behave like private companies – being self-interested and acting in ways that best meet their self-interests. Individualism applies to institutions in the form of 'autonomy' and through 'deregulation' policies. Autonomy equates to institutional individualism, with each site encouraged to create the best circumstances and outcomes that it can. Institutionalized individualism via autonomy or deregulatory policies and practices save governments money and reduce governments' overall responsibility for education. Authority is assumed at the local level and decisions are based on local needs. Institutional autonomy is justified on the basis that it produces higher education performance because decisions regarding budgeting, resourcing, staffing, and learning programming are made at the local level (Caldwell, 2016). Through their own efforts, education institutions will be winners or losers.

For example, autonomous schools such as those in Australia, the UK, or New Zealand follow mandated policy stipulations but not roadmaps on how to achieve corporate strategic goals. Devolved authority conveys self-determination within broad parameters, but following government strategy, curriculum and mandated testing arrangements remain obligatory. Funding that was once the preserve of central/systemic bureaucratic experts to disperse and oversee is now delivered directly to institutions – they are empowered to be responsible for resourcing requirements. Education institutions are free to control budgets, allocate resources to areas of local need, and employ their own staff. The neoliberal implication is that education institutions should be free to develop their own distinctive characteristics to increase responsiveness to their particular clientele.

Autonomy provides freedom for each institution to develop its own unique charter and distinctive marketing strategies. Individualized marketing denoting 'point-of-difference' or a market niche and any distinctive specialisms means that marketing, advertising, branding, slogans, corporate livery, and public relations have become new burgeoning facets of education business leadership.

Self-managed education institutions are governed by their own boards/councils assuming roles of local employer and organizational oversight including greater responsibility and liability. The neoliberal rationale is that localized authority empowers parents and community stakeholders and encourages them to take a greater level of interest and responsibility for the education of their children, taking some responsibility from government while also lodging a closer level of accountability. In some Australian states, 'independent–public' school councils/boards can choose to be incorporated (exposing them to greater public regulatory scrutiny), thereby being able to extend local, autonomous decision-making to even higher levels.

In schools, for example, autonomy, deregulatory practices, and the removal of red tape is justified as an effective means by which school improvement can occur. And concomitantly, broadening students' and parental choice is also justified as an appealing solution to continual accusations of a crisis in educational standards. These neoliberal maneuvers have become progressively more entrenched since the last decades of the twentieth century.

Autonomous, deregulated institutions have to be responsible and accountable, with their performance defined, controlled, and measured by policy regimes demanding transparency and constant improvement. While neoliberal 'freedoms' for individual education institutions delivers diversity for greater choice, it also entails greater risks, especially financial and governance risks.

Other forms of individualism include merit selection in employment (used to employ or promote the best person for a job rather than following traditional pathways favoring seniority or employment longevity) – a form of competitive individualism to enhance quality and improvement.

Effects and Consequences

Education leaders' work has increased in scope and complexity as work that was once undertaken by government bureaucracies is transferred to individual institutions to be conducted at the local level. Leaders' work has intensified, their jobs require long hours and impinge heavily on personal time, while stress is a growing problem amongst both leaders and educators (see for example, Bottery, 2004; Starr, 1998). School autonomy may enable localized decision-making regarding budgeting and staffing and programming, but it also intensifies the work of education leaders in ways that detract from their so-called 'core business' of teaching and learning (Starr, 2007).

Counter-intuitively, however, education reforms espousing autonomy actually reinforce and expand centralized power – with central control over strategy, policy, and education direction, the official curriculum, the overall investment in education, and determination of the means and substance of a range of regulatory, compliance, and performance accountabilities. Targets expressed as key performance indicators are pushed down to education leaders while many leaders are expected to do more with less – particularly with budgets. Hence, autonomy shifts responsibility for outcomes and blame for any problems to the local level – and yet there is no actual power shift to the local level – core power is retained at the central level (see Starr, 2015). In addition, there are criticisms about current education bureaucracies' command-and-control, hierarchical approaches, and coercive power for change.

Education is of such national importance that the state does not want to relinquish the reins. It needs control over the policy process, including policy 'implementation' at the local level.

Hence, policy is a private matter for the state – often developed with insufficient or no consultation or collaboration with practitioners who will be charged with enacting policy. This is a form of suppression to generate control with least resistance. Policymakers have also introduced the means by which 'consumer choice' and 'market competition' spur individual institutions to lift their game in comparison with others (irrespective of contextual differences and inequities) – topics that are discussed in Part II of this book. But implicit in all these mechanisms is an assumption that professionals cannot be trusted (Strathearn, 2000).

With a focus on merit selection for staff, leaders are now contracted on a limited tenure basis. This is both a risk management strategy but also a means of ensuring leaders are kept on their toes and focused on strategic improvement – or they will lose their jobs to competition.

Whereas individualism is valorized for parents and students, neoliberal policies do not support individualism within the teaching profession. Accountabilities, audits, testing regimes, and standardized curricula all control teachers and limit teacher autonomy. Teachers and education leaders are expected to be compliant and accommodating of political mandates for policy reforms. Individuals are less likely to have the courage to speak out against policy or accountability impositions for fear of losing their jobs or being sidelined. For educators, agency is constrained and restricted while their professional choices are tightly controlled.

Education authorities may argue that their people (employees) are their prime assets, but in reality, employees in education often don't perceive such warm sentiments or engagement. There are elements of feeling distanced while expectations are considered to be unrealistic and unresponsive to real-life needs. Individuals working intensively are increasingly finding their work to be atomistic, with repercussions good and bad borne alone by the individual worker.

Individualism cuts at the very heart of education which promotes collegiality, dialogue, and debate, and the canvassing of many standpoints. Importantly, work atomization also undercuts democratic processes of any kind. Educators complain that they are losing control of their 'professionalism' (see for example, Stroud, 2018).

Institutional autonomy is appreciated and supported by the majority of education leaders who like freedom in decision-making, although their comments are tempered with concerns about systemic constraints on this autonomy (see Chapters 11 and 15; see also Starr, 2015). There are further concerns that institutional autonomy in a climate of competition (see Chapter 6) can undermine collegiality across institutions. Exacerbating this criticism is the fact that intensified work encourages a myopic leadership focus within the limits of the institutional gates, leaving little time for anything beyond the immediate (see Chapter 10).

Education leaders see that the primacy of neoliberal sovereignty is making education more highly competitive across its many realms. Individualism literally encourages single-mindedness and self-interest – an 'I'/'me' as opposed to 'we'/'us' orientation to life – resulting in less collaboration and cooperation amongst institutions, students, educators, and education leaders. But there are contradictions and paradoxes within the 'individualism' push including traditions around age-based learning progression and the state's heavy reliance on standardization, including standardized testing, which calibrates and reduces individual differences into a standardized scale. In fact, the huge diversity amongst individuals is ignored by standardized curriculum, testing, and progression (see Starr, 2015).

Expectations about individuation raise the expectations of parents and governments, yet educators argue that these stakeholders have little understanding of educational realities. For example, in some contexts there are behavior problems amongst students (Letters to the Editor, *The Times*, 2018, p. 28), meeting students' welfare needs may be required (such as providing a breakfast program), while traditional education architecture mitigates against teachers working in teams to better attend to myriad individual student needs.

Concluding Remarks

Institutionally and amongst individual people, a focus on competitive individualism is underpinned by the notion of 'survival of the fittest.' Hence, institutions appealing to consumers and responding to consumer needs gain enrollments and subsequent per capita funding benefits, and the individuals who exert most effort and demonstrate superior outcomes will achieve and reap high rewards. Inherent in this thinking is an acceptance of inequity and inequality within education and society generally – as indicated by Adam Smith:

Civil government, so far as it is instituted for the security of property, is in reality instituted for the defense of the rich against the poor, or of those who have some property against those who have none at all.

(Adam Smith)

The focus on individualism has many downsides. Leaders view it as having created unfortunate human realities – alienation and increasingly personal anxieties – while encouraging some negative human traits: hedonism, narcissism, and selfishness. Leaders report increasingly polarized views amongst students and parents, a growing lack of respect and tolerance for views that do not concur with personal views, and a lack of courtesy and respect in political debates that undermine notions of both compromise and consensus (an issue discussed further in Chapter 14).

The focus on the individual creates public policy pressures for other neoliberal mantras, such as the emphases on choice and competition, showing how all features of neoliberalism are inextricably linked. These themes are explored in the following chapters.

Note

1 The term 'instruction' is inherently problematic from a critical perspective. It is suggestive of traditional chalk-and-talk, didactic teaching. However, given the word's current widespread usage, acceptance and understanding, I use it – reluctantly – here

References

Bottery, M. (2004). *The challenges of educational leadership.* London, England: SAGE.

Caldwell, B. (2016). *The autonomy premium: Professional autonomy and student achievement in the 21st century.* Camberwell, VIC: ACER Press.

Campbell, J. (with Bill Moyers). (1988). *The power of myth.* Documentary Series. USA: PBS.

De Gramont, A. (1991). *Albert Camus:Between hell and reason: Essays from The Resistance newspaper, 'Combat', 1944–1947.* (Selected and translated by A. de Gramont). Hanover, NH: University Press of New England, p. 12.

Fromm, E. (2011). *The revolution of hope: Towards a humanized technology.* New York, NY: Lantern Books.

Gonksi, D. (Chair) (2018). *Through growth to achievement: Report of the review to achieve educational excellence in Australian schools, March 2018.* Canberra, ACT: Commonwealth of Australia.

Hewitson, G. (2001). Feminist economics: Interrogating the masculinity of Rational Economic Man. *Journal of Economic Issues, 35*(1), 219–221.

Machiavelli, N. (2009). *The prince.* London, England: Vintage Publishing.

Mises, L. von (1969). *Socialism: An economic and sociological analysis.* London, England: Jonathan Cape, p. 97.

Productivity Commission (2016). *Introducing competition and informed user choice into human services: Identifying sectors for reform.* Canberra, ACT: Australian Government. Retrieved November 30, 2017 from www.pc.gov.au/inquiries/completed/human-services/identifying-reform/report/human-services-identifying-reform-overview.pdf

Rand, A. (1964). *The virtue of selfishness: A new concept of egoism.* New York, NY: New American Library.

Smith, A. (1776). *The wealth of nations, Book V, Chapter 1, Part 11 On the expense of justice.* London, England: W. Strahan & T. Cadell, p. 207.

Spencer, N. (2012). Machiavelli's The Prince, part 7: The two sides of human nature. *The Guardian*, May 7, 2012. Retrieved April 3, 2017 from www.theguardian.com/comm entisfree/2012/may/07/prince-machiavelli-human-nature

Starr, K. (1998). Power and production in local school management. *South Australian Educational Leader*, 9(4), 1–12.

Starr, K. (2007). Capacity building for the Principalship: Will leadership development solve the problem of Principal disengagement? *The International Journal of Knowledge, Culture and Change Management*, 6(8), 189–198.

Starr, K. E. (2015). *Education game changers: Leadership and the consequence of policy paradox.* Lanham, MD: Rowman & Littlefield.

Strathearn, M. (2000). The tyranny of transparency. *British Educational Research Journal*, 26(3), 309–321.

Stroud, G. (2018). *Teacher: One woman's struggle to keep the heart in teaching.* Crows Nest, NSW: Allen & Unwin.

The Times Letters to the Editor (2018). The elephant in the classroom: Misbehavior. *The Times*, September 28, 2018, p. 28.

4

PRIVATIZATION

The neoliberal precept of individualism implicitly embraces and supports privatization and private ownership. Privatization dismantles large-scale government investment in the public sphere – in line with precepts of small government and the rolled-back or minimal state. In other words, privatization enables governments to divest themselves of funding, provision, and management responsibilities and hand them over to the private sector. Private companies and institutions can be for-profit or not-for-profit, but either way, the private sector is considered to be more efficient and effective than publicly owned and operated enterprises.

Privatization is promoted as another aspect associated with individualism – with the privatized institutions being the favored model for government education provisioning (see for example, DeVos in Stossel, 2018). Private provisioning provides greater institutional diversity for choice and enhances a sense amongst citizens that they must take responsibility for their own education. Hence, there are private education institutions – some dependent on private income and philanthropic donations as well as government grants (such as independent schools in Australia), and a newer 'for-profit' education sector – the fastest growing post-secondary education sector in the USA (Deming, Goldin, & Katz, 2013).

Privatization in education comes in many guises, amongst them:

- legislative deregulation to remove barriers or impediments to private operations in the education market
- consultants (employed through tendered contacting) instead of permanent public servants – to provide briefings and advice, or undertake research, reviews, or evaluations for governments or education systems. (The assumption being that private consultants are objective and not self-serving, their services are efficient and timely, and their short-time contractual engagement

enables flexibility and saves the costs associated with full-time, permanent bureaucrats housed in permanent premises.)

- the sale of public education assets or services to private companies and providers
- outsourcing services once controlled by government (anything from cleaning, maintenance and transportation, to delivery of specialized services such as speech therapy, professional learning, and training), enabling further workforce flexibility and cost savings
- public-private partnerships, whereby governments collaborate with the private sector to provide public facilities (including schools and shared facility complexes)
- the creation of a new class of teachers who do not hold education qualifications (see LaLonde, Brewer, & Lubienski, 2015)
- user-pays or consumer contribution schemes, such as student loan schemes to fund university tuition
- private agencies who find students or staff for education institutions and education institutions for students (especially international full-fee-paying students).

These types of practices are examples of both the savings governments can make as they withdraw from direct public provisioning, as well as the state's changed role and responsibilities under neoliberal policies promoting privatization.

However, private education is not new. In previous centuries before public education became social policy, the only forms of education available were those provided by private providers. And in reality, schools exist on a continuum of 'publicness' with traditional public schools at one end of the spectrum and for-profit charter schools operated by education management organizations (EMOs) at the other (Oberfield & Henig, 2017).

The continuum demonstrates various positions from traditional local schooling to complete privatization, from not-for-profit to for-profit provisioning. There is as much institutional diversity within private and public sectors as there is across them.

Privatization in education is still in a phase of intense development, so comparisons will continue to emerge. Oberfield and Henig (2017) point out, however, that the level of private funding in education strongly influences the nature of education programs offered, the working conditions of teachers and education leaders, and stakeholder relationships.

Privatization is often justified through assertions that publicly funded education has failed. Neoliberals suggest that education has been captured by its 'providers' (provider capture) who are reluctant to change or improve. Persistent neoliberal reproaches suggest that education:

- is resistant to change
- is held back by conservative bureaucracies with little incentive for improvement
- is too controlled by education unions

- is unresponsive to public expectations and therefore to market impetus
- standards are too low and/or dropping
- ill-prepares students for the workforce
- shows little or no observable improvement in light of its increasing expenditure (it provides an inadequate return on investment).

The championed solution is to hand education over to the private sector whose impetus derives from market forces to achieve superior outcomes. Implicit is the view that successful institutions and companies deliver on consumer needs and 'customer' expectations of continual improvement and high achievement levels (see for example, DeVos in Stossel, 2018; Riggan, 2012). For example, Riggan (2012), reporting for the American Enterprise Institute (a conservative think tank), found that the private sector has high sensitivity to constructive criticism (especially in the case of newcomers in the for-profit education market) because their commercial survival depends on the positive perceptions of independent customers, investors, and shareholders. Positive satisfaction levels enhance reputations, and drive growth and future custom.

A good example of privatized and autonomous education is that of charter schools in the USA. A publicly funded school can be become a charter school, often through parent 'trigger' systems legitimized through state-based legislation. Parents can take control and trigger the conversion of a neighborhood school into a charter school. Charter schools are managed by private companies with private investors who profit from them. The view is that poorly performing schools run by school districts are hindered by factors such as top-down, remote district management, inflexible teacher unions and collective bargaining agreements, and staff seniority rules placing the interests of teachers and administrators ahead of children and parents (see Chubb & Moe, 1990).

Parent trigger laws circumvent difficult governance arrangements such as drawn-out and cumbersome district negotiation processes or disagreements with voters during school board elections (see Lubienski & Lee, 2016). Thus, charter schools are designed to overcome mediocrity and bypass bureaucratic red tape by providing schools with autonomy from district regulation and 'provider capture,' even though funding is provided by school districts.

Parents can enroll their children in the charter school of their choice rather than being assigned a school placement via strict zoning regulations. This creates a market incentive for innovation and responsiveness or charter schools risk losing parent support and students and, therefore, funding.

Charter schools can operate without interference from teacher unions, operating with contracted, non-permanent teachers whose ongoing employment is contingent on results – success being determined by improved students' results in standardized tests.

Charter schools are supported by powerful advocates, including the Melinda and Bill Gates Foundation (which invests heavily in education) and the Walton

Family Trust (founders of the Walmart store chain) (see for example, Denvir, 2013; DeVos as cited in Stossel, 2018), while Denvir (2013) reports that privately funded lobby groups actively campaign against teachers and their unions in support of increased private management in education.

Some school districts are now entirely operated under private management through outsourcing agreements with the full consent of parents, forcing the closure of many public schools.

Critique

Critics dispute the idea that privatizing education is the silver bullet that guarantees higher results. Both private and public education sectors show a huge variation amongst their institutions. Differences in students' academic performance are much more pronounced within rather than between sectors, whether charter schools, public schools, or other independent private schools (Lubienski, 2013). And there are charter schools that lag behind demographically comparable conventional public schools in terms of academic performance (see Miron & Urschel, 2012). Socio-economic factors and a range of other variables influence communities and have subsequent effects on their schools.

There are concerns that constant criticism of public schools and teachers stem from ulterior, neoliberal motives towards privatization. As Denvir (2013) claims from a U.S. perspective:

> The so-called school reform movement declares that public education has failed American students. But in reality, it is the policies of brutal austerity, relentless standardized testing, and teacher bashing that ensure failure – and promote privatization as the only solution. And so the beast is starved: fewer resources, fewer teachers, fewer aides to make schools safe and a worse education. Better yet, the more teachers employed in typically non-union charters, the weaker the political movement to defend public schools.

The gamesmanship is part of an ongoing battle over who will control public education dollars, and to what end – a game of institutional catallaxy (see Chapter 2). Denvir (2013) argues that political discourse in the U.S. is overpowered by a 'reform' agenda seeking to re-invent public schools in the image of corporate America. Self-described reformers (well-organized think tanks, philanthropic organizations, media outlets, bloggers, lobby and advocacy groups, or 'intermediary organizations') propose busting teachers' unions, heightening the stakes in standardized testing, and pushing districts to spend a growing share of their shrinking budgets on privately managed charters. Hence, a charter school movement that seeks wholesale privatization of school districts while opposing oversight of under-performing schools poses an existential threat to public education (Denvir, 2013; LaLonde et al., 2015; Strauss, 2013).

A further criticism of privatization in education concerns the rise of the 'for-profit' sector with its primacy in the profit motive and subsequent negative effects. There are many examples of private education providers cutting corners, engaging in dodgy or illegal practices, who dupe their 'customers' while dumbing down education and reducing its quality and service (see for example, Hil, 2012; Leahy, 2015; Morton & Brown, 2016).

There are also criticisms about *sub rosa* (secret) contracting surrounding private involvement or provisioning in education. Such contracts are commercial in-confidence – private, confidential, even though public monies from taxpayers are also involved.

The pursuit of custom and customer satisfaction may detract from education itself. Lubienski (2005), for example, found that when faced with competition, schools use money for promotional rather than educational purposes to leverage their position in the marketplace.

Lastly, the preference for private consultants over traditional education officials or education practitioners to create savings meets concerns about private 'commercial-in-confidence' contracts and lists of 'preferred providers.' Policymakers may gain a sense of legitimacy through the use of supposedly arms-length, 'objective' private means – especially where there are fears that policy reforms may be unpopular in the education sector – but in reality these are expensive exercises that may ensure further contracted engagements by telling governments what they want to hear (see for example, Berkovic, 2017).

In sum, privatization is a major means by which neoliberalism has been entrenched in education. The effects on policy, practice, and provision are changing the role of the state, perceptions about, and the very nature of, education.

References

Berkovic, N. (2017). $10b to outsource bureaucracy. *The Weekend Australian*, December 29, 2017. Retrieved January 3, 2018 from www.theaustralian.com.au/national-affairs/10bn-bill-to-outsource-bureaucracy/news-story/e959b7e30351d35e0df30fbd5c536629

Chubb, J. E., & Moe, T. M. (1990). *Politics, markets and America's schools*. Washington, DC: Brookings Institute Press.

Deming, D., Goldin, C., & Katz, L. (2013). For-profit colleges. *Harvard Scholar*, 23(1), 137–163. Denvir, D. (2013). The solution to US public schools is not corporate America. *The Guardian*, June 24, 2013. Retrieved February 20, 2017 from www.theguardian.com/commentisfree/2013/jun/24/us-public-schools-budget-crisis

Hil, R. (2012). *Whackademia: An insider's account of the troubled university*. Sydney, NSW: NewSouth Publishing, University of New South Wales Press Ltd.

LaLonde, P., Brewer, T. J., & Lubienski, C. (2015). Teach For America and Teach For All: Creating an intermediary organization network for global education reform. *Education Policy Analysis Archives*, 23(47), April 20, 2015. Retrieved April 4, 2017 from https://files.eric.ed.gov/fulltext/EJ1070361.pdf

Leahy, M. (2015). Reforming vocational education: It's time to end the exploitation of vulnerable people. *The Conversation*, December 16, 2015. Retrieved April 4, 2017 from https://theconversation.com/reforming-vocational-education-its-time-to-end-the-exploitation-of-vulnerable-people-51396

Lubienski, C. (2005). Public schools in marketized environments: Shifting incentives and unintended consequences of competition-based educational reforms. *American Journal of Education*, 111(4), 464–486.

Lubienski, C. (2013). Privatizing form or function? Equity, outcomes and influence in American charter schools. *Oxford Review of Education*, 39(4), 498–513.

Lubienski, C., & Lee, J. (2016). Competitive incentives and the education market: How charter schools define themselves in metropolitan Detroit. *Peabody Journal of Education*, 91(1), 64–80.

Miron, G., & Urschel, J. L. (2012). *Understanding and improving full-time virtual schools*. Boulder, CO: National Education Policy Center, School of Education, University of Colorado. Retrieved March 31, 2018 from https://files.eric.ed.gov/fulltext/ED533960.pdf

Morton, R., & Brown, G. (2016). No kidding, the last laugh's on day-care cheat who stole $3.6m. *The Australian*, November 25, 2016, p. 1.

Oberfield, Z. W., & Henig, J. R. (2017). *Are charters different?: Public education, teachers, and the charter school debate*. Boston, MA: Harvard Education Press.

Riggan, M. (2012). *Private enterprise in American education. Special Report 5. Between Efficiency and effectiveness: Evaluation of for-profit education organizations*, April 2012. Washington, DC: American Enterprise Institute.

Strauss, V. (2013). How closing schools hurts neighborhoods. *The Washington Post*, March 6, 2013.

Stossel, J. (2018). *Reason: Interview with Betsy DeVos*, May 8, 2018. Retrieved March 1, 2018 from www.youtube.com/watch?v=ydVKyDgw_SM

5

CHOICE

Choice is the enabler of individualism. Individuals need choices to ensure their needs are met and to pursue their interests and preferences. Choice empowers individual 'consumers' by personalizing decisions about goods, services, associations, and life activities. Without choice, people cannot express or exercise their individual freedoms. Choice is a democratic right, entailing options and diversity.

Neoliberals endorse the right of sovereign 'consumers' to make choices in every aspect of life – in family and working life, including in education. Having choice in education provides alternatives to suit individual interests and preferences, whether it be in the choice of education institutions, courses, or programs.

Taking schools as an example – a choice of schools gives parents control over their child's education with individual preferences being influenced by school type, location, academic performance, courses, programs, extra-curricular activities, pedagogical approaches, price, facilities and resources, philosophical orientation, or alignment with particular affiliations as in the case of faith-based institutions. Parents' choices include judgments and perceptions about 'quality' (programs, teachers, pastoral care, leadership) and reputation, which can be influenced by the biases and choices of family or friends.

School choices reflect parents' beliefs and ideas about the purposes of education – whether education is a property right (owned by individuals for the benefit of individuals) or a personal right (the rights of every individual that benefits everyone in society) or a mixture of both. Allen and Burgess (2014) argue that the following factors incentivize choice in schooling:

- strong academic results (including standardized test and exam results)
- proximity to home
- a school's reputation based on student behavior

- the socio-economic composition of the student enrollment
- formal but also informal comparative information about the school (from league tables, reviews, prospectuses, but also from personal social networks)
- the ability of siblings to enroll
- values affiliation, including faith-based alignment.

Through their choices parents can affect the kinds of ideas and classmates their children encounter since schools attract like-minded parents and students. In other words, a 'birds of a feather flock together' kind of social engineering can occur, which is designed to scaffold beliefs and enhance supportive social networks. Inherent in choices are individual beliefs about society and the 'good' life (see, for example, Bryk, Holland, & Lee, 1993; Coleman, Hoffer, & Kilgore, 1982; Coleman, 1988). And schools can market themselves to appeal to certain consumer preferences.

However, it is still the case that most parents choose a neighborhood school through convenience, the lower costs and transportation time involved, and because their children's classmates will most likely live nearby.

In many Anglophone countries there has been bi-partisan political support for school choice to provide scope and diversity in the education 'marketplace.'

Rationalizing Choice

Neoliberal proponents view school choice as an equity issue, since it provides all parents from poor or affluent areas with the opportunity of enrolling their child in a high-quality school. Fundamentally such a position accepts the impossibility of achieving equal quality in education – in teaching or resourcing (see for example, Boyd, Lankford, Loeb, & Wyckoff, 2005; Nechyba, 2006; Peske & Haycock, 2006; Sirin, 2005) – a criticism of neoliberal public provisioning of any kind. Neoliberalism tolerates inequities as a natural outcome of individuals' choices in life.

Choice theory suggests that individuals' preferences act as market indicators and the market responds accordingly by adjusting supply to meet demand. The market reads consumers' needs, demands, and expectations, and 'service providers' respond, and in so doing, compete for custom and preference – in the case of education, for enrollments and, therefore, funding. Hence, there is strong inter-complementarity between neoliberal choice and competition, with every education institution becoming an individual competing unit. Competition for enrollments in turn promotes innovation and other entrepreneurial activities towards improvement. Choices, therefore, are believed to influence and incentivize development and advancement, and have a positive effect on education.

School choice frustrates traditions such as enrollment zoning regulation, which guarantees a place for every child living within a defined catchment area, and mitigates against the notion of the 'local school.' Choice advocates, therefore, push for deregulation – in this example, for open admission policies to stimulate and enhance choice and options for improvement (see Ball, 2018).

The free market view is that traditional provisioning is monopolistic and inefficient, captured by 'providers' (educators and education leaders), with little or no incentive to improve and with little consequence for poor performance. From a neoliberal perspective, private organizations are perceived to perform better than publicly run systems controlled by permanent public officials who rob individuals and schools from making independent decisions based on consumer demand (see for example, Chubb & Moe, 1990). Neoliberal market theory suggests that economic benefits derived through market competition include higher productivity, superior 'outputs,' and a greater return on investment.

From this perspective, consumer choice enhances education's 'successes' and roots out its failures – the winners and losers – identified through supply and demand theory (see for example, Friedman, 1955). Choice sorts schools through their levels of sponsorship – in other words, education institutions "need to remain competitive to survive" (ISCA, 2017). If choice is taken to its logical conclusion, schools that do well in the battle for enrollments may easily become over-subscribed (full to quota with waiting lists of potential enrollees). Non-competitive institutions will either improve to re-gain market confidence, or consumers will 'vote with their feet' and withdraw enrollments. 'Failing' institutions will also lose the faith of governments, become unviable, and be forced to close (see for example, Guerra, 2018; NEPC, 2017).

'Successful' schools are primarily calibrated through student achievement outcomes, measured through formal high-stakes 'objective' standardized testing regimes which have become the measure of schools' productivity and overall performance amongst OECD countries.

Individual choices, however, have broader consequences. Governments facing competing demands have to make decisions that may not suit all individuals or institutions, but they can distance themselves somewhat from resourcing decisions, since the neoliberal principle of choice effectively shifts decision-making into the hands of consumers. Resource allocation rests on the choices of independent players, so in subtle ways, school choice is intertwined with notions of public accountability.

Making rational choices depends on individual consumers having access to transparent information – such as comparative data – so they can make optimal judgments to suit their preferences and circumstances. Comparative school performance data provides parents with assurance that they are doing the best for their children by choosing the most suitable and appropriate option. Choice advocates argue that for the education market to work, funding allocations have to follow their choices. For example, the Brookings Institute argues that:

> ...parents should be afforded the maximum degree of choice, provided with valid information on the performance of the education programs that are available, and have their preferences for education programs reflected in the funding of those programs.
>
> *(Greene et al., 2010, p. 4)*

Being inextricably linked to consumer power, choice theory also seeks to empower local consumers, by ensuring education institutions have autonomy to meet market needs. Hence, education choice is not only an important feature of individual freedom but it is entwined with institutional autonomy (or institutional sovereignty). The 'benefits' of school choice are considered more effective when combined with school autonomy alongside strong accountability mechanisms to ensure quality (see for example, Wößmann, 2007). These accountabilities include governance oversight at the immediate institutional level. Parents join institutional education leaders as the new operatives of education, with leaders being answerable to school boards or councils.

Autonomous schools are also 'choosers,' and, in many jurisdictions, can choose their own staff, and make spending choices and internal decisions about programs and pedagogy. Institutional autonomy is presumed to incentivize student achievement, school performance, innovation, cost-effectiveness, efficiency, and diversity in education provision.

School autonomy – or institutional individualism – is inextricably bound with notions of education being a private rather than a public matter. Autonomous and privatized schools are presumed to be more cost-efficient and of higher quality (see Chapter 3; see also, for example, Rizvi, 2016). Hence, choice theorists encourage private education and independent–public schools. This equates with notions of 'small government' as well as preferences for deregulation and the removal of governmental red tape. Hence deregulated education markets have enabled a wide range of providers to enter the marketplace, including a rapidly growing 'for-profit' sector. Endorsement for choice, autonomy, and privatization is expressed by the Brookings Institute thus:

> Arguments for school choice include improving school quality and efficiency through competition among schools for students; enhancing opportunity for students from disadvantaged families who may otherwise be trapped in ineffective schools; and spurring innovation through the greater administrative autonomy likely to exist in schools of choice.
>
> *(Greene et al., 2010, p. 1)*

There are many examples across the world of government encouragement for the exercise of consumer choice in schools, such as:

- The USA's 2001 *No Child Left Behind* (Elementary and Secondary Education) Act which exposed low-performing schools so that enrollments could be transferred to high-performing schools
- Australia's *My School* website, which publishes comparative data about every school in the nation
- Charter schools and parent trigger legislation (see Rogers, Lubienski, Scott, & Welner, 2015)

- The UK's school performance tables and Ofsted (school inspection) reports to assist parents in researching and comparing "the quality of teaching in schools" (Gov.UK, 2018).

As sovereign individuals are free to make choices in exercising their self-interests, so institutional autonomy enables schools to determine their niche market positioning and to make decisions to suit their targeted 'clientele.' To inform consumers, school promotion and marketing (branding) are encouraged. In this way, choice also creates market diversity in the sector to enable wider choices to meet equally diverse needs. Choice also applies to teachers and leaders who have agency in deciding where they work – where to sell their labor power – so staff too can determine which employer will best meet their self-interests.

These efforts illustrate a reimagined role of the state. Local authority over education services and operations is the direct responsibility of education institutions and their governing authorities. Governments' role is to control overarching policies, curriculum frameworks and national/state education budgets, while facilitating independence and competition at the local level.

In summary, choice proponents support:

- choice for everyone in all areas of education
- diversity of education provisioning to increase options for choice
- open admission/enrollment systems
- transparent institutional accountability with comparable reporting of institutional performance
- funding that follows enrollment choices
- institutional autonomy so each institution can respond to market demands and expectations
- flexible provisioning
- the closure (non-funding) of unpopular 'failing' schools (see for example, De Vos in Stossel, 2018; Greene et al., 2010).

Choice in education demands diversity in type and delivery design. A few examples in the schooling sector are described below.

Government Schools

Students are guaranteed a place in, and can attend, their local government provided and funded school. These are elementary, primary, or secondary schools, but sometimes alternatives are available such as selective schools (who choose their students, usually based on high academic results), technical or vocational schools, or schools catering for students with special needs. These schools are free to attend, albeit with the usual school-imposed fees or levies, but the major cost is borne by local tax payers.

Autonomous Government-Funded Schools

These are government-funded schools granted total autonomy. Examples include independent-public schools operating in some Australian states (e.g. over 80% of Western Australian government schools are independent-public schools), while other jurisdictions operate policies of 'default autonomy,' handing more authority and responsibility to schools and their governing bodies away from bureaucratic oversight from local education authorities.

The UK education system offers a wide range of school choices funded by government (and chosen by school communities but with diminished support from local authorities). For example, there are sponsored, chain or converter academies, and free schools that are faith based or offering specialisms, as well as university technical colleges, studio schools, and presumption schools.

The USA's charter schools are independently run, publicly funded schools that are exempted from many rules and regulations. They have more autonomy in exchange for increased accountability (see Elmore, 2003). Typically, if charters receive more applications than they have vacancies, enrollment may rely on a lottery.

Private/Independent Schools

Private or independent fee-paying schools are less restricted and can determine most aspects of their operations without direct oversight by government bureaucratic strictures. Private schools may be part of an education system affiliated with a church or faith, but they can also be standalone institutions operating totally independently without any form of systemic support and relying primarily or solely on privately sourced revenues, mostly through fees paid by parents. (Compliance with state-approved curriculum and testing arrangements is expected, and they are usually licensed to operate subject to state-sponsored review processes.) They may also receive some government funding (as is the case in Australia).

Schools Offering Alternative Approaches

This includes institutions following specific pedagogies or philosophies such as Steiner Waldorf and Montessori schools, or schools such as A. S. Neill's Summerhill School (Neill, 1960).

Home Schooling

Individual freedom gives parents the right to educate their children at home, with teaching provided by the parent/s or someone appointed by the parent/s. The number of students being home schooled is increasing (Locke, 2017; Un, 2016; Urban, 2018).[1]

Virtual/Cyber Schools/e-Learning

Virtual education (mostly for-profit) is cited as being the fastest growing education sector in the USA (Miron & Urschel, 2012), and includes virtual charter schools. Virtual schools meet neoliberal tenets of choice and efficiency. They are cost and labor efficient. They do not require a campus, permanent staff, or extra resources. Virtual education is anytime, anywhere, on any device, and offers economies of scale. Online provisioning is appealing to governments as an innovative way of expanding education reach while saving on most of its costs.[2]

Vouchers

The ultimate case for choice comes down to voucher systems which have been promoted for decades by free market liberal advocates as the best and fairest form of consumer empowerment. Vouchers are pronounced as an equitable and portable education funding mechanism enabling an equivalent per capita funding for each child. Voucher systems enable parents to choose any school, anywhere, in any education system with governments writing the check.

The USA's education savings accounts are a type of voucher whereby parents receive a percentage of the funding required to educate a child in a public school to be spent instead in the private sector. Voucher systems are rare, however, although they exist in a few U.S. states and are regularly discussed as a viable funding option in school choice and funding debates (see for example, The Friedman Foundation for Educational Choice/EdChoice, 2017).

Critique

Choice opponents believe that putting schools to market to compete and meet individual rather than collective interests serves only to advantage some individuals at the expense of others. Choice undermines the common weal and increases social disparities.

In reality some individuals have many more choices than others, especially families with higher incomes (see for example, Choy, 1997). Factors such as rurality, distance, as well as familial or socio-economic circumstances are significant, as are related issues such as costs, a lack of transportation, or time to travel. Hence, the mantra of choice is empty when for many, a lack of alternatives means no choice at all. The effects of school choice are most clearly demonstrated in resourcing inequalities, with choice decisions hitting hardest on the poorest schools. As Greene et al. (2010, p. 2) explain, opponents believe choice:

> ...will stratify students by family background, result in niche schools that do not convey the nation's common heritage, provide taxpayer support for religious instruction, and nullify the advantages of standardization in

curriculum, teacher preparation, and management that accrue when schooling systems are designed to deliver a common educational experience across
a universe of schools. Opponents of choice also argue that many traditional
public schools perform superbly and that those that do not can be improved
through better resource allocation and management.

Choice proponents, on the other hand, suggest that what is on offer for free is
disparate in terms of quality and reputation: "[the]... reality of public schooling is
that the quality of schools is substantially correlated with geography and parental
income" (Choy, 1997; Greene et al., 2010, p. 2). The current correlation between
parents' high socio-economic status and enrollments in schools in locations where
house prices are high cannot be denied (Allen & Burgess, 2014). So, the pro-choice
question is: why should parents settle for the local offering if it isn't good enough?
This concern is espoused by the USA's Secretary for Education, Betsy DeVos, who
explains why she considers the traditional public education system a "dead end":

America falls further behind, too many kids are denied an opportunity, too
many kids get substandard educations, the status quo remains, change is
thwarted, and everyone loses. Let me give you a real world example of what
I'm talking about, and I would like you to think about this as if we were
talking about your own children. Here are your two choices. Alpha School is
a high-performing school, with graduation rates ranging from 70–90 percent,
depending on the year. Beta School is a low-performing school, with graduation rates hovering around 50 percent. If you were given the choice
between Alpha School and Beta School for your children, which would you
choose? If you chose Alpha School, then in Washington, D.C., you chose a
private or charter school for your kids. If you chose Beta School, then in
Washington, D.C., you chose the traditional public school.

(cited in Strauss, 2016)

Similarly, Caplan (2018) argues that 'ubiquitous' 'useless education' is a waste of time
and money. Opponents, however, endorse a vision of every school being a quality
school, irrespective of location or socio-economic demographics (see for example,
Teese, 2011). Pro-public advocates push for needs-based funding policies to reflect
schools' contextual differences as a means by which the most disadvantaged students
can receive the most government support in attempts to reduce inequities (see for
example, Gonski, 2011).

There is research evidence demonstrating parents' increasing reliance on publicly
available, comparative data sets about schools, particularly standardized testing
results and league tables (Allen & Burgess, 2014). Yet these data sets are highly
unreliable and a very crude measure of what schools actually achieve – a matter
discussed in more detail later in this book. But a negative consequence is that parents' choices based on high-stakes test scores can incentivize schools to admit high-

performing students rather than those whose learning needs are more resource intensive (Burgess, Propper, Slater, & Wilson, 2005).

Choice outcomes result in poorer schools taking the lion's share of responsibility for students with the greatest needs (Choy, 1997).[3] This is laudable but unfair if student outcomes are under par and the school is punished and subsequently under-resourced. Schools deemed to be 'failing' due to low test scores also pay the price of low reputation or closure. School closures usually occur in the poorest districts with the fewest options, which diminishes options even further, making the lives of the neediest even more difficult (see for example, Lee & Lubienski, 2017; Strauss, 2013). These activities can result in populations being further segregated along social, cultural, racial, and economic lines. Such divisions are undesirable for communities, societies, and nations, yet neoliberalism engineers such outcomes.

Critiques of school choice raise controversies about for-profit education, where profits go to investors (shareholders), where students and their learning are not the prime concerns, and where institutions promise more than they deliver (see for example, Knee, 2016). Independent schools that are faith based are also criticized by some for being in violation of the separation of powers (church and state) (see for example, Taylor, 2017).

For a range of valid reasons, critics argue that the 'maximum utility' assumptions within rational choice theory do not hold up. In reality, education is a field about which everyone has an opinion and therefore many non-rational decisions abound. Wide-ranging standpoints are based on equally diverse information from formal and informal sources – or lack thereof. 'Rationality' cannot be guaranteed in choice making in education or anything else.

Also along these lines, choice critics argue that while choice is an individual matter, 'herding' is also a choice and the more common instinct in human nature – that is, people are social beings and tend to do as others close by do, with private thoughts or observations often being secondary considerations (Baddeley, 2009). Herding infers a benefit – safety in numbers – and individuals are likely to go along with a majority view because it is riskier and uncomfortable being considered contrarian, unusual, or an outlier to populist thought (see Baddeley, 2017).

Teaching quality always appears in parent choice debates (see for example, De Vos in Stossel, 2018). The assumption is that the 'best' teachers are in the highest-performing schools. However, this belief ignores the obvious – schools considered to be the 'best' are usually located in wealthy suburbs, where students reap the rewards of their social advantages and achieve to higher levels without having to contend with social disadvantages. Pupils enrolled in the wealthiest schools are not more intelligent; they and their parents often simply have a greater wherewithal to support learning and achievement. Schools in such circumstances reap rewards of higher sponsorship, higher funding, and more fortuitous reputations. Meanwhile teachers in disadvantaged schools must meet a broader range of students' learning and social needs (Choy, 1997).

Importantly, it is true that within every school in every sector and of every type, there are good, bad, and mediocre institutions (see Lubienski & Lubienski, 2013). Choice and type does not guarantee quality and 'success.' It is also impossible to satisfy demands for all choices – for a huge range of reasons, many choices will remain unmet (Allen & Burgess, 2014) – the 'invisible hand' of the market will always be distorted to some degree in education.

Parents' choices in schooling demonstrate different visions of education and society and the differing value sets that underpin them. Advocates for choice want more tailored or bespoke services and provisioning to meet their personal preferences. Pro-choice proponents valorize the market as the best means of meeting individual needs, raising quality, and enhancing the lives of all citizens, albeit with outcomes being different and diverse – but consider that everyone will benefit nonetheless. Opponents are concerned that neoliberalism's emphasis on choice is breaking down long-held beliefs about the secular nature of public education. They view the pursuit of the market and self-interest in education as undermining, de-stabilizing, and enfeebling its most important purposes of acting for the common good (a matter discussed in the final chapters).

Notes

1 Reasons for home schooling are many, but common explanations include dissatisfaction with existing formal school provisions; children's experiences of bullying, mistreatment, or their dislike of schools; the desire for one-on-one attention; or a distrust in formal education systems (which includes dissatisfaction with programs, teaching staff, teaching methods), or disagreement with policy requirements such as compulsory vaccinations. The state allocates funds to schools based on enrollment numbers, but these funds are not available to parents who decide to school their children at home. So, in most jurisdictions, home schooling incurs a saving for governments but a cost to parents. Home schoolers consider that this situation is inequitable when they also have to bear costs associated with lost income (if a parent is the teacher) or hiring another adult to teach their children at home.

2 Many commentators consider e-schooling to be the most contentious and prolific rival to traditional schooling seen to date – an education game changer (Greene et al., 2010). However, the quality of online provisioning is inconsistent (Miron & Urschel, 2012).

3 Choy (1997), for example, found that public school populations are generally larger as are class sizes than in private schools. Their enrollment is more racially and ethnically diverse, and they have greater numbers of students with special learning needs or behavior difficulties

References

Allen, R., & Burgess, S. (2014). *School performance and parental choice of school: Secondary school analysis. Research report, January 2014.* London, England: Department of Education. Retrieved April 4, 2017 from https://assets.publishing.service.gov.uk/government/up loads/system/uploads/attachment_data/file/275938/RR310_-_School_performance_a nd_parental_choice_of_school.pdf

Baddeley, M. (2009). *Herding, social influence and economic decision-making: Socio-psychological and neuroscientific analyses.* London, England: The Royal Society Publishing. Retrieved April 30, 2018 from http://rstb.royalsocietypublishing.org/content/365/1538/281

Baddeley, M. (2017). *Behavioural economics: A very short introduction.* Oxford, England: Oxford University Press.

Ball, S. (2018). Commercialising education: Profiting from reform! *Journal of Education Policy,* 33(5), 587–589. Retrieved July 1, 2018 from www.tandfonline.com/doi/full/10.1080/02680939.2018.1467599

Boyd, D., Lankford, H., Loeb, S., & Wyckoff, J. (2005). Explaining the short careers of high-achieving teachers in schools with low-performing students. *The American Economic Review,* 95, 166–171.

Bryk, A. S., Holland, P. B., & Lee, V. E. (1993). *Catholic schools and the common good.* Cambridge, MA: Harvard University Press.

Burgess, S., Propper, C., Slater, H., & Wilson, D. (2005). *Who wins and who loses from school accountability? The distribution of educational gain in English secondary schools* (September 2005). CEPR Discussion Paper No. 5248. Retrieved April 4, 2017 from https://papers.ssrn.com/sol3/papers.cfm?abstract_id=837284

Caplan, B. (2018). *The case against education: Why the education system is a waste of time and money.* Princeton, NJ: Princeton University Press.

Choy, S. (1997). *Public and private schools: How do they differ?* Washington, DC: National Center for Education Statistics, U.S. Department of Education. Retrieved April 4, 2017 from https://nces.ed.gov/pubs97/97983.pdf

Chubb, J. E., & Moe, T. M. (1990). *Politics, markets, and America's schools.* Washington, DC: Brookings Institution Press.

Coleman, J., Hoffer, T., & Kilgore, S. (1982). Cognitive outcomes in public and private schools. *Sociology of Education,* 55, 65–76.

Coleman, J. (1988). Social capital in the creation of human capital. *American Journal of Sociology,* Supplement 94, S95–S120.

Elmore, R. (2003). Accountability and capacity. In M. Carnoy, R. Elmore, & L. S. Siskin (Eds.), *The new accountability: High schools and high-stakes testing* (pp. 188–202). New York, NY: Routledge.

Friedman, M. (1955). The role of government in public education. In R. A. Solo (Ed.), *Economics and the public interest* (pp. 123–144). New Brunswick, NJ: University of Rutgers Press.

Gonski, D. (Committee Chair) (2011). *Review of funding for schooling.* Canberra, ACT: Australian Government.

Gov.UK (2018). *School performance tables and Ofsted reports.* London, England: UK Government. Retrieved April 4, 2018 from www.gov.uk/education/school-performance-tables-and-ofsted-reports

Greene, J., Loveless, T., MacLeod, W. B., Nechyba, T., Peterson, P., Rosenthal, M., & Whitehurst, G. with Croft, M. (2010). *Expanding choice in elementary and secondary education: A report on rethinking the federal role in education.* Washington, DC: Brown Center on Education Policy at Brookings, Brookings Institute.

Guerra, J. (2018). *We live here: What happens to students when failing schools close? State of Opportunity Report.* Detroit, MI: Michigan Radio, University of Michigan. Retrieved April 4, 2018 from http://stateofopportunity.michiganradio.org/post/we-live-here-what-happens-students-when-failing-schools-close

ISCA (2017). *Parents and school choice.* Retrieved July 26, 2017 from http://isca.edu.au/about-independent-schools/parents-and-school-choice/

Knee, J. (2016). Why for-profit education fails. *The Atlantic,* November 2016 issue. Retrieved April 30, 2018 from www.theatlantic.com/magazine/archive/2016/11/why-for-profit-education-fails/501140/

Lee, J., & Lubienski, C. (2017). The impact of school closures on equity of access in Chicago. *Education and Urban Society*, 49(1), 53–80.

Locke, S. (2017). Home schooling rising fastest among students with special needs as parents look for new directions, August 28, 2017, *ABC News*. Retrieved April 30, 2018 from www.abc. net.au/news/rural/2017-08-28/homeschooling-debate-amid-rising-numbers/8829992

Lubienski, C., & Lubienski, S. T. (2013). *The public school advantage: Why public schools outperform private schools*. Chicago, IL: University of Chicago Press.

Miron, G., & Urschel, J. L. (2012). *Understanding and improving full-time virtual schools*. Boulder, CO: National Education Policy Center, University of Colorado Boulder.

National Education Policy Center (NEPC) (2017). *Closing low-performing schools is a failing reform strategy*. Boulder, CO: NEPC, School of Education, University of Colorado. Retrieved April 4, 2018 from https://nepc.colorado.edu/newsletter/2017/05/closing-low-performing

Nechyba, T. (2006). Income and peer quality sorting in public and private schools. In E. Hanushek & F. Welch (Eds.), *Handbook of economics of education* (Vol. 2, pp. 1327–1368). Amsterdam, The Netherlands: North Holland.

Neill, A. S. (1960). *Summerhill: A radical approach to child rearing*. New York, NY: Hart Publishing Co.

OECD (2012). *Equity and quality in education: Supporting disadvantaged students and schools*. Retrieved April 1, 2018 from www.oecd.org/edu/preschoolandschool/50293148.pdf

OECD (2013). *Education policy outlook: Australia* (June 2013). Retrieved April 1, 2018 from www. oecd.org/edu/EDUCATION%20POLICY%20OUTLOOK%20AUSTRALIA_EN.pdf

Peske, H. G., & Haycock, K. (2006). *Teaching inequality: How poor and minority students are short changed on teacher quality*. Washington, DC: The Education Trust.

Rizvi, F. (2016). *Privatization in education: Trends and consequences*. Education Research and Foresight Series, No. 18. Paris: UNESCO. Retrieved April 4, 2018 from https://unes doc.unesco.org/ark:/48223/pf0000246485

Rogers, J., Lubienski, C., Scott, J., & Welner, K. G. (2015). Examining the parent trigger as a strategy for school reform and parental engagement. *Teachers College Record*, 117(6), 1–36.

Sirin, S. R. (2005). Socioeconomic status and academic achievement: A meta-analytic review of research. *Review of Educational Research*, 75, 417–453.

Stossel, J. (2018). *Reason: Interview with Betsy DeVos*, May 8, 2018. Retrieved March 1, 2018 from www.youtube.com/watch?v=ydVKyDgw_SM

Strauss, V. (2013). How closing schools hurts neighborhoods. *The Washington Post*, March 6, 2013.

Strauss, V. (2016). To Trump's education pick, the U.S. public school system is a 'dead end'. *The Washington Post*, December 21, 2016. Retrieved July 26, 2017 from www.washing-tonpost.com/news/answer-sheet/wp/2016/12/21/to-trumps-education-pick-the-u-s-publi c-school-system-is-a-dead-end/?noredirect=on&utm_term=.e0ce74adc81d

Taylor, J. E. (2017). The Supreme Court, religion and the future of school choice. *The Conversation*, July 10, 2017. Retrieved April 30, 2018 from https://theconversation. com/the-supreme-court-religion-and-the-future-of-school-choice-80588

Teese, R. (2011). *From opportunity to outcomes: The changing role of public schooling in Australia and national funding arrangements*. Melbourne, VIC: Centre for Research on Education Systems, University of Melbourne.

The Friedman Foundation for Educational Choice (now EdChoice) (2017). *What is school choice?* Retrieved July 26, 2017 from www.edchoice.org/school-choice/wha t-is-school-choice/

Un, S. (2016). Why more parents are home schooling their children, September 3, 2016. *MarketWatch*. New York, NY: MarketWatch. Retrieved April 30, 2018 from www.marketwatch.com/story/why-more-parents-are-home-schooling-their-children-2016-09-01

Urban, R. (2018). Unhappy parents embrace home schooling in record numbers. *The Australian*, April 30, 2018. Retrieved April 24, 2018 from www.theaustralian.com.au/national-affairs/education/unhappy-parents-embrace-home-schooling-in-record-numbers/news-story/3b25b650cb194736b63b6a2902c1332d

Wößmann, L. (2007). International evidence on school competition, autonomy and accountability: A review. *Peabody Journal of Education*, 82(2–3), 473–497.

6

COMPETITION

Competition encourages challenge and contest in the free market. Competition is synonymous with a game or rivalry involving competitors, contenders, or adversaries. There is competition for customers, 'share of wallet,' resources, financial reward, prestige and recognition, for grades or a placing in a game or sport, or for a higher position on league tables. Competition conjures up thoughts of winning and losing, gaining advantage or supremacy – sometimes through effort, sometimes by chance, by auctioning, bartering, or currying favor. It is the counter-narrative to cooperation, alliance, or mutuality.

Neoliberal competition is presumed to encourage self-motivation and industry, while the outcomes of competition are determined by the market. Without competition, it is believed, individuals lack incentive to improve and are not as motivated to perform to the highest possible levels. In neoliberalism, competition is presumed to produce positive benefits: higher levels of quality and efficiency, improved effort and performance towards goal achievement, while serving as a market indicator to meet 'consumer' preferences.

Competition drives the practices and programs deemed popular by demand. As innovation, improvement, and entrepreneurialism encourage new developments and rewards, other competitors are motivated to emulate, so competition encourages the spread of good ideas and practices. Hence, competition involves market players striving to improve and meet market expectations in the hope of garnering business and support, which in turn aids consumer choice. This is the invisible hand of the market in operation, benefiting all – 'providers' and 'customers' – as people engage in the game of catallaxy (see Chapter 2).

To aid choice in education the publication of transparent and comparable performance data provides 'consumers' (students or parents/guardians) with an easy means of determining their most desirable institutions, while others will be motivated to replicate 'best practices' in order to better achieve and compete.

To stimulate individualized performativities, competition is thus further aided by mandated vertical, externally mandated accountabilities. Measured performance controlled by external authorities is perceived to sharpen focus on goal attainment towards improved outcomes. These kinds of neoliberal practices are legitimated by the state as means of promoting competition and empowering consumer choice.

Amongst market proponents, competition's potential is impeded by government policy interventions such as public funding, grants, subsidies or sponsorships, sanctions, levies or excises, or restrictive regulation, all of which are believed to distort market signals and operations. A further distortion is when there is no competition, for example, when one organization has market monopoly or when just a few producers create oligopolies which concentrate supply and provide limited choices for demand.

In basic terms, competition in education pits individuals and education institutions and systems against others. Competition is encouraged between institutions within an education sector and with those in other sectors, while individual agents compete against others from outside and within their enrolling or employing institution. Therefore, the neoliberal view is that education institutions should be autonomous and freestanding in order to engage in competition without unnecessary restriction. They should be responsible for the enrollment outcomes of competition and funding so received, while individual employees should compete for positions, tenure, appraisal outcomes, and remuneration (based on performance) to ensure the best for the job. Competition in education is usually subtler than this crude description would suggest, yet governments can exert quite strident policy measures to produce competition's indicators – reviews and results (which become rankings) – while students can compete aggressively for grades, enrollment admission, or scholarships.

Competition is global as well as local. Nations compete on aspects such as enrollment and completion rates, as well as achievement outcomes, aided and encouraged by international agencies such as the OECD. A seemingly obsessive international focus on comparisons, increased transparency, and accountability heightens consumer awareness about education offerings and the range of providers across the world, which infiltrates discourses and perceptions about 'excellence' and 'quality.' Further, rankings and ratings drive the commodification of education itself, which in Australia, for example, is the nation's third largest export earner.

Competition between education institutions primarily revolves around student enrollments and student achievement results. The results of enrollment competition ultimately depends on consumer choices which determine levels of financial support, which, in return, influence all other resources, from people to plant to consumables. Competition for enrollments is presumed to make education institutions more responsive to local needs. Hence, per capita funding models in education reward those institutions attracting higher enrollment numbers and become a market mechanism for resource allocation based on choice.

Traditionally, education institutions did not have to 'compete' for anything, let alone enrollments. But neoliberal policy emphasizing competition turns tradition 180 degrees, with enrollment or 'catchment' zones criticized for being constraints to competition, and concomitantly, impediments to consumer choice.

Providers are presumed to compete first for custom and funding and then for higher reputations through achievement outcomes and improved and innovative practices. Involvement with other institutions and the business sector are encouraged in these endeavors.[1]

The most strident market mechanism to entrench enrollment competition are voucher systems in the schooling sector, whereby parents take a government-funded voucher of a certain value in exchange for enrollment in any school of their choice. This runs against the idea of the local school as schools are at liberty to chase and choose their own admissions, in competition with each other.

Hence, enhancing enrollment numbers has spurred new competitive behaviors in education – enrollments can be 'gamed.' For example, education institutions have:

- changed their business models to attract international full fee-paying international students
- expanded their likely enrollment catchment through the provision of transportation
- introduced specialist subjects or services (such as re-entry schemes to encourage adults to return to study)
- opened campuses in other suburbs or even overseas
- instituted cooperating 'sister' programs across schools, states, and nations
- attracted students of high academic worth via scholarships (called 'cream-skimming')
- avoided quotas and space limitations by making courses available only online (which also aids efficiency)
- engaged in marketing campaigns and expanded public relations activities
- engineered enrollment enticements such as providing laptops or tablets
- offered quicker, easier qualifications (Leahy, 2015).

Some states are placing more credence in the neoliberal free market as the most efficient arbiter of resource allocation by ushering in policies of privatization and deregulation to open market access to new, non-traditional players (including for-profit providers), thereby increasing competition as well as expanding options for consumer choice.

Some staunch neoliberals have suggested that to enhance competition to its fullest capabilities, education funding mechanisms in schools should be based on students' results, or a model that takes both student enrollment numbers and student achievement scores into account, rather than on a traditional per capita basis (see for example, Anderson & Boyle, 2015). This assumes that low-achieving schools would be incentivized to raise students' scores through bonus reward schemes – a 'needs-based' model augmented with demands for improvement. For example, schools receiving higher levels of funding could spend more on resources that positively impact student achievement – additional teachers or teacher aides, for example. Such thinking suggests that without significant deregulation of current schooling systems, choice, efficiency, improvement, and competition are thwarted in achieving their true and fullest market effects (Allen & Burgess, year unkown).

Competition practices in education continue to proliferate and expand, from enrollments and grades and rankings, to measured retention rates and levels of satisfaction so that these too can be touted to secure a market edge (see for example, OECD, 2014).

For governments the goal of competition in education is enhanced institutional improvement, international economic competitiveness, greater productivity, and more effective and efficient human capital development.

Critique

Like its neoliberal accomplices – individualism and choice – the obvious downside to competition in education is the inevitable fall-out of 'failures.' Individuals and education institutions do not operate on a level playing field, and competition is unfairly weighted towards the fortunes of the already advantaged – the winners in competition. Higher levels of resourcing go to institutions demonstrating the best results in competition – 'successful' or 'strong' institutions receive greater funding and many associated advantages, meaning resources often go to those who need them the least (see for example, Anderson & Boyle, 2015; Teese & Polesel, 2003).

Market competition opens up the likelihood of a vicious cycle in which low-performing institutions are punished for their failure – entrenching inequities and divisions (see Lubienski, 2013). Education policy encouraging competition creates systemic stratification, with some institutions being 'residualized' because they can't compete – their custom comes from those with fewer choices and reduced social and/or economic means (see for example, Henry, 2001) or whose geographical location prevents high resourcing levels (such as rural locations). Poorer institutions reliant on government funding often experience both inadequate funding and budget cuts (Thompson, Crampton, & Wood, 2012). Hence, competition policies elide context as a factor that impedes or enables competition in education.[2]

Competition is individualized. It undermines collegiality and collective responsibility, while weakening the notion of an education 'system.' Competition thereby creates stresses around performativity and work atomization as individuals compete rather than cooperate in collegial teams. Competition also serves as a disincentive for high-performing educators and leaders to serve in 'poorer-performing' institutions that could use their expertise. For students, competition is intensified through comparative standardized testing, while for educators, competition is heightened through international websites promoting anonymous comparative judgments, such as *rate your teacher.com.*

Anglophone nations commodify education and clamber for the market custom of full-fee-paying international students, encouraging neoliberal forms of 'academic capitalism,' while on a world scale these practices may be viewed as a type of education imperialism or 'neocolonialism' (see for example, Ross & Gibson, 2006).

Competition through deregulation can have opposite effects than those purported by market advocates – it can force up price and drive down quality, especially when private, for-profit providers have profit rather than education as their main goal. When nefarious education outlets fail in competition the market doesn't come to the rescue – in such circumstances, consumers suffer. Competition reform can result in a 'race to the bottom' (Wheelahan, 2016). And individual institutions can also endorse practices viewed as irregular or undesirable.

For example, in deregulated higher education systems some institutions have lowered admission standards to capture students who would not have otherwise met requirements for admission or implemented alternative access schemes which are criticized for their 'dumbing-down' potential (see for example, Hil, 2012; Ting, Bagshaw, & Munro, 2017). Some deem such practices to be cheating while it could also be viewed as opening up the market to greater choice and custom. Hence, while enrollment pressures are presumed to enhance quality, they can also result in practices simply designed to increase 'market share' by putting issues of surviving or thriving before education credence.

To enhance chances, some individuals are prepared to pay to get ahead of the pack and gain advantage: for example, coaching for scholarship examinations or tests, supplementary programs, and cram schooling. Competition and the 'consumer appetite' for it has encouraged the development of a vast shadow education industry, much of it unregulated, which operates around formal education provisioning (Starr, 2012).

Competition is accused of bringing out the worst in human behavior – 'one-upmanship' and winning at all costs. Competition with others can be so strong it can encourage unscrupulous behaviors – individuals may cheat – but high stakes competition in education caters for cheats too, with a burgeoning industry in fake assignments with outsourced 'mill writers' or contracted plagiarism (see Chlopicki, 2017; Holman, 2017; Usborne, 2017).[3]

Labor market liberalization has encouraged new 'consumer behaviors' and extended and intensified all forms of credentialism – crucial for individual displays and 'proof' of worthiness as well as aiding individuals in competition for jobs.

Education has traditionally been viewed as a great equalizer and means of bridging social differences, for enabling social mobility and raising living standards. Competition in education sorts and streams and, thereby, does the opposite. Equity and fairness are impossible aspirations when competition is designed to set individuals apart, purportedly through their own efforts and then through the market's reward systems. Education has always had difficulties achieving a semblance of equity, but what has always been a bad situation is made worse by an intensive focus on competition. Social cohesiveness and education equity give way to social fragmentation and widened inequalities.

Notes

1   One increasingly popular means by which traditional enrollment constraints have been overcome is through institutions cooperating or federating to produce an alliance of institutions under one administration (such as teaching schools alliances in the UK, which take responsibility for teachers' 'training' and professional development). This 'one-provider' model is presumed to positively motivate many sites for improvement, thereby enhancing their chances and outcomes in competition.
2   In the USA, for example, school funding is dependent on revenues earned from local property taxes. In poorer areas, there are fewer funds for schools that often require additional learning support for students. Wealthier locales have more money to spend on education for children from wealthier parents. And the same applies when wealthy college institutions are able to tap into larger pools of alumni funds (sponsorship, donations, and endowments) than their poorer counterparts.
3   Other examples of cheating include 'click farms' in efforts to improve reputations and ratings on social media via 'likes,' 'friends,' or 'followers' (Business Insider, 2017).

References

Allen, R., & Burgess, S. (n.d.). *The future of competition and accountability in education.* Retrieved June 13, 2018 from www.bristol.ac.uk/media-library/sites/cmpo/migrated/documents/competition.pdf

Anderson, J., & Boyle, C. (2015). NAPLAN data and school funding: A dangerous link. *The Conversation,* August 20, 2015. Retrieved April 4, 2017 from https://theconversation.com/naplan-data-and-school-funding-a-dangerous-link-46021

Business Insider (2017). Thai police raid 'click farm', find 347,200 SIM cards. *Associated Press,* June 13, 2017. Retrieved July 17, 2017 from www.businessinsider.com/ap-thai-police-raid-click-farm-find-347200-sim-cards-2017-6/?r=AU&IR=T

Chlopicki, K. (2017). Most staff suspect students of cheating. *Campus Review,* October 5, 2017. (Reference available through libraries but otherwise requires personal subscription.)

Henry, M. (2001). *Policy approaches to educational disadvantage and equity in Australian schooling.* Paris, France: International Institute for Education Planning/UNESCO.

Hil, R. (2012). *Whackademia: An insider's account of the troubled university.* Sydney, NSW: NewSouth Publishing, University of New South Wales Press Ltd.

Leahy, M. (2015). Reforming vocational education: It's time to end the exploitation of vulnerable people. *The Conversation,* December 16, 2015. Retrieved April 4, 2017 from https://theconversation.com/reforming-vocational-education-its-time-to-end-the-exploitation-of-vulnerable-people-51396

Lubienski, C. (2013). Privatizing form or function? Equity, outcomes and influence in American charter schools. *Oxford Review of Education,* 39(4), 498–513.

OECD (2014). *Education at a glance, 2014.* Paris, France: OECD Publishing.

Ross, E. W., & Gibson, R. (Eds.) (2006). *Neoliberalism and education reform.* Cresskill, NJ: Hampton Press, Inc.

Starr, K. (2012). *Above and beyond the bottom line: The extraordinary evolution of the education business manager.* Camberwell, VIC: ACER Press.

Teese, R., & Polesel, J. (2003). *Undemocratic schooling.* Melbourne, VIC: Melbourne University Publishing.

Thompson, D. C., Crampton, F., & Wood, R. (2012). *Money and schools.* New York, NY: Routledge.

Ting, I., Bagshaw, E., & Munro, K. (2017). Uni offers 2017: University ATAR minimum entry marks continue to decline. *The Sydney Morning Herald,* January 18, 2017. Retrieved January 20, 2017 from www.smh.com.au/education/uni-offers-2017-university-atar-m inimum-entry-marks-continue-to-decline-20170118-gttz6h.html

Usborne, S. (2017). Essays for sale: The booming online industry in writing academic work to order. *The Guardian,* March 4, 2017. Retrieved March 11, 2018 from www. theguardian.com/education/2017/mar/04/essays-for-sale-the-booming-online-indus try-in-writing-academic-work-to-order

Wheelahan, L. (2016). Patching bits won't fix vocational education in Australia – a new model is needed. *International Journal of Training Research, early online.* doi:10.1080/ 14480220.2016.1254368

7

IMPROVEMENT, INNOVATION, AND ENTREPRENEURIALISM

Neoliberal emphases on continual improvement, innovation, and entrepreneurialism – or "the new spirit of capitalism" (Ampuja, 2016) – demands 'onwards and upwards' creative progressivism, organizational agility, flexibility, and out-of-the-box thinking, in contrast to Keynesian social democratic bureaucratized practices denounced as cumbersome, slow, self-serving, and unresponsive. For education, the shift has meant a change from providing workers for an industrialized workforce to harnessing human capital development to enhance students' talents and learning achievements to benefit post-industrial economies in uncertain times.

The drive for improvement and innovation intensifies as post-industrial democracies face new economic challenges as a result of globalization, including the loss of manufacturing and traditional agricultural industries due to cheaper imports, taxes, and sources of off-shore production. A consequence is a significant emphasis on continual improvement and innovation to drive the development of an 'innovation economy,' a 'knowledge-based economy,' and a 'knowledge society' to better meet the needs of advanced capitalism.

In neoliberal terms, innovation and continually improved quality stimulates economic growth and raises consumer expectations and standards, thereby creating social and economic improvements for all. Innovation and improvement in education have received increasing levels of attention over the past three decades because education is seen as a prime mover in these efforts. A consequence is a tighter grip on education by the state, to steer and control education and knowledge production towards its market ambitions.

Innovation and improvement are intertwined with individualism, and educators must find the keys to unlock the talents and interests of every student so that each can reach their highest learning potential for the good of themselves and the economy (see Biesta, 2017). Continual improvement towards higher results and the fostering of creative new ideas are new policy expectations because these are key to national prosperity in the 'global innovation race' (see for example, Innovation and Science Australia, 2017).

Improvement in education policy aims for constant progress, development, amelioration, and transformation. Improvement is described in policy terms as 'betterment' and 'value enhancement,' 'advancement,' and as a 'corrective' to 'assure' quality and compliance. Education improvement policies speak to 'excellence,' 'empowerment,' fuller expressions of 'community engagement,' 'professionalism,' and the re-casting or re-invention of existing practices (see for example, Department of Education and Training, 2018).

For three decades education has taken on the business process of 'continual improvement,' which puts its practices, processes, and outputs under the microscope to weed out inefficiencies and 'failures' and enhance outputs. 'There is always room for improvement' and individuals and individual institutions can and should 'do better' and strive for greater results. Continual improvement is the aim for all aspects of education, from programming, pedagogy, and learning achievement, to education leadership, business, and administration, and including intangible elements such as ensuring positive learning cultures, community building, and reputation 'management.'

At all levels of education, policy discourses are strident about continual improvement – this is non-negotiable – and measured and reported primarily through comparative results and rankings. A good example is the Australian state of Victoria's 'improvement model' named FISO (Framework for Improving Student Outcomes) with its focus on excellence in teaching and learning, 'professional leadership,' a positive climate for learning, and community engagement in learning (based, however, on traditional, linear change models) (Department of Education and Training, 2018).

Innovation is a related concept in education policy and aims to promote discovery, bright and new ideas, and advance new solutions, while fostering a spirit of originality and creativity. Innovation is both a process and an outcome. The antonym of innovation is 'exnovation,' which has both positive and negative connotations – 'best in class' requiring no need of improvement, or, in regressive terms, meaning that the best option is taking a step in the opposite direction or when de-adoption (abandonment) is the soundest decision.

Disruptive innovation successfully changes the ways in which we work, live, and play, and challenges the status quo. As such, governments are placing their bets on the knowledge, skills, and dispositions they see as key to future innovation and national economic development, hence the current focus on STEM subjects (science, technology, engineering, and mathematics), while computer coding is considered mandatory learning and imperative in the new economy (see for example, Hamilton-Smith, 2016 Ricci, 2015; Obama, 2016).

In neoliberal terms, national prosperity and growth comes from innovation and invention combined with enterprise and entrepreneurship. Free market neoliberalism relies on innovators to be entrepreneurs in finding solutions to market problems, producing higher quality, better products and services, greater competitiveness, cheaper production, and identifying opportunities for growth and productivity. 'Entre' refers to newness – to 'entering' or appearing for the first time. Thus, entrepreneurialism is about innovative ideas combined with initiative and the making of opportunities and being the first to bring them to market. It emphasizes start-ups, commercialization, and associations with business and industry in promoting chance and opportunity, while inherently involving elements of risk and challenge.

Incentivizing improvement and innovation in education has been encouragement for business, industry, and 'end-user' partnerships to enhance the commercialization of discovery, research, and invention (while sharing the risks involved); policy support schemes for innovative small businesses and start-ups; the introduction of targeted grants; tax incentives, and the removal of red tape and regulatory restrictions (see for example, Read, 2017).

Generally educators don't take their good ideas to market (although they may promulgate them through professional associations, journals, or conferences). The not-for-profit sector tends not to envision its ideas as saleable commodities or attempt to profit from them. Hence, the word 'intrapreneur' appeared in education during the 1980s to refer to and encourage creative and innovative employees with good ideas.

It is hoped that the neoliberal imperative for performance improvement and creative efforts towards innovation will pervade the subjectivity of students, educators, and education leaders, with such endeavors shaping personal and professional histories. Individuals are expected to internalize the need for improvement and personal effort through which come rewards. This expectation to meet policy ambitions is directed through key performance indicators and performance appraisals, comparative assessments, benchmarks, and rankings, designed to aid a sense of personal mission. Hence, 'performativity' towards improved results pervades professional work activities and the personal thoughts of educators and education leaders (Ball, 1994), and in many cases, their employment depends on it. Policy pursuits manipulate identities as students, educators, education leaders, and employers are subtly and cannily trained to be keenly focused on extrinsic value through the education 'enterprise.'

Innovation and improvement also influence 'customer' choice. Hence, innovative organizations that constantly improve are more likely to appeal to 'customers' and are less likely to be overtaken by competitors. Consumers receive information about improvement and innovation through transparent comparative data, the marketing efforts of institutions, or through word-of-mouth. Successful institutional innovations and improvements not only receive greater 'consumer' support and reputation, but also motivate other individuals and institutions to improve in order to compete. Going full circle, competition spurs the emulation of innovations and improvements while notions of 'best practice' add to this stimulus (see for example, McGowan, 2018). The suggestion is 'if you are standing still, you are going backwards.'

From a neoliberal perspective, education has not been proactive enough in improving or innovating. For example, DeVos argues that education lacks a spirit of innovation and entrepreneurialism:

> We are the beneficiaries of start-ups, ventures, and innovation in every other area of life, but we don't have that in education because it's a closed system, a closed industry, a closed market. It's a monopoly, a dead end. And the best and brightest innovators and risk-takers steer way clear of it. As long as education remains a closed system, we will never see the education equivalents of Google, Facebook, Amazon, PayPal, Wikipedia, or Uber. We won't see any real innovation that benefits more than a handful of students.
>
> *(cited in Strauss, 2016)*

Sentiments like this are behind the neoliberal policy push for improvement, innovation, and entrepreneurialism in education. But also pervading the improvement push is the neoliberal perception that the private sector is more innovative and open to improvement than the public sector (just as the private sector is presumed to be more efficient [cost-effective] and agile; see for example, Chubb & Moe, 1990; DeVos in Stossel, 2018). While private enterprise is assumed to take a proactive stance towards innovation, the opposite is assumed of public sector organizations which are condemned as slow and often having to be coerced into change, improvement, and development (see for example, Hawley Mills & Baroody, 2011; Hoxby, 1996; McGrath Schwartz, 2011; Riggan, 2012).

Comparable data from both sectors, however, reveal fundamental and vast differences in the factors motivating innovation, barriers to innovation, the nature of innovations pursued, approaches to innovation, and in the ways innovation is measured. For example, Kay and Goldspink (2016) found that public sector workers often attempt to innovate even when there are no overarching inducements to do so, but fear of scrutiny means many innovations fail to be enacted. Accountabilities and hierarchical line management systems of approval and compliance often stall or thwart innovation attempts. Many lack confidence in pursuing innovations that are not aligned with strategy and hence not considered to be priorities. Tasks outside usual job specifications are considered too risky in a highly risk-averse, accountable policy environment. And work intensification means educators often don't have time to focus on the new.

This suggests that education authorities and organizational policies are getting in the way, mitigating what might have been successful innovations for improvement – and this is despite policies pushing for innovation and creativity, autonomy, distributed leadership, and individualized responsibility. However, Kay and Goldspink also found that experienced leaders were more confident in taking risks and sidestepping impediments, and as a result were more likely to achieve successful innovation than their less-experienced peers. This gives some credence to the notion of institutional autonomy.

Public sector institutions are more strongly influenced by political and systemic maneuvers (from governments and education departments/authorities) and swayed by public expectations and sentiments often incited by the media. And, according to Kay and Goldspink (2016, pp. 4–5), the stakes are higher:

> The market provides the private sector with a greater range of possibilities to extract reward from the risks it takes... By contrast, the level of public and media scrutiny under which the public sector innovates – due to it being in the business of producing public good – is inevitably and significantly higher. 'Good enough' in the public sector is not 'good enough' if it involves even a small adverse impact and an associated negative news headline... the rewards for public sector agents are arguably low or nil, while the risks for even small mistakes have very real, immediate and lasting (political) consequences.

The authors call, therefore, for vastly different thinking and approaches in the public sector if innovation is to be fostered.

International organizations such as the OECD calibrate the outcomes of improved education performance (including in monetary terms). The countries at the top of the OECD rankings are inevitably in focus as others try to extract their 'formulas' for success in the hope of climbing international educaiton league tables.

Critique

It might be assumed that goals for improvement, creativity, and discovery could not be criticized. In many ways, these have always been embedded in the very concept of education – or why bother being 'educated?' And there will always be individuals and institutions who can and should improve. Criticisms, therefore, are about:

- the ways in which policymakers go about their push for improvement
- misguided policy priorities concerning what is to be improved
- how improvements should be made
- the rationale for change, or, 'improvement for what purpose' and 'in whose interests?' and,
- foreseeable or unintended policy consequences.

The evidence behind policy is rarely exposed or, if it is, the veracity of evidence is simply assumed. As indicated elsewhere in this book, much policy 'evidence' can be criticized as poor or 'bad' science: for example, based on small or skewed samples, elision of context and other essential information, or based on no firm evidence at all.

Critics of the neoliberal focus on innovation and entrepreneurialism in education suggest that knowledge, teaching, and learning are being exploited by the market as something to be bought and sold (see for example, Ball, 2003; Burawoy, 2011; Naidoo & Jamieson, 2005). Commodified and commercialized education is tied to extrinsic motivations rather than the intrinsic motivation educators are trying to inculcate in students.

If knowledge creation and discovery has most weight when it can be commercialized and contributes to productivity and economic growth, corporations are often the biggest beneficiaries. Corporate and business interests are often put first when policy encourages closer links with education institutions to ensure development and innovation, but also to ensure graduates are 'job ready' – as determined by business and industry and reducing needs for on-the-job training. And government priorities for higher education research are geared largely towards economic goals (see for example, Australian Government, 2018). Research that has little or no commercial value will likely go unfunded.

Improvement and innovation are valorized, with institutional successes becoming quality 'benchmarks.' The trouble with emulation in hopes to 'copy' and thereby raise 'quality' and repeat recipes for success is that it ignores enormous contextual and philosophical differences (see for example, Reid, 2007), leads to standardization and sameness, and operates against the neoliberal notion of diversity for choice.

Reich (2010) exposes the rise and influence of what he calls 'paper entrepreneurs'– trained in accountancy, finance, and the law, paper entrepreneurs advise the polity and push for innovation and entrepreneurialism via policy. These entrepreneurs-once-removed guide both governments and corporate leaders and dominate policy substance and direction, including in the social sphere, but produce nothing tangible themselves. Embedded in this assertion is a sense of policy entrepreneurialism, which is expensive and unproductive. Hopes lie within intention and the capacity to influence and infiltrate neoliberal subjects with the aid of inducements like the appraisal of performance against strategic goal achievement.

Despite incentives, however, there are conflicting education policy aims that inhibit innovation: for example, mandatory risk management policies ensure a limited and low appetite for risk that can stultify experimentation and originality, while the pursuit of efficiency and standardization can be barriers to exploration and discovery (Kay & Goldspink, 2016; Starr, 2015).

Improvement is a one-way street – its focus is on institutions and the individual educators and education leaders within them. Control is hierarchical. Those devising policy and the direction of education are not accountable to those mandated to enact policy decisions.

An inherent assumption behind much of the innovation and entrepreneurial push is that education investment must yield profitable and productive returns. The simple pursuit or learning for the sake of it is not enough.

References

Ampuja, M. (2016). The new spirit of capitalism, innovation fetishism and new information and communication technologies. *Journal of the European Institute for Communication and Culture*, 23(1), 19–36.

Australian Government (2018). Science and research priorities. Canberra, ACT: Australian Government. Retrieved May 4, 2018 from www.science.gov.au/scienceGov/ScienceAndResearchPriorities/Pages/default.aspx

Ball, S. (1994). *Education reform: A critical and post-structural perspective*. Buckingham, England: Open University Press.

Ball, S. (2003). The teacher's soul and the terrors of performativity. *Journal of Education Policy*, 18(2), 215–228.

Biesta, G. J. J. (2017). *The rediscovery of teaching*. New York, NY: Routledge.

Burawoy, M. (2011). Redefining the public university: Global and national contexts. In J. Holmwood (Ed.), *A manifesto for the public university* (pp. 27–41). London, England: Bloomsbury.

Chubb, J. E., & Moe, T. M. (1990). *Politics, markets and America's schools*. Washington, DC: Brookings Institute Press.

Department of Education and Training (2018). *FISO improvement model*. Melbourne, VIC: Victoria State Government. Retrieved August 1, 2018 from www.education.vic.gov.au/school/teachers/management/improvement/Pages/improvement-model.aspx

Ford, C. (2015). Department of disgrace. *The Monthly*, August 2015. Retrieved April 1, 2017 from www.themonthly.com.au/issue/2015/august/1438351200/catherine-ford/department-disgrace

Hamilton-Smith, L. (2016). Learning curve: Coding classes to become mandatory in Queensland schools. *Australian Broadcasting Corporation News*, February, 2017. Retrieved April 1, 2017 from www.abc.net.au/news/2016-11-17/coding-classes-in-queensland-schools-mandatory-from-2017/8018178

Hawley Mills, K., & Baroody, K. (2011). *Restructuring schools for high performance: A primer for state policymakers*. Watertown, MA: Education Research Strategies.

Hoxby, C. M. (1996). How teachers' unions affect education production. *The Quarterly Journal of Economics*, 111(3), 671–718. Retrieved June 14, 2018 from https://doi.org/10.2307/2946669

Independent Broad-based Anti-Corruption Commission (2017). *IBAC investigation exposes $2 million TAFE training scam and issues at V/Line*. Melbourne, VIC: IBAC Victoria.

Innovation and Science Australia (2017). *Australia 2030: Prosperity through innovation: A plan for Australia to thrive in the global innovation race*. Canberra, ACT: Australian Government.

Kay, R., & Goldspink, C. (2016). *Public sector innovation: Why is it different?* Sydney, NSW: Australian Institute of Company Directors. Retrieved September 3, 2017 from http://aicd.companydirectors.com.au/~/media/cd2/resources/advocacy/governance-leadership-centre/pdf/05493-1-pol-glc-public-sector-innovation-research-paper-a4-may16_web.ashx

McGowan, M. (2018). 'Too much control': Pasi Sahlberg on what Finland can teach Australian Schools. *The Guardian*, January 7, 2018. Retrieved January 12, 2019 from www.theguardian.com/australia-news/2018/jan/07/pasi-sahlberg-finland-teach-australian-schools-education

McGrath Schwartz, D. (2011). Sandoval bill would put teachers on one-year contracts, change layoff system. *Nevada Territory*, April 16, 2011. Retrieved January 31, 2017 from https://lasvegassun.com/news/2011/apr/16/sandoval-bill-would-put-teachers-one-year-contract/

Naidoo, R., & Jamieson, I. (2005). Knowledge in the marketplace: The global commodification of teaching and learning in higher education. In P. Ninnes & M. Hellsten (Eds.), *Internationalizing higher education* (pp. 37–51). Heidelberg, The Netherlands: Springer.

Obama, B. (2016). Teach all students computer coding. *Your Weekly Address*, January 30, 2016. Retrieved April 1, 2017 from www.youtube.com/watch?v=agAJOQ5FKpU

Read, L. (2017). *Research Innovation 2017: Building meaningful partnerships for improved collaboration and research commercialisation.* Sydney, NSW: IQPC.

Reich, R. B. (2010). *The paper entrepreneurs are winning over product entrepreneurs (A thirty year retrospective).* Robert Reich blog, April 2, 2010. Retrieved April 1, 2017 from http://robertreich.org/post/491676652

Reid, A. (2007). An anatomy of the attacks on Australian education. *Principia*, Autumn2007, 5–7.

Ricci, C. (2015). Coding education in schools: Crucial as English and Maths – or is it? *The Age*, May 30, 2015. Retrieved April 1, 2017 from www.theage.com.au/education/coding-education-in-schools-crucial-as-english-and-maths–or-is-it-20150529-ghct42.html

Riggan, M. (2012). *Private enterprise in American education. Special Report 5. Between efficiency and effectiveness: Evaluation of for-profit education organizations*, April 2012. Washington, DC: American Enterprise Institute.

Starr, K. (2015). *Education game changers: Leadership and the consequence of policy paradox.* Lanham, MD: Rowman and Littlefield.

Stossel, J. (2018). *Reason: Interview with Betsy DeVos*, May 8, 2018. Retrieved March 1, 2018 from www.youtube.com/watch?v=ydVKyDgw_SM

Strauss, V. (2016). To Trump's education pick, the U.S. public schools system is a 'dead end'. *The Washington Post*, December 21, 2016. Retrieved October 3, 2017 from www.washingtonpost.com/news/answer-sheet/wp/2016/12/21/to-trumps-education-pick-the-u-s-public-school-system-is-a-dead-end/?utm_term=.eda16d334af9

8

EFFICIENCY

Efficiency is about making optimal use of time, money, effort, and resources to increase productivity, while minimizing wastage. Efficiency is the relationship between one or more 'inputs' (resources or processes), and one or more 'outputs.' Efficiency is promoted as improving accountability for public monies, while also enhancing public management and promoting transparency to aid informed consumer choices. Efficiency, is not so much about saving time (as the word used to more regularly imply), as it is about saving money – currently, educators associate 'efficiencies' and 'efficiency drives' with cost-savings exercises.

Efficiency gains in education are measured by costs ('inputs') to outcomes ('outputs') ratios. 'Inputs' are people, money, and time; 'outputs' are both educational and those related to education business outcomes. Efficiency increases as output to input ratios improve.

Efficiency gains can be measured in every education institution, every sector, every state. Efficiency methods and measurements are multidimensional, although governments and policymakers have tried to establish consistent national norms and processes for analyzing and comparing efficiency gains. Efficiency 'performance' information or comparative 'evidence' shapes strategic planning, policy priorities, budget processes, and resource allocation decisions.

Efficiency is inextricably linked with productivity (see Chapter 9), ROI (return on investment), and VFM (value for money) assessments, and is a major factor in decision-making about strategy, budgets, funding, and resource allocation.

Resourcing levels or 'inputs' differ in every education institution and the same applies to 'outputs.' Some education institutions are reliant solely on government/local tax revenues. Others are lucky enough to attract private funds, alumni support, gifts, donations, and bequests, or have significant assets to enable investment income. And there are huge cost differentials across contexts in education provisioning and course delivery. For example, courses requiring expensive equipment or infrastructure cost more per student to deliver, some students require extra resources to meet their learning needs, and geographical location is another huge factor (see for example, Starr, 2015b). In some cases, such differentials are covered fully or partially with student or parent contributions, such as tuition fees, with all forms of private investment in education increasing its efficiency.

Efficiency is encouraged through activities such as price benchmarking and transparent, comparative measurements and reporting, with reviews and audits also intended to incentivize 'results-oriented' cultures (see Chapter 9).

Budgetary pressures have motivated governments to minimize public sector costs to make them 'efficient,' while also raising their effectiveness or 'productivity.' In other words, from governments' perspectives, efficiency is about containing or reducing the costs of education while instituting measures to extract the highest standards and service quality. Efficiency in education is pursued through activities such as:

- automation and digitization (with AI promising huge future efficiency gains)
- de-centralization or policies promoting institutional 'autonomy'
- 'outsourcing' services to 'private providers'
- organizational 'downsizing' (reducing 'headcount' and therefore, payroll costs)
- 'flexible' 'human resource management' practices (including casual employment and short-term labor contracts)
- strengthening competition amongst education 'providers' (argued as lowering costs and improving 'quality' – including public and private 'providers')
- charging service 'users' for service delivery costs ('user-pays' principles)
- expanding scales of operation/economies of scale
- resource sharing and 'prosumption' (Curristine, Lonti, & Joumard, 2007; see Starr, 2012; 2015a).

In education, there are other ways in which efficiency gains have been made that are not included in textbooks. Education leaders, for example, improve efficiency and productivity levels by working many more hours than those for which they are paid. (The payment exchange – payment for labor [hours worked] equations – are therefore skewed.) Tenure and performance-based pay are current hot topics, while commercialization and the exploitation of intellectual property are newer forms of efficiency in education.

Efficiency in education has been aided by changes in the ways education programs are funded. For example, many automatic block funding mechanisms have been replaced by competitive grants schemes, requiring formal grant applications to be prepared with arguments convincing enough to persuade funding assessors. This practice has come alongside funding reductions, stricter targeted funding mechanisms, and harsher requirements for reporting and auditing.[1]

Exercising greater efficiencies in education has put a focus on activities such as risk management, 'human resource management,' regulations and accountability frameworks, and cultural change – these being the responsibility of institutional leaders.

Efficiency measures have been aided by discourses criticizing education for being 'inefficient,' 'unproductive,' too costly and 'uneconomical,' too cumbersome and restrictive, too slow, unresponsive, with too many duplicated services, with its funding not tied to performance or improvement targets. Its practices have been condemned as 'protectionist,' with teacher unions and strong collective bargaining cultures constraining efficiency gains by further entrenching 'provider capture' and a 'closed shop' mentality.

Efficiency proponents want to see budgets, resource, and funding allocations based on performance measurements with appropriate rewards (such as bonuses, increased funding, and public recognition) and sanctions (such as funding restrictions, increased auditing oversight, and public criticism) (see for example, Curristine et al., 2007). The argument is that in this way, public monies can be distributed or re-distributed for the greatest effect.

Neoliberal efficiency activities are underpinned by the principles of 'efficient' taxation to minimize the taxes paid by individuals while also minimizing bureaucratic intervention or excessive centralized administration – i.e. 'small government' or the 'rolled-back' state.

However, efficiency processes undertaken by governments are also criticized for deficiencies, including a lack of long-term planning for reforms, and inadequate and inconsistent measurement instruments with concomitant effects on the quality of information and the decisions therefore made – with Curristine et al. (2007) also citing the problems of getting politicians to use efficiency data in policy decision-making, the need for reform practices to be more adaptive to changing circumstances, and for incentives to motivate politicians and bureaucrats to change their 'inefficient' behaviors (see also Bouckaert & Peters, 2002).

Neoliberal arguments about inefficiency also hit up against those of education leaders who have to cut the coat to fit the cloth, with severe funding shortfalls being common criticisms (see for example, Chokshi, 2018; Marsh & Adams, 2017). Operating margins in education institutions are usually low and cash flow is often precarious. And if there is a relationship between 'inputs' and 'outputs,' then improving outcomes will most likely entail increasing resource 'inputs.'

Like all neoliberal tenets, efficiency issues and debates are politically and economically inspired and have substantial social and cultural impacts.

Note

1 What is not factored into this efficiency measure is the time expended in application writing exercises, in the decision-making of grants panels, and the time associated with mandatory program effectiveness and expenditure evaluations to ascertain VFM (value for money).

References

Bouckaert, G., & Peters, B. G. (2002). Performance measurement and management: The Achilles' heel in administrative modernization. *Public Performance and Management Review*, 25(4), 359–362.

Chokshi, N. (2018). More than 90% of US teachers spend their own money on school supplies, survey finds. *Independent*, May 18, 2018. Retrieved August 1, 2018 from www.independent.co.uk/news/world/us-teachers-money-school-supplies-survey-strikes-a8356466.html

Curristine, T., Lonti, Z., & Joumard, I. (2007). Improving public sector efficiency: Challenges and opportunities. *OECD Journal on Budgeting*, 7(1), 1–41. Retrieved August 1, 2018 from www.oecd.org/gov/budgeting/43412680.pdf

Marsh, S., & Adams, R. (2017). Headteachers warn parents: There is not enough money to fund schools. *The Guardian*, September 27, 2017. Retrieved October 15, 2018 from www.theguardian.com/education/2017/sep/27/headteachers-tell-parents-you-are-still-in-a-postcode-lottery

Starr, K. (2012). *Above and beyond the bottom line: The extraordinary evolution of the education business manager.* Camberwell, VIC: ACER Press.

Starr, K. E. (2015a). *Education game changers: Leadership and the consequence of policy paradox.* Lanham, MD: Rowman & Littlefield.

Starr, K. (2015b). Small rural school leadership: Creating opportunity through collaboration. In S. Clarke & T. O'Donoghue (Eds), *School leadership in diverse contexts* (pp. 43–56). London, England: Routledge.

9

PRODUCTIVITY

Productivity goes hand-in-glove with efficiency – it measures the ends produced from means and aims for constant improvement gains. In neoliberal terms raising productivity involves mobilizing resources (time, people, money, infrastructure, equipment, and utilities) or 'inputs,' to raise the quantity and/or quality of 'outputs.' Productivity focuses on positive developments – gains, increases, and improvement – but also identifies negative trends. It is about finding the means to secure greater return on investment (ROI) and value for money (VFM).

For governments, the three Ps of economic growth are population, participation, and productivity. Population is required for ongoing consumption to keep the economy going (for governments – via sales tax receipts from consumer spending on goods and services). Employment equals 'participation.' Having high population participation in the paid workforce produces income tax receipts and reduces 'under-utilization' – underemployment or unemployment. Workforce participation comes with associated costs for government, including training and education costs (although individuals also pay). Hence, the population creates costs for governments – costs associated with infrastructure, essential social services, law and order, and defense. Consumption and participation thus serve and enable individuals and governments – both depend on it. But the gold standard of growth is productivity. Productivity concerns attaining greater 'outputs' with the same (or reduced levels of) resourcing – 'inputs.' If governments can extract greater outputs without incurring extra costs, then productivity becomes a national priority. Measured in economistic terms, a productive citizenry contributes to a nation's economic outputs and international economic competitiveness. Productivity is a major means by which nations aim to achieve economic growth – they want it 'faster, cheaper, and better.' In short, Australia's Productivity Commission defines productivity as a supply-side measure aiming to minimize inputs and waste, and maximize outputs, efficiency (costs and time), quality/value, and demand.

Education is viewed by governments as a prime means of raising national productivity. Education is at the base of all occupations and is a major contributor to productive innovation and inventions. Further, governments want a highly educated population so that individuals are able to look after themselves throughout their lives and pay their own way rather than relying on government welfare. There is a strong economistic tenor behind national productivity statistics which focus on getting the maximum productivity out of 'human capital,' in this case from learning, including workforce knowledge, skills, and qualifications.

Productivity in education includes several types of activities:

- increasing enrollments
- reducing staff to student ratios
- increasing international full-fee-paying student intakes
- improving graduation/course completion rates
- improved student/parent satisfaction survey results
- increasing research outputs and research impact
- expanding research or commercial grants
- labor increases per 'unit' (i.e. per person), e.g. student completions per staff member.

There are pursuits closely aligned with 'efficiency' (cost savings) to reduce expenditure, eliminating wastage to make resources more productive. There are also output measurements quantifying effort and achievements against pre-set goals (such as key performance indicators) and the time taken to achieve them. Productivity also measures aspects of education such as student learning achievement outcomes, graduate employability and 'job readiness,' research quantum, or the commercial value of partnerships and innovations (factors that can be measured relative to spending to calculate productivity increases or decreases).

Any Google search of 'productivity' will come up with equations to calculate productivity – usually something like, 'productivity = outputs (measurable achievements) over inputs (resources invested).' This relates to ROI (return on investment) – with the added incentive of achieving 'efficiency'. Hence, it is simple to see that any productivity improvements mean doing more with the same level of 'inputs' or having an equal or higher productivity rate with fewer inputs. For example, in education, retention rates, number of graduates, or standardized test improvements without a budgetary increase represent a productivity increase. Productivity increases can also occur through reducing costs and through workforce flexibility (agility) to extract greater returns from current levels (or decreased levels) of resourcing. The whole productivity exercise is about increasing the efficiency by which resources are converted to measurable, improved outputs.

Productivity is inextricably bound with the concepts of efficiency (the best cost) and effectiveness (quality). Efficiency equates with cost savings, achieving the lowest level of investment to undertake operations and achieve goals, and doing the same or better with less. Effectiveness equates with quality and goal achievement. In education, governments and education authorities want to see improved outcomes/achievements alongside greater efficiencies to achieve maximum value for money (VFM).

By its very nature, productivity concerns output measurement and comparisons. It is based on 'evidence,' used amongst other measures for 'evidence-based' policymaking (see Biesta, 2017). Indications of 'quality' are clearly associated with productivity measurement (such as leaders' key performance indicators which focus their work to produce both professional and market rewards), while governments have instigated 'quality' indicators through setting standards for learning, teaching, and education leadership.

Productivity agendas have placed every aspect of education under the fiscal microscope, requiring leaders' responsiveness to governmental strategic goals and attention to a range of accountabilities. Australia's Productivity Commission, for example, collects data about education funding and income, assets and liabilities, resourcing levels, accountability for expenditure, and resource management practices – and compares this information with international data sets. The Productivity Commission seeks to "deliver good student outcomes at a reasonable cost," raise the quality of teachers and education leaders, and strengthen the use of evaluation, with an overriding consideration being the country's position and outcomes compared to other nations via formal standardized testing regimes (Australian Government, Productivity Commission, 2012). Productivity data are used to inform education funding levels, further reforms, and policy agendas – usually categorized by level and sector (early learning, schools, higher education, and vocational education).

Productivity measures, along with various forms of accountability, are designed to provide strong impetus for continual improvement. Time-management programs, strategic prioritizing, and the introduction of key performance indicators and targets are all measures undertaken to motivate productivity. On top of day-to-day work activities, they spur what Ball (1994) refers to as 'performativity' because the efforts and results of education leaders and others are also measured, with strategic plans and key performance indicators shaping work priorities and 'outputs.' National productivity agendas in education are focused on priorities determined by governments and government departments, and are expected to be delivered by education leaders on top of local priorities for change.

Governments and education authorities measure productivity in terms of overall institutional improvement against past performance, or against pre-set standards, usually applicable to all institutions within a given jurisdiction, to enable comparisons in their sector within the same district, state, nation, or internationally. Productivity measures have also spurred the introduction of work allocation models, changing 'standards' and output targets.

Productivity measures are turned into benchmarks and performance indicators to compare levels of local, national, and international outputs against inputs. For example, a school can benchmark its spending on 'human resources' with schools of similar enrollment size to gauge the average expenditure on staff. Thus, education performance indicators of efficient and optimal resource usage are used to justify funding increases or decreases.

Hoxby (2003, p. 309) suggests several ways in which schools can increase productivity:

> In the short term, administrators who are attempting to raise their school's productivity to respond to competition have only certain options. They can induce their staff to work harder; they can get rid of unproductive staff and programs; they can allocate resources away from non-achievement-oriented activities (self-esteem) and toward achievement-oriented ones (math, reading, and so on). In the slightly longer term, they can renegotiate the teacher contract to make the school more efficient. If administrators actually pursue all of these options, they may be able to raise productivity substantially.

Calculations of the productivity of education have, therefore, material consequences, and also influence education policy responses.

Some of the improvements achieved in education that have had a huge impact on national productivity include:

- the rapid 'massification' of secondary and tertiary education (this expansion has democratized education, enabling broader participation rates)
- there are more students enrolled at all levels of education than ever before
- all education sectors now enroll a more diverse student population than ever before
- the number of international students continues to increase rapidly
- more individuals extend their education to higher levels (often paying for tuition and incurring student fee debts)
- student retention rates beyond the legal school-leaving age have increased
- teachers 'individualize' each student's program to cater for specific needs and interests, often without extra support
- students with special learning needs are now included and integrated in general classrooms
- in higher education, the number of graduates continues to increase, including those with postgraduate degrees
- commercial partnerships have produced savings
- research and discovery has aided innovation and continual improvement
- the quality and number of academic publications is measured and demonstrates continual growth
- online courses have enabled much larger (sometimes huge) student intakes.

Education is now more accessible, diverse, and inclusive; it is focused on results, continual improvement, and is focused on students' learning – it is 'productive.'

Recent suggestions for further productivity include ideas such as education facilities being open all hours for public usage; further deregulating university admissions and fee systems, enabling institutions to set enrollment quotas and charge rates to suit their needs; streamlining compulsory professional learning via online, DIY, self-marking programs; replacing students' real-life learning experiments and experiences with virtual simulations; providing foundational discipline knowledge in all institutions by one generic online program for everyone; and replacing end-of-year teacher holidays with requirements for professional learning or industry placements (see for example, Squires 2002).

The long-term private benefits of education are also calculated in terms of costs and return on investment. From an economic perspective, education provides many benefits for individuals, with higher qualification levels in education positively affecting longevity, health, wealth, employment, levels of social capital and political participation, personal security, financial independence, social mobility, home ownership, and pension levels. There are also benefits for the whole of society. The more educated a nation, the:

- greater its social cohesion
- lower its levels of unemployment
- lower its incarceration levels
- lower the dependence on social welfare
- greater the levels of volunteering
- higher the levels of interpersonal trust (see for example, OECD, 2014).

Education is literally life-changing, and it is clearly essential to national productivity in numerous ways.

Despite continual productivity gains, the neoliberal perspective rails against traditional education practices – from funding to work practices. Education is perceived as inefficient, unproductive, or under-productive. Traditional education arrangements – expensive campuses with 'idle' (unproductive) spaces, tenured and unionized educators, intensive resources and support services, heavily regulated and inflexible procedures – are viewed as past their 'use-by' date. They are seen to tie up too much capital with a low return on investment – in short, they are 'unproductive' and not as effective as they could be. As described in earlier chapters, the neoliberal perspective is that education performs better when it is put to market to compete for custom and funding, when individuals are empowered to choose, and when education institutions have flexibility to tailor their offerings, choose and change their staff, with autonomy to improve as they see fit without bureaucratic hindrance.

As an example, Squires (2002) argues that publicly funded education institutions have for too long been hampered by regulatory and reporting mandates that are inappropriate for modern-day businesses. They absorb too much time, reduce efficiency, and require the employment of a greater administrator to educator ratio than could be tolerated or sustained by private businesses (expenditure on administration reduces funding for education pursuits – education's 'core business').

Hoxby (2003) argues that greater competition in education will produce the productivity increases as seen in other sectors. For example, Hoxby found that the introduction of non-traditional health providers in the United States increased productivity (more patients, fewer health professionals), and resulted in greater efficiency (lower costs) and higher outputs (general wellbeing and life expectancy). Similarly, competition in the transport industry increased productivity – transportation became faster and cheaper, and delivery options were more individualized. Of course, there are always at least two sides to every story, and in this case, there are many criticisms, the most obvious being the negative effects on workers and the workforce in these sectors, and the effects on 'customers' (see for example, Collins, 2016; Kaplan & Haas 2014). In education, however, Hoxby argues that public debate has been dominated by concerns about allocation distribution across populations, which hinders and detracts from productivity measurement in light of competition.

Others suggest that:

- students are unproductive because a large percentage of them are disengaged (Goss & Sonnemann, 2017)
- billions of dollars are wasted in thousands of unproductive, low-capacity school districts – while even some of the most affluent schools also show poor productivity (Boser, 2014)
- teacher evaluations (performance appraisals) are unproductive because bureaucratic red tape prevents the removal of 'under-performing' teachers (Berns, 2011)
- teachers should be employed on one-year contracts to make it easier to remove unproductive teachers (McGrath Schwartz, 2011)
- choice expands 'provider' options and incentivizes education productivity because higher-performing institutions gain students from unproductive rivals (e.g. Hoxby, 2003)
- teacher unionism has a negative influence on school productivity as based on the costs of inputs and the effects on outputs (Hoxby, 1996).

Governments supporting neoliberal social policy ideals are increasingly taking note of such sentiments. Education costs continue to rise while student achievement results are criticized as declining, which presents nations with "a productivity challenge" (Odden & Busch, 1998, p. 4). Cheered on by a disparaging media, they lament 'dropping' standards that are indicative of falling human capital productivity which undermines national economic advantages and growth. In other words, from a human capital perspective, what happens in education has macroeconomic effects on jobs, national income, trade, and living standards.

Productivity debates inevitably raise questions about who pays for education. In contrast to the 'producer economy' practices established during the last century, a market-based, neoliberal policy environment encourages individual responsibility through user-pays principles, alongside a quality and value proposition presumed to be enhanced by market competition and choice. Education can be paid for through public taxes – by raising taxation or by re-directing funds from other competing areas of public funding, or it can be paid for by the individuals who use education services, or there can be a co-payment system which is a combination of these two sources.

Critique

Education's productivity gains such as those mentioned above are substantial and have occurred in a relatively short period of history, yet they are rarely acknowledged by governments or policymakers who expect continual productivity increases and efficiency 'dividends.'

Also elided from public discussion is the fact that productivity improvements often occur during periods of decreasing public investment (inputs) in education. Education leaders argue that raising productivity outputs is contingent on having sufficient inputs in the first place and cutbacks and rising costs must be acknowledged. Headteachers in the UK, for example, complain that seven years of budget cuts have left school budgeting in crisis, affecting special needs provisioning, student counseling services, class sizes, curriculum choices, equipment purchasing, and forcing staff redundancies (Lightfoot, 2018). Further, funding is described as an unfair "postcode lottery," which is a common complaint in many countries where education funding is not needs-based (Marsh & Adams, 2017).

A commonly expressed opinion in education is that productivity is achieved by 'working smarter not harder' (a Google search will provide ample examples) – since further 'inputs' are usually not an option. Of course, anyone would cede such benefits. But smart educators and education leaders are working harder and longer hours through necessity – they say they are working harder, irrespective of smarter, efficient procedures or improved technological capability. (Technology has, in fact, made their work a ubiquitous aspect of their lives.) Educators now assume responsibility for tasks previously undertaken at the state level, or by previous employees deemed 'surplus to requirements' through re-engineering or other workforce flexibility/productivity drives, including increasing DIY online form-filling that once employed administrative staff. Work demands on education leaders increase continually, but if individuals are working harder, it is presumed to be their own fault (see for example, Ball, 1994). Much work required of leaders takes time and effort away from education itself.

Calculating productivity is increasingly complex and its pursuit paradoxically takes time, resources, and leaders' attention away from the main game – learning, teaching, research, and service. Productivity accountabilities – output audits, quality audits, and mandated data collection – have created the need for increasing numbers of administration employees, alongside official compliance auditors at central levels, so in many ways it could be said to have decreased efficiency and institutional productivity. Productivity reporting is another mandate that, ironically, mitigates against productivity.

Students are viewed in terms of 'inputs' (costs) and 'outputs' (primarily formal test results). There are concerns that productivity measures are very easy to engineer since their focus is so narrow -- education institutions might, therefore, waive efficiency or effectiveness measures in their favor. For example, to raise effectiveness they may preclude weak students from taking standardized tests (encouraging them to stay away that day) or they may heighten enrollment requirements to take only high-achieving students. And while productivity demands improvement, some 'improved' outputs may not indicate educational improvements. It's possible, for example, to increase the number of graduates by reducing educational rigor and quality, or to raise test scores through selective enrollment.

Measuring education outputs is not as simple as measuring the outputs of a manufacturing industry, for example. In neoliberal policy, education is referred to as a service 'industry' – a people-centered 'enterprise.' It is heavily context specific – with incredible diversity, many goals, and complicated by numerous expectations from a wide range of stakeholders. Taking context into account would make productivity much more difficult to measure comparatively.

Instruments such as standardized testing, student satisfaction surveys, graduate destination surveys, and output calibrations such as research quantum outputs, demonstrate that productivity measurement in education is crude and focused on only minute aspects of the entire enterprise. Consequently, productivity as a concept in education receives a very poor reception amongst educators. It means ramping up efforts to improve quality measures but without consideration being applied to influential contextual factors.

More telling is what outputs are not measured and what cannot be measured. How, for example, can the value of any student's education be measured in terms of productivity, considering education's multiplier effect – the impact of the knowledge and skills they learn; the beliefs, dispositions, and values they acquire; the influence they may have on other individuals, groups, communities, industries, and society in general? Other significant considerations include each student's inherent capabilities or level of motivation and effort, or levels of private funds or efforts that may have contributed.

Hence, in many countries, attempts to calibrate the productivity of teaching staff have met with numerous complications, including attempts to change to reward-based or institutionally decided remuneration systems (as has happened in the UK). Elsewhere, powerful teacher unions have successfully persuaded employing bodies that many educators (and others) contribute directly and indirectly to any student's achievement outcomes. These factors also have an impact on 'human capital' and build 'human resource' capability. In this respect, productivity measures in education can only ever be "partial" (Morris, 2002).

One of the reasons behind this 'partiality' is that productivity activities are almost always quantitative (supposedly 'objective') in nature – the qualitative side of change (which can elucidate contextual details and explanations) is rarely explored. This raises questions about whether the ideas of educators and education leaders are valued, and/or whether subjective information from numerous contexts is simply too difficult to measure and quantify (although such data can provide critical information as to why productivity is high or low).

Unfortunately, data sets and statistics simply don't and can't provide the full story about education or any education institution. Context matters, but one-size-fits-all auditing practices for productivity do not collect information that might provide the contextual reasons and explanations for particular outcomes. Quantitative measurement is often presumed to be more scientific and reliable, but without intensive, contextual information, such data often misses critical aspects of the whole picture.

In sum, productivity is constituted by measurement apparatuses that substantiate new, observable leadership practices and responses – all of which have implications for education. Equating 'outputs' numerically rather than more broadly and holistically produces practices that fundamentally change the direction, focus, and function of education.

References

Australian Government, Productivity Commission (2012). *Schools workforce: Productivity Commission research report, April 2012.* Canberra, ACT: Australian Government.

Ball, S. (1994). *Education reform: A critical and post-structural perspective.* Buckingham, England: Open University Press.

Berns, D. (2011). Teacher evaluations called unproductive. *Las Vegas Sun*, April 20, 2011. Retrieved January 31, 2017 from https://lasvegassun.com/news/2011/apr/20/teacher-evaluations-called-unproductive/

Biesta, G. J. J. (2017). *The rediscovery of teaching.* New York, NY: Routledge.

Boser, U. (2014). *Return on educational investment: A district-by-district evaluation of U.S. educational productivity, July 2014.* Washington, DC: Center for American Progress.

Collins, M. (2016). Did regulation work? *Industry Week*, October 26, 2016. Retrieved August 1, 2018 from www.industryweek.com/regulations/did-deregulation-work

Goss, P., & Sonnemann, J. (2017). *Engaging students: Creating classrooms that improve learning.* Grattan Institute Report No. 2017–2001, February 2017. Carlton, VIC: The Grattan Institute.

Hoxby, C. M. (1996). How teachers' unions affect education production. *The Quarterly Journal of Economics*, 111(3), 671–718. Retrieved June 14, 2018 from https://doi.org/10.2307/2946669

Hoxby, C. M. (2003). School choice and school productivity: Could school choice be a tide that lifts all boats? In C. Hoxby (Ed.), *The economics of school choice* (pp. 287–341). Chicago, IL: University of Chicago Press. Retrieved June 14, 2018 from www.nber.org/books/hox03-1

Kaplan, R. S., & Haas, D. A. (2014). How not to cut health care costs. *Harvard Business Review*, November 2014. Retrieved August 1, 2018 from https://hbr.org/2014/11/how-not-to-cut-health-care-costs

Lightfoot, L. (2018). Headteachers to petition Downing Street: "There's nothing left to cut". *The Guardian*, September 25, 2018. Retrieved October 15, 2018 from www. theguardian.com/education/2018/sep/25/headteachers-p etition-downing-street-budget-cuts

Marsh, S., & Adams, R. (2017). Headteachers warn parents: There is not enough money to fund schools. *The Guardian*, September 27, 2017. Retrieved October 15, 2018 from www.theguardian.com/education/2017/sep/27/headteachers-tell-parents-you-are-sti ll-in-a-postcode-lottery

McGrath Schwartz, D. (2011). Sandoval bill would put teachers on one-year contracts, change layoff system. *Nevada Territory*, April 16, 2011. Retrieved January 31, 2017 from https://la svegassun.com/news/2011/apr/16/sandoval-bill-would-put-teachers-one-year-contract/

Morris, K. (2002). Productivity in higher education. *Business / Higher Education Round Table*, Issue 15, November 2002, 18–22.

Odden, A., & Busch, C. (1998). *Financing schools for high performance: Strategies for improving the use of educational resources*. San Francisco, CA: Jossey-Bass Publishers.

OECD (2014). *Society at a glance 2014: OECD social indicators*. Paris, France: OECD Publishing. Retrieved July 23, 2018 from https://read.oecd-ilibrary.org/socia l-issues-migration-health/society-at-a-glance-2014_soc_glance-2014-en#page1

Squires, R. (2002). Productivity in the higher education sector: A consulting engineer's perspective. *Business / Higher Education Round Table* (B-HERT News), Issue 16, November 2002, 13–14.

10

PERFORMATIVITY

Introduction

Performativity is a complex phenomenon involving many tangible and intangible facets. Fundamentally, performativity concerns extracting greater labor productivity and outputs, making judgments and comparisons about work 'quality,' and inculcating a strong sense of duty within individual employees to motivate their efforts towards attaining organizational goals and needs. In the case of education leaders, the aim is for institutional objectives and aspirations to become the prime focus, over and above personal motivations or ambitions. There is also an expectation is that leaders will instill the same dedication in all education employees.

Performativity embodies individualism, enterprise, productivity, efficiency, competition, improvement, innovation, and entrepreneurialism. It aims to motivate and influence goal achievement, superior outcomes, and excellence, while consolidating a uniform organizational approach to align 'product,' people, and processes with strategy. Ball (2003, p. 216) describes performativity as:

> ...a technology, a culture and a mode of regulation that employs judgements, comparisons and displays as means of incentive, control, attrition and change – based on rewards and sanctions (both material and symbolic). The performances (of individual subjects or organizations) serve as measures of productivity or output, or displays of 'quality', or 'moments' of promotion or inspection. As such they stand for, encapsulate or represent the worth, quality or value of an individual or organization within a field of judgement.

Some aspects of performativity are formalized and overt, externally imposed and motivated, while others are covert – instilled in the psyche of individuals so they are self-motivating. Performativity thus has inwards and outwards effects, operates from within and without, and affects minds, attitudes, actions, and behaviors. It concerns self-control, self-direction, and self-governance (Foucault, 1981) and puts restraints around work conduct considered inappropriate or unimportant.

Performativity instills both positive and negative emotions and feelings, and invades leaders' subjectivities day and night (Ball, 2000). Performativity is promoted through work targets, key performance indicators, or other means by which performance is judged and rated. Performance-related exercises are forms of accountability. Corporate accountabilities are the responsibility of leaders who assume oversight (and often a level of liability) for their own performance, the performance of others, and the institutions they lead.

Performativity thus structures power relations and is a new form of both socialization and the moral order within the neoliberal 'professionalism' and 'managerialism' based on greater regulation, compliance, and accountability (Ball, 2005). Leaders' performance and institutional outputs are 'managed,' 'assessed,' 'appraised,' or 'reviewed' by others – and usually many others – students and their parents ('clients' or 'customers'), governing boards or councils, education authorities, governments and government instrumentalities, private companies (as in the case of standardized testing), the media, and internationally by agencies such as the OECD. 'Performance outcomes' and 'outputs' are gauged in many ways, but when it comes to education leaders, generally everyone has a view.

Performativity is key to the personal effort of the neoliberal subject who is continually learning in order to retain currency in the employment market. It is instrumental in creating 24/7 work cultures, over-scheduling, work intensification, and the erosion of professional life into 'personal' times and spaces – or 'life overload' (Haig, 2018). Daily work, impending work, and future employment prospects and opportunities are shaped by performative calibrations.

Performativity is embodied in the neoliberal subject as individuals respond to intentions, expectations, and regulation in everyday education practice (Ball, 2016). It is the means by which education is regulated and 're-formed' through its own practitioners to re-work education cultures (Ibid.). Performativity both informs and 'reforms' education practice while pervading the self, the meaning and purposes of education, what education leaders do, how, and when (Ball, 2000). It involves impression management and reputation management – observable behaviors and what is 'seen' to have been done and achieved (Ibid.).

Performativity concerns meeting or exceeding job requirements and pleasing 'line managers' who are the formal determiners and raters of performance – some of whom are known, some whom are unknown and invisible – hence performativity can involve a degree of concealment, facelessness, and confidentiality.

Governing bodies are responsible for determining institutional strategic goals (within overarching systemic strategic frameworks), monitoring their enactment and organizational progress, and reviewing their effectiveness. Hence, governing councillors also bear responsibility for performative accountabilities while becoming another level of reporting for education leaders. Education governance, therefore, serves as a site of compliance within individual institutions, as well as a closer point of scrutiny and assessment of institutional and leadership performance.

Externally, performance is gauged via numerous audit, review, testing, and reporting regimes – a topic discussed in the following chapter. Increasingly, quantitative data analyses of leadership 'performance' outcomes are taking precedence over qualitative evaluations.

Performance criteria become performance outcome ratings. Performance reviews or appraisal mechanisms determine work quality on a continuum from 'success' to 'failure,' and hence are both seductive and dangerous in the possibilities they elicit (Foucault, 1983). For example, enrollment growth may indicate success and boost a leader's career prospects while declining student numbers could be interpreted by assessors as a sign of failure (Allen & Burgess, year unknown, p. 7).

Performance development, appraisal, and calibration encapsulate a set of inextricably correlated aims: centralized control over 'service provisioning,' minimization of foreseeable risks, 'efficiency' enhancement, and the max-imization of outputs, 'effectiveness,' and impact.

The leadership functions under scrutiny focus on improvement of institutional outcomes (primarily student achievement outcomes), effective staff engagement, relationship management, innovation and ideas for development, 'customer/ consumer' services, and the student experience.

Performative Instruments in Education Leadership

Performative requirements and expectations are embedded in texts such as job descriptions and person specifications, enterprise agreements, strategic plans, and through activities such as performance appraisals, professional reviews, and surveys (for example, 360° evaluations, institutional inspections, and annual institutional reporting regimes). Through these means education leaders are constantly aware of being monitored, evaluated, and 'surveilled,' with expectations of 'adding value.' These are scaffolded by employment practices such as probationary periods, limited tenure employment contracts, performance-based pay or bonus schemes, compul-sory registration requirements (such as registration to teach), professional learning obligations, or mandated training hours.

A further aspect of education work that bolsters performativity concerns neoliberal employment and work practices. Education work is increasingly 'flexible' and destabilized, having changed from a mostly permanent workforce to one more contingent and short-term (with part-time or temporary workers filling previously permanent positions). Job classifications are reduced in number while job descrip-tions have expanded in scope, requiring cross-skilling and cross-training to ensure the fewest number of employees possess the greatest number of necessary skills (Smith, 1997). Neoliberal employment in education is less hierarchical in structure and increasingly efficient (cost-effective), with duties being blurred and fluid across the workforce. Education work itself requires more intensified effort which, for education leaders, extends through longer hours of the day and all days of the week. Temporary or part-time workers have been the most disadvantaged as their status shifts from 'core' to 'peripheral,' while a further noticeable consequence is sharper gender and race hierarchies within education. With limited tenure employment contracts, careers in education leadership are less stable and more likely to be of short duration. Through all these means, education 'reforms' are presumed to be achieved to aid productivity and efficiency.

Leadership Performance Enhancement and Assessment

Myriad data sets about institutional outcomes are gathered from individuals, classrooms, courses or year levels, individual education sites, education administrative districts, as well as nationally and internationally. Education authorities are "awash with data" (Anderson, Turnbull & Arcaira, 2017, p. 1).

However, metrics focused on education leaders are becoming normalized as performative accountabilities. In the schooling sector, for example, all kinds of information are seen to reflect on the effectiveness of principals – their on-the-job appraisal/evaluations include assessments of student achievement data collected through standardized testing; student behavior data, such as the number of suspensions or exclusions; surveys relating to student, teacher, and parent satisfaction levels; retention and completion rates; budgetary efficiency and effectiveness; to name a few.

A growing range of leadership 'tracking' data and analytics instruments[1] have emerged that are designed to promote leadership capability and labor productivity, while concomitantly embedding performance requirements and expectations in leaders. Such instruments are marketed as delivering opportunities for 'doing more with data,' aiding 'evidence-based' decision-making, improving methods of data collection, while overcoming previous methods that were problematic (such as relying on third-party, word-of-mouth references and endorsements, or being subject to nepotism such as through 'old boys' networks).

Data is considered to provide solid 'evidence' of performance for decisions about future work activities and leadership development. The Australian Institute for Teaching and School Leadership (AITSL), for example, ties data tracking to institutional success, saying that "[s]uccessful jurisdictions and schools are increasingly using data and metrics to track and report on leadership development achievements, and to inform decision-making on future actions and investments." AITSL suggests that leadership 'success' can be measured through a number of (very linear) steps:

- collectively identifying and articulating the objectives of leadership development strategies
- implementation
- identifying appropriate metrics and measurement methods

- tracking progress over time
- assessing success
- ongoing review to address areas for future development.

In practice, AITSL proposes these measures be augmented by instruments such as 360° feedback evaluations, self-reflection tools, internal performance and development processes, and externally administered psychometric assessment tools.

Anderson et al. (2017, p. 3), talking about the principalship, argue the performative benefits thus:

> ...we have seen that a commitment to managing the principalship more intentionally helps spur greater attention to information—and, in turn, better information presents new opportunities for shaping principal placement, support, and succession planning. Compelling displays of information are helping district leaders take advantage of their opportunities to address issues of school leadership.

Along these lines, leadership 'pipelines' or 'leadership tracking systems' (LTS) have recently been introduced in some school systems as means of augmenting leadership development and performance appraisal, heightening leadership performativity. Leadership pipelines are repositories of high-level, longitudinal data sets about individual leaders designed to manage all aspects of their performance. Pipelines generate 'business intelligence' by gathering, mining, tracking, analyzing, reviewing, and storing data over time.

Pipeline data sets start with locating, preparing, and selecting leadership 'talent'; making decisions about 'talent' development and support (using assessments of past experience, identifying individual strengths ['signature assets'] and 'growth areas'); evaluating leadership performance; monitoring career progression, through to succession planning. Proponents also propose sharing individuals' longitudinal data with those who run education leadership courses and training programs to enable further streamlining and alignment.

Pipeline data focuses leaders' attention on the improvement priorities that assessors and policymakers want to see. The word 'intentionality' is used to explain pipeline effects enabling school districts to "manage" and "actively shape the caliber" (*Ibid.* p. 1) of education leaders by assessing and making judgments about each leader on whom they have accumulated data.

While focused on individuals, aggregated data can detect and diagnose real-time systemic trends and patterns to understand what is transpiring, or can be used to make calculations, forecasts, probabilities, and predications for the purpose of improving leader decisions and actions. Pipelines are promoted as 'early warning alerts' to identify problems or needs 'sooner rather than later.' Hence, they are promoted as having the capacity to unearth data gaps or data that have previously gone unseen or unnoticed and which, therefore, have not been acted upon for improvement (Bienkowski, Feng, & Means, 2012). Pipelines overcome traditional issues of education administration being siloed into specialized sections, often using different data systems, with no data sharing. Pipelines and instruments with functionalities like them bring data sets together, being both accountability instruments and improvement motivators, performing quality checks, identifying anomalies and outliers, raising red flags, rectifying errors, and reducing 'incidents' and incident levels.

Pipelines are presumed to be quick and efficient measures of leadership effectiveness while "unleashing the power of information" (Anderson et al., 2017, p. 2). Further, they can be customized to suit various contexts and priorities, with choices as to how data are gathered and presented.

A further aim is for education systems and education leaders to be 'data informed and focused,' 'concentrating on delivering,' 'stepping up' and 'ramping up efforts,' to 'selectively groom and grow potential leaders,' so that education leadership work 'serves important [higher policy] purposes' (see Anderson et al., 2017).

Pipelines are promoted as motivating individual leaders towards higher levels of achievement, while determining areas of strength and areas requiring improvement. Numbers are codes and abstractions that are assumed to be 'impartial,' 'dispassionate,' 'systematic,' 'scientific,' 'methodical,' 'reliable,' 'efficient,' 'consistent,' 'valid.' Presenting the quantum of education leadership work in numerical form is depicted as an 'objective,' fair and logical way of determining how people are 'performing.'

As developments in algorithms, analytics, and data mining continue to proliferate, it is clear that the impact on education leadership will be even more impactful than is already the case. Being developed are autonomous intelligent machines that will make determinations based on personal data to 'profile' the characteristics of individual leaders. Profiles are presumed to predict likely future behaviors, some of which may be deemed in need of adaptation, change, or development. In future it might be the case of comply with profile recommendations (and undertake learning and actions for change) or leave (lose one's employment). It is easy to see, however, how various leadership decisions and actions can be easily tracked, with leaders' habits, relationships and associations, and time usage being recorded and assessed through profiling exercises.

Critique

While justified as in terms of improvement, performativity embraces accountability mechanisms that control, 'manage,' evaluate, and judge education leaders' work. Education leaders may not be aware or give consent about the data collected about them. They do not always make decisions about the data gathered, the means by which they are collected, the ways in which data are analyzed or interpreted and reported, or the purposes for which data will be used, how they are used, or by whom. Further, education leaders rarely have the opportunity to provide feedback to systemic leaders or immediate line managers – performative exercises are not a two-way street. They serve the interests of those with the authority to make assessments and judgments – and may not serve the interests of leaders, particularly if leaders are not involved in the development of assessment instruments and if there is no means of providing explanations and reasons for the actions, decisions, and reasons under scrutiny.

Some leaders resent their work being 'surveilled.' They perceive the ways in which performance is judged and calibrated as signaling a lack of trust, while there are also concerns about judgments being made by others who do not perform education leadership work and the technical instruments by which measurements are made and performance is calibrated. Education leaders may not perceive the data collected and dissected as the most valuable in determining their 'on-the-ground' assessments of what needs to be done, why, and when. There is a strong sense that measures only cover so much, but not the full extent of leaders' work – and perhaps avoid what leaders considered to be the most important aspects of their roles (which will be different in every context).

Performativity keeps people on the 'straight and narrow,' on a 'short leash.' Performative data are used to compare and contrast, so inevitably some form of scaling or ranking occurs, and there is nothing leaders can do about it. External bodies who devise measurement mechanisms, and those that control them, have often never been leaders of education institutions, yet their decisions have a huge impact on those who do, as well as their leadership practices.

Audit and compliance practices are individualized – they apply to individuals who are required to account for their productivity towards attaining key performance goals, and to individual institutions, whose outputs are compared with other institutions to provide indications of 'quality.' In both instances, standardized measurement instruments are used to make comparisons but fail to take account of contextual or circumstantial matters. Data may evade explanatory information – for example, there may be demographic reasons behind enrollment decline – hence, leadership is not always instrumental in outcomes. Contextual factors have an effect and an impact on performance, but 'what matters is measured' – peripheral matters are inconsequential to the compilation of assessments, ratings, and rankings, even if they do have a bearing on outcomes. Hence, some aspects of education are relegated to 'peripheral' status.

Unfortunately, despite acknowledging the distributed nature of education leadership, performance measurement practices focus on individuals and usually those with formal titles. Education leaders can and do have impact, but it is unfair and impractical to measure leadership 'success' by focusing on a sole leader when so many other people and variables are involved in producing institutional outcomes – education requires teamwork and education institutions rest on a 'leadership at all levels' approach. Implicit in this practice is a sense that only one individual is responsible and liable for outcomes, hence performative measures often embrace a very traditional conception of leadership – the single, heroic, all-powerful, all-knowing leader (see Starr, 2011).

Measurement metrics are mechanistic in their approach and myopic in their scope. The messiness, 'impromptu-ness,' and unpredictability of the daily quotidian in education cannot be factored in or captured.

Performativity can heighten leader anxiety and create a sense of insecurity, instability, and self-doubt. There is a sense of always being judged, daring not to put a step wrong. Job satisfaction and morale can be affected and a sense of alienation can over-ride confidence in personal capabilities and convictions. The result, according to Ball (2016), is inauthentic practice that erodes professional judgment and 'intuition,' and inauthentic relationships that undermine professionalism.

One of the biggest responsibilities borne by education leaders concerns their own job – including their work experiences and longevity in a leadership role. Education leadership positions are usually limited tenure contracted positions covering a set time period, with renewal or dismissal at the end of the contracted period (often three or five years). This fact alone brings home the enormity of the responsibility for institutional performance outcomes which have a knock-on impact on personal livelihoods and professional reputations.

Implications can be significant. For example, the School Improvement Grant (SIG) Program, part of the *No Child Left Behind Act* in USA (2001–2015), made assessments on school outcomes and leadership performance to identify:

- turnaround schools (where staff were fired and a new principal and staff appointed)
- transformation schools (the principal was fired and a series of structural strategies and curriculum changes implemented and monitored, with rewards and sanctions for subsequent success or failure)
- restart schools (the school was closed and re-opened under charter school management)
- school closure (all students were transferred to higher-achieving schools).

Trujillo and Renee (2015) reported that of 1,600 schools receiving SIG funds, 74% were transformation schools and 20% were turnaround schools, demonstrating the vulnerability of leaders, as well as teachers and schools.

This is a misdiagnosis of the root causes concerning socially, politically, economically, and culturally infused contexts. It is easy to put 'failure' down to ineffective teachers and principals and to label institutions as 'failing,' but education offers no level playing field and context plays a huge part in determining education outcomes, but there is little or no accounting for context. Performance accountabilities reduce a complex endeavor involving millions of uniquely different individuals and education sites to a numbers game, with the effect being to "shock, interrogate, shame… and abstract individuals from their contexts" Taubman (2009, p. xi). The 'failure' is structural failure, including the failure of assessors who elide this well-established and researched fact. 'No excuses' policy measures are narrow and error-ridden measures of education success and effectiveness.

Amazingly, education systems don't appear to learn from their mistakes, which is particularly disappointing when education is supposed to encourage critical and deep thinking, creativity, originality and, importantly for this example, trust and faith in the professionalism of practitioners as learners, thinkers, and problem-solvers. Processes that do not include sufficient recognition of leaders' reflections on experience (information that is not collected) means that it is education systems that fail, over and over.

While providing some useful data for schools, official data collections are not the only forms of information available and, many would contend, not the most important information on which to base the most appropriate decisions for learning, teaching, and leadership development. Performance accountabilities, however, embody the unintended consequence of distracting professionals and taking them away from the tasks they would normally deem to be of greater importance and greater educational impact, while changing the nature and substance of leadership work (Ball, 2000).

Performative regimes are exogenous impositions and forms of control that convey a lack of trust amidst extrinsic motivators in the form of rewards and sanctions designed to incentivize and extract optimal performance. However, performance outcomes appear to never be enough – improvement is 'continual.' The stakes are higher with outstanding ratings becoming harder to achieve.

Complex social realities and processes cannot be reduced to numbers and statistics. Like other forms of accountability (see Chapter 10), the irony about performativity is its attempt to control individuals and individual 'autonomous' institutions, which runs counter to neoliberalism's prime principle and valorization of sovereign individualism.

Note

1 For in-depth definitions of terms such as learning analytics and data mining, see Bienkowski et al. (2012).

References

Allen, R., & Burgess, S. (n.d.). *The future of competition and accountability in education.* Retrieved June 13, 2018 from www.bristol.ac.uk/media-library/sites/cmpo/migrated/documents/competition.pdf

Anderson, L. M., Turnbull, B. J., & Arcaira, E. R. (2017). *Leader tracking systems: Turning data into information for school leadership.* (Report commissioned by The Wallace Foundation, New York, NY, June 2017.) Washington, DC: Policy Studies Association, Inc.

Australian Institute for Teaching and School Leadership (AITSL) (2018). *Leading for impact: Australian guidelines for school leadership development,* December 2017. Melbourne, VIC: AITSL.

Ball, S. J. (2000) Performativities and fabrications in the education economy: Towards the performative society. *Australian Educational Researcher, 17*(3), 1–24.

Ball, S. J. (2003). The teacher's soul and the terrors of performativity. *Journal of Education Policy*, 18(2), 215–228.

Ball, S. J. (2005). *Education policy and social class: The selected works of Stephen J. Ball.* London, England: Routledge.

Ball, S. J. (2016). Subjectivity as a site of struggle: Refusing neoliberalism? *British Journal of Sociology of Education*, 37(8), 1129–1146.

Bienkowski, M., Feng, M., & Means, B. (2012). *Enhancing teaching and learning through educational data mining and learning analytics: An issue brief.* Washington, DC: US Department of Education.

Foucault, M. (1981). *The courage of truth: Lectures at the College De France 1983–43.* London, England: Palgrave Macmillan.

Foucault, M. (1983). On the genealogy of ethics: An overview of work in progress. In H. Dreyfus & P. Rabinow (Eds.), *Michel Foucault: Beyond structuralism and hermeneutics* (pp. 229–252). Chicago, IL: University of Chicago Press.

Haig, M. (2018). *Notes on a nervous planet.* Edinburgh, Scotland: Canongate Books Ltd.

Smith, V. (1997). New forms of work organization. *Annual Review of Sociology*, 23, 315–339.

Starr, K. (2011). Principals and the politics of resistance to change. *Educational Management, Administration and Leadership*, 39(6), 646–660.

Taubman, P. M. (2009). *Teaching by numbers: Deconstructing the discourse of standards and accountability in education.* New York, NY: Routledge.

Trujillo, T., & Renee, M. (2015). Irrational exuberance for market-based reform: How federal turnaround policies thwart democratic schooling. *Teachers College Record*, 117(6), 1–34. Retrieved May 8, 2017 from www.tcrecord.org/Content.asp?ContentID=17880

11

ACCOUNTABILITY

Education is a public and private 'good' and, given its expense and importance in the lives of individuals, communities, and nations, it is understandable and reasonable to expect accountability for practice and quality. Governments and other authorities need to ensure that education delivers. It is also understandable that overseeing bodies wish to find reliable means of determining how education systems are performing. In education institutions, accountability/audit/testing/compliance/regulatory practices are focused on the education program and outcomes in teaching and learning, or on activities concerning education business and governance.

Consumers of education also have rights and expectations about the service/experience they will encounter. Transparency and accountability mechanisms serve as a safeguard to protect and uphold standards, to meet consumer needs and expectations. Consumer rights and expectations incur responsibilities for education leaders and all employees, with accountabilities in place to provide governments and the public with a measure of assurance.

Accountability policies and practices in education are extensive, varied, and inescapable. There are numerous accountability regimes operating in education, each focused on differing components and embedding specific forms and degrees of surveillance and sanction. Accountabilities are intended to provide organizational and systemic efficiency; ensure ethicality; and provide 'evidence' to inform policy, and improvements to practice. Standards and performance levels represent a baseline of accepted outcomes – the norm, the average, and encapsulate notions of conformity and uniformity – to provide a level of certainty and assurance. They serve purposes of risk aversion, compliance, regulation, monitoring, and control, and produce the metrics and analytics – the 'facts' – to enable comparison, encourage competition, and enhance consumer choice.

The word 'accountability' encompasses such a large range of activities that the plural form is used here – 'accountabilities.' Accountabilities are official measures of systemic, institutional, or individual performance. They are mandated by education authorities and bureaucracies with the imprimatur of the state, are inextricably linked, and are controlled by 'objective,' third parties. Accountabilities hold individual education leaders to account, and while they come under a range of guises, they continue to grow in scope and consume leaders' time, energy, and thoughts.

Within education institutions, corporate governance and leadership accountabilities concern adherence and alignment with government legislation, systemic policy decisions, corporate mission and vision statements, and strategic plans – these are the methods by which central bureaucracies attempt to ensure consistency, quality assurance, and public accountability across education sectors. In short, accountability instruments and processes aim for 'delivery' improvements from costs and compliance, to provisioning, programs, personnel, and outcomes.

While accountability policies and processes make transparent certain aspects of education for the purposes of conformity and for making judgments about worth or quality, they also change education cultures towards neoliberal goals by instilling a sense of cultural control (Smith, 1997).

Education accountabilities have often incurred similar responses in policy and practice across the developed world. The OECD, for example, collects and compares international quantitative data and it justifies this role in terms of ensuring education systems achieve greater efficiency, effectiveness, and equity.

Accountability regimes are regarded as an efficient and effective way of managing education systems. A high premium is placed on data to monitor and measure compliance, progress, and outcomes, and technological capability changes the way data are collected, stored, and used.[1] Accountability mechanisms are usually, therefore, technical and quantitative in nature and use multiple methods of calibration – metrics, analytics,[2] competencies, standards, profiling, rubrics, grades, ratings and rankings, scorecard systems. Accountabilities come in the form of compliance regulations, standing orders, audits, mandated testing regimes, evaluations and appraisals, reviews and reports. They are presented as 'objective,' 'disinterested,' 'impartial,' 'dispassionate,' 'systematic,' 'scientific,' 'methodical,' 'reliable,' 'efficient,' 'consistent,' and 'valid' means of measuring, monitoring, and reporting on the quantum and quality of the activities and outputs of education. At their root, accountabilities represent a baseline of accepted outcomes – the norm, the average, and encapsulate notions of conformity and uniformity. Policy responses are an outcome of the slicing and dicing of data so derived.

Technological forms of regulation/compliance checking/monitoring continue to expand. Big data and its uses continue to expand, and as machine learning and robotic technologies advance, many different ways of collecting and analyzing data will emerge, on top of new ways of learning. For example, it is now commonplace in education to use social network analyses and web scraping (harvesting) in employment selection processes.

Numbers, codes, and other abstractions of education (in all its complexity) are applied because they are purported to have many benefits that are interlinked with neoliberal aims. They primarily aim for alignment, improvement, and 'transformation,' and they measure institutional or individual progress towards these aims. Accountabilities also aim to achieve increased efficiency and effectiveness while providing transparent information for 'clients' or 'customers' to exercise market choices and make judgments based on individual self-interests. Accountabilities are believed to incentivize for 'quality' as individual institutions became the core unit of change and responsibility, and as employees ('human resources') and students strive for 'excellence.' Education data is published in transparent forms to enable consumers to make comparisons and choices. Transparency and accountability mechanisms safeguard and uphold standards to meet the expectations of authorities and the public.

Transparency and accountability policy mechanisms put the onus on individuals and individual institutions to do the right thing and be seen to be doing the right thing so that the public's rights are protected. Accountabilities are, therefore, performative in that they focus on the individual institution from which further assessments and measurements about leadership productivity and effectiveness are extracted. Results compare individual institutions with concomitant assumptions about the abilities and effectiveness of education leaders.

Ultimately, however, the state's interest is in ensuring education meets its neoliberal remit concerning continual improvements to aid national economic growth, competitiveness, and productivity. Governments make election promises about education and accountabilities they will put in place to ensure policy is achieved and improvements are monitored. Within neoliberal policy regimes, education has to be attuned to the needs of the political economy, business, and industry, and have a focus beyond benefits to individuals. Bennett, as cited in Matters (2006, p. iii) argues:

> To keep jobs and to maintain current living standards, governments need to constantly improve the skill levels and productivity of their existing workforces. But to guarantee that future living standards are maintained, those governments must also ensure that today's students are educated to the highest achievement standards possible. And [education institutions] must be held accountable for that achievement if those standards are to be met.

Education systems and institutions are continually repositioning themselves to be more adaptive to change, responsive to 'customers/consumers' (students and parents), and to drive improvements across all functions of education delivery and business.

Educators hold positions of responsibility and trust, so to raise the stakes the UK government, for example, publishes the outcomes of hearings against teachers and issues orders prohibiting certain individuals from teaching for unacceptable behaviors – misconduct being defined as "unacceptable professional conduct and conduct which may bring the profession into disrepute" (Teaching Regulation Agency, 2018). Naming and shaming is part of transparency and accountability regimes and serves to keep everyone on track.[3]

Types of Accountabilities

These are vertical and horizontal accountabilities. Vertical accountabilities are externally imposed and controlled and include official compliance and regulation requirements, as well as audits, testing, and reviews. Vertical accountabilities are scaffolded with further mandates including regulations regarding generating, retrieving, managing, storing, using, and destroying data, as well as the time limits for data storage. There are also accountabilities for data accuracy, information being up-to-date, compliance with International Information Standards, privacy assurances, and protocols being adhered to for both temporary and permanent records.

Horizontal accountability is far more important and includes data that are relevant for internal institutional purposes designed to increase professionalism and meet local needs, including data about teaching and student learning. Horizontal accountabilities – which are often not compulsory – have the greatest impact on students and their learning and institutional improvement.

Data derived from mandated vertical accountabilities are used to produce rankings at international, national, district, institutional, and individual levels. For example, school students are tested against their national and international peers. Academics are caught up in research output metrics, whether they wish to be or not. Ranked data are often used inauthentically and turned into league tables. For example, high-stakes standardized student testing regimes are expected to raise the stakes, and the creation of league tables to aid comparison and promote competition and improvement.

Vertical accountability regimes are not simply a mechanism of "coercive" surveillance (Shore & Wright, 1997), but provide means by which the state can regulate, observe, investigate, inspect, and intervene. The aim is for education systems and education leaders to be 'data informed and focused,' 'concentrate on delivering,' to 'step up' and 'ramp up efforts,' and to 'selectively groom and grow potential leaders' so that education leadership work serves important [higher policy] purposes (see Anderson, Turnbull, & Arcaira, 2017). Vertical accountabilities are prescriptive, authorized, and enforced and, combined with the full gamut of consequences – positive and negative – they are hence highly significant to every education institution and the lives of all education leaders. There are significant costs for 'poor performance.' For example, speaking from a U.S. schooling perspective Trujillo and Renee (2015, p. 4) remind us that "[s]tandardized test scores are still the main means for identifying schools for intervention, and punitive sanctions for underperformance remain central to the federal program."

Education data collected in the name of accountability typically include:

- student learning (mostly gauged through standardized literacy, numeracy, science, mathematics tests)
- student retention and course completion rates
- satisfaction levels – surveys of students, parents, and staff members
- absenteeism statistics
- behavior records (student suspensions, exclusions, expulsions)
- graduate destinations and employability data
- student exit/transfer data
- enrollment statistics, including enrollment diversity data
- financial audits
- the quantum of research outputs graded by 'quality'
- competitive research income, including commercial income
- compliance checks
- risk assessments
- occupational health and safety management audits
- education reviews
- performance planning and performance appraisals
- policy reviews.

New accountabilities follow new governments and occur when new policies or funding models are announced – so accountabilities change regularly.

Critique

Accountability is the means by which authorities maintain power and influence over autonomous institutions and individuals – they are "the poison pill" of neoliberalism – "the means by which the few control the many" (Evers, 2018, personal correspondence).

Accountabilities are non-negotiable and implicitly embrace a sense of being answerable, duty-bound, obligated, 'weighed up,' compared, and kept in check. However, antonyms also provide telling insights, with non-compliance being a 'transgression,' 'violation,' 'infraction,' and denoting insubordination, recalcitrance, disobedience, nonconformity, ungovernability, unruliness, with offenders being 'out of line,' 'bending the rules,' and 'making waves.'

There are some obvious downsides of accountability regimes from the perspective of education leaders. Accountabilities of all kinds are time-consuming, and mostly serve external, extrinsic needs and not internal priorities. In addition, they take leaders' focus from teaching and learning and are making leadership roles more complex.

Having to pay attention to various high-stakes accountabilities has incurred a dual role for leaders, who have to keep an eye on the business side of the institution as well as the education side. Many have observed the paradoxical effect of this duality – while expectations for education outcomes and student achievement have risen, the time and focus leaders are able to dedicate to teaching and learning has been eroded by expanding business and compliance accountabilities (Starr, 2015). Many leaders admit to having delegated much of their education-focused work to others in order to keep abreast of the gamut of tasks now under their remit (Starr, 2009). All are adamant, however, that education leadership work appears to have been changed irrevocably as a result (see for example, Starr, 1999).

External mandates fail to acknowledge or consider context and contextual influences that have a profound impact on education and its outcomes. Regulatory regimes rarely take a proportionate perspective – all education institutions are charged with the same remit and requirements irrespective of their size, the complexity of their program/s, community, or the subsequent levels of risk they have to manage. There is an implicit refusal to acknowledge huge differences in education provisioning – education is not a level playing field, but accountabilities unfairly determine those who will be rewarded in education and the 'failing' institutions to be penalized (including forced closure – with calculations about opportunity costs for individuals and communities never being part of the equation). To make adjustments for context and social needs appears too difficult for policymakers and education's assessors, hence simple, one-size-fits-all measures are rolled out. External assessments and measurements dependent on whittling complexity across contexts down to a numbers game, however, are not 'the facts.' They do not consider education institutions as socio-political and normative contexts. Performance and learning standards are simply that – abstractions about an average.

Statistics are also inherently unreliable to greater or lesser degrees. Data reporting may contain mistakes and can be manipulated, intentionally or unintentionally. Responsible persons may under-report or elide certain information. Every statistical sample is subject to a level of standard error and uncertainty. There can be sampling and measurement errors and faults in assumptions underlying analysis. Data storage and privacy may not be adequate.

Proponents of the 'jaggedness principle' criticize one-size-fits-all assessments, since no one is average, no one is normal, and further, notions such as 'above' or 'below' average, are equally problematic. The infinite variability of human beings, each individual's strengths and weaknesses, their unique behavioral predispositions, and diverse responses to life situations ensures that one-dimensional rankings arrived at through averages are seriously flawed. Simply put, standards and averages are flawed because they are one-dimensional and ignore context and complexity (Rose, 2015).

As Rose (2015, p. 10) points out, "from the cradle to the grave you are measured against the ever-present yardstick of the average, judged according to how closely you approximate it or how far you are able to exceed it." Further:

> Most of us know intuitively that a score on a personality test, a rank on a standardized assessment, a grade point average, or a rating on a performance review doesn't reflect your, or your child's, or your students' or your employees' abilities. And yet the concept of average as a yardstick for measuring individuals has been so thoroughly ingrained in our minds that we rarely question it seriously." (*Ibid.*)

However, the discourse used by comparative data collectors and assessors around accountabilities is very risk-averse around their own practices – they refer to 'inferences,' 'estimates,' 'approximations,' 'conceptual limitations,' 'sampling uncertainty,' 'uncertainty zones,' 'error risk,' 'unweighted mean,' 'time distortions,' 'missing data,' 'unreliable estimates,' 'reliability thresholds,' 'likelihood,' 'restrictive assumptions' – which provide their own evidence as to the statistical capriciousness and untrustworthiness. But, there are no escape clauses for education institutions.

The OECD, for example, claims to provide "an authoritative compilation of key international comparisons of education statistics" (2014, p. 34). More valid, however, may be its sub-national comparisons, for example, between the various states or provinces of a country (in most federated countries, responsibility often resides at the state level). Large regional variations may be reported, but international statistics would elide such nuances. It would be possible, for example, for a low-scoring country to demonstrate some high-performing regions within it, and vice versa.

Shanghai, China was the highest performer in PISA results in 2012 – it is one city in China and not representative of the whole country, but this one city is compared with entire countries, including both rich and poor nations such as Qatar and Peru (both low-ranking OECD performers). The OECD reports that one in three Korean students is a top performer in mathematics, but in countries like the United Kingdom and Norway, students perform below the OECD average.

Data are abused by being used for inauthentic and disingenuous purposes – to compare, make unfair judgments, and create league tables. When they attempt to provide comparisons across nations and the enormous contextual differences that entails, they are on shakier ground than policy decision-makers give them credit for. As Campbell (1979, p. 85) argues:

> Achievement tests may well be valuable indicators of general school achievement *under conditions of normal teaching aimed at general competence*. But when test scores become the goal of the teaching process, they both lose their value as indicators of educational status and distort the educational process in undesirable ways.

For students' learning, for example, this means more time and curriculum emphasis is spent in preparation for standardized tests. Learning areas not included in standardized tests have become less important. The arts, humanities, languages, health and physical education are now peripheral to mathematics/numeracy, the sciences, technology, English/literacy. Further, these are subjects promoted as government policy priorities – usually referred to as STEM subjects (science, technology, engineering, mathematics).

Covington (2000) identifies two major motivations for learning amongst students. The first is the motivation to please parents and teachers, impress peers, and achieve high grades – referred to as a 'performance orientation.' Another group of students are more interested in achieving competence, understanding, and enjoying and appreciating their learning experiences – referred to as a 'mastery orientation'. This is slower and is more about achieving a 'personal best' rather than achieving against the scores of others. The former can rely on rote learning, which can dampen real learning, whereas the latter fosters real engagement, creativity, risk-taking, and inquiry.

Decades of education research demonstrates that students engage more fully in their learning when they see a real purpose in it; when it is authentic, intrinsic to their interests, and when they have some purchase on how it is achieved – and the opposite is also true (Leithwood et al, 2004). A focus on grading, assessing, and testing reinforces the performance orientation and snuffs out the mastery orientation which is natural in young children (Leithwood et al, 2004). The most negative effects of testing which ranks students is that it serves to disengage even more those who are already most at risk in their schooling (Leithwood, 2001).

We can focus on more authentic forms of assessment – i.e. assessment that measures the achievement of criteria or goals, best achieved through an inquiry practice into topics of significance to the students and perhaps completed through cooperative teamwork. This is about making learning meaningful, more interesting, and utilizing the strengths of all students rather than having them complete abstract tasks for competitive assessment against others.

Education leaders consider mandated accountabilities to be overbearing – very bureaucratic, managerial, cumbersome to administer, too time-consuming, and often complicated and difficult to read, while online formats are criticized for being 'clunky,' faulty and unreliable (see for example, Dabbagh, 2018; McGowan, 2018).

A few problem cases serve to justify even stricter standards, more comprehensive reviews, audits and reporting, and tighter monitoring. However, criticisms further surround the ability of certain education institutions to avoid levels of accountability and sanctions for poor performance, to influence the state's judgments through their ability to mobilize political capital (Nespor & Voithofer, 2016).

Data are presented in technical ways that may not be easily accessible or understandable and there is even evidence that some educators feel insecure about reading and using data (Earl, 2005). Further, those who receive and interpret external data take an individual's and institution's 'story' out of their own hands – they paint a picture of 'success' or otherwise that will never be the true picture because they cannot provide all details, variables, and qualitative explanations. In other words, measurement mechanisms represent 'facts' but fail to capture the full picture – the salient details that would make them authentic and meaningful.

Education institutions have gone about 'institutionalizing' and formalizing corporatized accountabilities using similar methods and instruments internally in efforts to coerce staff at all levels to comply and engage with strategic goal achievement; instigating internal reviews; performance appraisals; self-assessment tools; peer review and feedback processes; targets, benchmarks, and models of 'best practice'; key performance indicators that serve to make individuals their own masters and jailers; and notions of decentralized autonomy (irrespective of re-centralized power and control).

Other changes to education work include constant reporting and providing 'evidence', while education workers are more likely to be employed as contracted employees (not permanently employed) or to work on a limited tenure basis if they are education leaders. None of these neoliberal practices were prevalent in education before the 1980s.

An ironic effect of pervasive accountabilities is the change to the education workforce in order to keep up with these time-consuming requirements. Funds that could be spent on resources more closely influencing students and their learning – teachers, for example – have been reallocated to a new and diverse range of leadership, middle management, and administration roles. These education employees must take account of the external policy and regulatory environment and institutional needs to focus on achieving obligatory requirements.

Corporatized accountabilities are criticized because of the lack of consultation behind their rationale, the processes entailed, the uses to which data will be used, or the potential outcomes they may have (including unintended consequences); a lack of take-up of and engagement in longer-term strategic plans within the organization, with realities often being too focused on short-term operational issues; and the waste of effort and energy required to adjust plans and processes when accountability impositions change (due to a change of government, for example).

Education leaders believe there is too little support and training for new roles and responsibilities even though neoliberal subjects are expected to be continually learning; increasing surveillance creates steeper organizational hierarchies of power and authority; while accountabilities increase pressures, demands, and workloads, referred to as 'excessive' and as 'work intensification' (see for example, Howse, 2017; Smith, 1997).

This leaves little time to think and be creative while always feeling the workload is insurmountable; there are increased levels of work-related stress and ill-health amongst education leaders, and a leadership succession, shortage and disengagement problem because people decide they do not want to do these jobs. A consequence is the 24/7 nature of the position, with much work conducted outside working hours during personal time. In short, accountabilities apply to everything and everyone except policy and policymakers. So whose interests do accountabilities serve?

Education's social purposes are opaque in policy, but the focus of accountabilities are clear demonstrations of the state's free market, neoliberal agenda. As the saying goes, 'what is measured is what matters,' and what matters most places economistic aims above traditional education goals. A natural effect is that being so weighty in their consequence and potential impact, education leaders place emphasis on accountabilities because they matter, which has important repercussions for leadership practice.

Some accountabilities are manipulable to some extent; others are impermeable. For example, an education institution has some wriggle room and can present itself in positive terms through compulsory annual reporting requirements, but the results of national standardized student testing regimes are incontrovertible. However, there is evidence that some education institutions – online, virtual institutions – appear to be able to control their presentations or avoid accountabilities that are expected of their traditional counterparts.[4]

Taubman (2009, p. xi) explains how accountabilities have reduced a complex field such as education to a numbers game, with the effect being to "shock, interrogate, shame… and abstract individuals from their contexts," arguing that education reduced to numbers is a result of market predation, with standards and accountabilities having impoverished education and led it astray. He poses a very apt question:

> Although most teachers and teacher educators disagree with its [accountability] excesses and can point out its failures, few of us know how to turn back what has happened or can point to alternatives. Many of us are bewildered as to how we arrived at a point where our teaching has been reduced to numbers – the numbers on test scores, the numbers on dollars attached to merit pay or to be made by profit hungry corporations, or the numbers of outcomes met. We wonder how we came to allow CEOs and politicians to determine what and how we teach, and how prescribed performance outcomes and scripted curricula rose to such importance. How did it happen that teachers and teacher educators came to talk about teaching and learning in ways that mimic how accountants, bankers, and salespeople talk about business?

Taubman's comment sums up some very common feelings amongst education leaders, which lead to pressing and essential questions: Who has access to power and resources? Who makes decisions? And, how are resources allocated and on what basis?

Campbell's law is apposite: "the more any quantitative social indicator is used for social decision-making, the more subject it will be to corruption pressures and the more apt it will be to distort and corrupt the social processes it is intended to monitor" (Campbell, 1979, p. 85).

To sum up, Leithwood (2001, p. 5) argues that:

> This does not mean that all accountability policies are worthless. It does mean, however, that without active advocacy, support, local refinement, and further development by educators..., there is little chance that such policies will enhance the educational experiences of [students].

The next part of the book looks at education leaders' comments on the matters contained in this chapter and the preceding chapters of Part I. The chapters in Part II reveal leaders' beliefs, perceptions, summations, and reactions.

Notes

1 The key challenge for the public sector is managing the security risks that these technologies pose in addition to issues concerning data ownership and control. While AI in the public sector is a little way off, advanced machine learning is fast becoming the means of linking data sets to assist policy conversations and future government initiatives.
2 Analytics – once a word used by insurance risk assessors – now penetrates all aspects of education.
3 Typical reports of teacher misconduct include: Presenting inappropriate curriculum content; Undertaking other paid employment outside education during periods of absence; Religious bias; Attending extremist marches/public meetings; Intolerant/inappropriate social media postings; Engagement in inappropriate chatrooms or accessing pornography; Sexual harassment; Inappropriate relationships with students; Drug or alcohol use; Criminal charges (e.g. assault); Non-disclosure of criminal behaviors of peers/colleagues (e.g. not acting on allegations of child sex abuse); Dishonest assessment practices or assisting students to cheat in tests or public examinations; Aggression and assault, including hitting students; Failure to cover examinable syllabuses; False claims on curriculum vitae; Misuse of confidential information/breach of privacy laws; Inadequate student supervision; Fraud, theft.
4 They are able to exercise 'accountability-immunity' through manipulating avatars in ways that avoid negative sanctions (Nespor & Voithofer, 2016). An avatar, used in this sense, refers to a virtual organization's digital representation of itself, which can be manifested and changed in terms that appeal to the state as needs be.

References

Anderson, L. M., Turnbull, B. J., & Arcaira, E. R. (2017). *Leader tracking systems: Turning data into information for school leadership.* (Report commissioned by The Wallace Foundation, New York, NY, June 2017.) Washington, DC: Policy Studies Association, Inc.

Campbell, D. T. (1979). Assessing the impact of planned social change. *Evaluation and Program Planning,* 2(1), 67–90.

Carney, S., Rappleye, J., & Silova, I. (2012). Between faith and science: World culture theory and comparative education. *Comparative Education Review,* 56(3), 366–393.

Chilcott, T. (2014). Move to restrict school rankings: NAPLAN inquiry seeks end of comparison data. *Courier Mail,* March 28, 2014, p. 15.

Covington, M. V. (2000). Goal theory, motivation and school achievement: An integrative review. *Annual Review of Psychology,* 51, 171–200.

Dabbagh, O. (2018). NAPLAN trials online testing in face of criticism. *SBS News*, August 30, 2018. Retrieved September 19, 2018 from www.sbs.com.au/news/naplan-trials-on line-testing-in-face-of-criticism

Earl, L. M. (2005). *Assessment as learning: Using classroom assessment to maximise student learning*. Thousand Oaks, CA: Corwin Press Inc.

Evers, C. (2018). *Personal correspondence*, July 29, 2018.

Howse, J. (2017). The corporatisation of New Zealand tertiary institutions: A decade of change. *Leading & Managing*, 23(1), 65–76.

Leithwood, K. (2001). 5 reasons why most accountability policies don't work (and what you can do about it). *Orbit*, OISE, University of Ontario, 32(1), 1–5.

Leithwood, K., McAdie, P., Bascia, N., & Rodrigue, A. (Eds.) (2004). *Teaching for deep understanding: Towards the Ontario curriculum we need*. Toronto, Canada: Elementary Teachers' Federation of Ontario.

Matters, G. (2006). *Using data to support learning in schools*. Camberwell, VIC: ACER Press.

McGowan, M. (2018). Education chiefs have botched Naplan online test, says Victoria minister. *The Guardian*, August 9, 2018. Retrieved September 19, 2018 from www. theguardian.com/australia-news/2018/aug/09/act-concerns-about-online-naplan-tests-rejected-by-minister-months-ago

Nespor, J., & Voithofer, R. (2016). "Failure" irrelevant: Virtual schools and accountability-immunity. *Teachers College Record*, 118(7), 1–28

Organization for Economic Cooperation and Development (OECD) (2014). *Education at a glance 2014: OECD indicators*. Paris, France: OECD.

Rose, L. T. (2015). *The end of average: How to succeed in a world that values sameness*. New York, NY: HarperOne.

Shore, C., & Wright, S. (2000). "Coercive accountability": The rise of audit culture in higher education. In M. Strathern (Ed.), *Audit cultures: Anthropological studies in accountability, ethics and the Academy*. London, England: Routledge.

Smith, V. (1997). New forms of work organization. *Annual Review of Sociology*, 23, 315–339.

Starr, K. (1999). *That roar which lies at the other side of silence: An analysis of women principals' responses to structural reform in South Australian education*. (Unpublished doctoral dissertation, University of South Australia, Adelaide, SA). Retrieved from http://search.ror. unisa.edu.au/media/researcharchive/open/9915955288701831/53111935600001831

Starr, K. (2009). Confronting leadership challenges: Major imperatives for change in Australian education. In L. Ehrich & N. Cranston (Eds.), *Australian educational leadership today* (pp. 21–38). Bowen Hills, QLD: Australian Academic Press.

Starr, K. E. (2015). *Education game changers: Leadership and the consequence of policy paradox*. Lanham, MD: Rowman & Littlefield.

Taubman, P. M. (2009). *Teaching by numbers: Deconstructing the discourse of standards and accountability in education*. New York, NY: Routledge.

Teaching Regulation Agency (2018). *Teacher misconduct: The prohibition of teachers, October, 2018*. London, England: Teaching Regulation Agency, UK Government. Retrieved January 12, 2019 from https://assets.publishing.service.gov.uk/government/uploads/system/uploads/attachment_data/file/752668/Teacher_misconduct-the_prohibition_of_teachers_.pdf

Trujillo, T., & Renee, M. (2015). Irrational exuberance for market-based reform: How federal turnaround policies thwart democratic schooling. *Teachers College Record*, 117(6), 1–34. Retrieved May 8, 2017 from www.tcrecord.org/Content.asp?ContentID=17880

PART II

An Ebbing Tide...?

Education Amidst a Formidable and Inhospitable Policy Logic

The foundational principles of free market neoliberalism described in Part I are inextricably interlinked. No single neoliberal tenet can be disentangled from another – each intimately influences, manipulates, and affects all the others to produce a complicated web of responses that infiltrate policy and transform practice, which have equally labyrinthine effects and consequences – some intended, others unintended.

This part of the book looks at these major effects and consequences. It consolidates over three decades of research probing questions related to neoliberalism and education. At its base are questions about 'What is going on here?' Why is neoliberalism in education – what is the rationale? How are neoliberal policies influencing and impacting on education in general and education leadership in particular, and with what consequences? What problems do neoliberal policies aim to solve? Whose problems are they? Whose interests do they serve? And lastly, 'How do education leaders explain and respond to neoliberal policy agendas in practice and what responses do they deem appropriate?'

Delving down the rabbit hole of neoliberalism to plumb its aims and purposes in education produces conclusions that appear unreal, implausible, and unbelievable, yet they are supported by national governments, powerful institutions (such as the OECD), and global corporations. As in *Alice in Wonderland*, the foundations upon which education systems and education policy are based appear "[c]uriouser and curiouser!" (Carroll, 2010). Similarly, Hutton declared that many would find serious explanations about neoliberalism too far-fetched as to be believable: "It surely cannot be true that the ideas around which... much of the world's... economy and society have been organised... are as flaky as this. The answer is that they are" (1995, p. 236).

The research responses upon which this book is based are not monolithic, but there is overwhelming agreement amongst education leaders on many points as to make them particularly relevant and noteworthy. Unambiguous issues and examples of neoliberalism's impacts surfaced repeatedly across time and contexts. This part of the book, therefore, consolidates and discusses the major themes that have emerged over many research projects with education leaders. It encapsulates their perceptions with the overarching theme being that education has lost its way and its ethicality in neoliberal times.

Of prime significance is that conversations with education leaders have produced no clear understanding of the purposes of education at the current time or where neoliberal policy pursuits will end up. The question of purpose cannot be adequately explained by leaders in education terms – it appears from reams of transcripts that education has no adequately explained or substantiated public purposes. Like the Hatter in Alice's Wonderland, the overwhelming response is similar: "I haven't the slightest idea!" (Carroll, 2010). Leaders are clear, however, that education's fundamental principles have changed, and these changes are for the worse.

Other education leadership researchers record similar findings, such as a study of Australian primary school principals which found that private (social mobility) and economic (social efficiency) policy aims were privileged above education's public (democratic equity) purposes:

> The findings overwhelmingly point to tensions between what... the principals, believe ought to be the purposes of education and what the strategies to achieve those purposes might be, and the realities of what is actually happening... the results indicate a major shift away from public purposes of education to those more aligned with private purposes. Many of the barriers to achieving a greater focus in schools on public purposes are seen to be related to external (to the school) issues, such as government policy decisions, differential funding and resourcing across school sectors and emerging community and societal factors.
> (Cranston, Mulford, Keating, & Reid, 2010a, p. 517; see also Cranston, Mulford, Keating, & Reid, 2010b)

These are all a far cry from the four pillars of education identified in earlier times by the Delors Report (UNESCO, 1996) being about 'learning to know,' 'learning to do,' 'learning to live together,' and 'learning to be.' And these kinds of findings are replicated across many countries.

Neoliberalism has proven to be increasingly robust and resilient. As globalization and the needs of capital change, so neoliberalism morphs and adapts, and governments provide a helping hand by progressively relinquishing social and economic responsibilities to market players. Respondents in this research have seen first-hand the impacts on communities as social security safety nets tighten, reduce, or dry up, and as individuals bear a new civic responsibility by accepting personal risks and consequences associated with their sovereign individual choices in the pursuit of self-interests and self-reliance. The rub lies in the take-up of free market neoliberalism by political economists and knock-on effects in public policy, including education policy. As Winston Churchill remarked, "We first design our structures, then they design our lives."

This part of the book delineates major themes within leaders' commentaries. Discussed are issues and dilemmas as well as opportunities raised by education leaders, as they enact education policy and both shape and respond to change. The summative themes that follow are, like neoliberalism's underlying tenets themselves, recursively and inextricably linked. They exert significant influence on the lived experience and perceptions of respondents.

Part II portrays leaders' hopes – the possibilities, alternative narratives, and courses of action for policy and leadership practice – which are rooted in a very different set of principles and morality. Questioned throughout the following chapters is neoliberalism's fitness for, and sustainability in, education, since the aggregation of leaders' views and perceptions is representative of a deep and widespread disquiet about current education policy and where education is heading.

Four major themes emerged across many research projects across the decades. These represent leaders' prime learnings and concerns: education has lost its way; equity has been diluted at a time when it's never been more necessary; rampant anti-educational sentiments have pervasive repercussions for, within, and beyond education; and education policy appears to have changed education leadership practice irrevocably. Part II ends with final summations and personal concluding remarks.

References

Carroll, L. (2010). *Alice's adventures in Wonderland*. London, England: Penguin Books.

Cranston, N., Mulford, B., Keating, J., & Reid, A. (2010a). Primary school principals and the purposes of education in Australia. *Journal of Educational Administration*, 48(4), 517–539. Retrieved August 3, 2018 from https://doi.org/10.1108/09578231011054743

Cranston, N., Mulford, B.Keating, J., & Reid, A. (2010b). Politics and school education in Australia: A case of shifting purposes. *Journal of Educational Administration*, 48(2), 182–195 Retrieved August 3, 2018 from https://doi.org/10.1108/09578231011027842

Hutton, W. (1995). *The state we're in*. London, England: Jonathon Cape.

UNESCO (1996). *Learning: The treasure within*. Report to UNESCO of the International Commission on Education for the 21st Century. Paris, France: United Nations Educational, Scientific and Cultural Organization. (Chair: J. Delors).

12

EDUCATION IS OFF COURSE

Education as a trusted social institution has taken a hammer blow from neoliberalism, which has succeeded in fundamentally altering its purposes, aims, values, practices, everyday discourses, and leadership. Neoliberalism has dismantled long-established understandings and traditions that were generally accepted for decades, such that education's remit is diametrically opposed to that of the not too distant past. This is a 180° turnaround from previous policy foundational understandings based on principles of democracy and the common good. Similarly, what constitutes 'quality' and 'success' are inversions of past conceptions – these are now individualized (and institutionalized) and limited in their focus.

During their working lives, many education leaders have witnessed two quite distinct dominant ideologies influencing education policy (as well as other public sector policy): one determining that freedom is best sought through democracy, collective participation, and the common good (including a social accord regarding public welfare), and the other resolving that freedom is best pursued through the market, sovereignty, and choice (a more private, individualized settlement), as is the current case.

Over the past three decades, education leaders have had to constantly adapt with both policy and practice becoming progressively more entrenched in neoliberalism, as education became a key plank in re-shaping society along market lines. In the process, education is now viewed as a public good as a consequence of enhancing individuals' rights, choices, and chances. Education's intrinsic, inclusive value for all individuals, communities, and societies has been altered to purposes that sort, select, and decide who is included, who is excluded, who is lauded, who 'fails.'

Neoliberal education policies are designed to better serve the needs of capitalism, with uppermost motivations being to improve national productivity and international economic competitiveness, while transforming citizens into independent, self-sufficient economic units. Free market neoliberalism is justified and advocated as the best available means of achieving greater education improvement, affordability, and responsiveness to 'stakeholders' – governments, communities, and individual 'consumers.' Just as privatized health systems offer consumers a choice of health insurance funds and health providers, education is so progressing. Concurrently, performance targets and monitoring have been consolidated centrally (despite notions of institutional autonomy and self-regulation) in attempts to yield greater control and certainty, higher performance, and budgetary efficiencies.

Education has been opened to competition, corporatized, commercialized, privatized, commodified, and marketized. However, governments do not justify or explain the economistic rationale behind market-oriented mechanisms in education or provide adequate evidence to validate the policy decisions they make. Similarly, long-term desired endpoints are rarely revealed. But policy goals and activities are reinforced by regular assertions from neoliberal proponents condemning education as failing in its mission, being too expensive, with falling standards and few incentives to improve, while 'consumers' are at the mercy of self-interested 'providers.'

Governments' priorities in supporting privatization and an enhanced role for the private sector in education, fiscal austerity, reductions in government spending, and the progressive transfer of education costs to the individual 'users' or 'consumers' have all had a part to play in fundamentally re-casting every aspect of education. The assumption is that education leaders will react and respond to market pressures – individualism, choice, competition, transparency, performance effectiveness, accountabilities, productivity, and efficiency – to improve education and its institutions by behaving in much the same way as private organizations. Education has been 'reformed' into another commodity to buy and sell in a competitive marketplace where the odds are tipped in favor of the most advantaged individuals and institutions.

Amongst education leaders, the sharp edges of neoliberal policy are perceived to be distorting education's rightful purposes, constraining its means and methods, harming its outcomes, and disrupting what were once commonplace sensibilities. Notions of market neutrality are not substantiated in leaders' comments. For example, students who are living with parents or caregivers can't be held accountable for their circumstances which will have a bearing on their education in general. Yet inherent in neoliberalism is the belief that individuals will choose, through their own decisions and efforts, whether they succeed or fail, and they will individually bear the consequences. Educators don't believe this is an acceptable end point. There are some students who need extra support to succeed and no one likes to see someone fail due to factors beyond their control.

Failure may be fine in business and there may be agreement that 'bad' businesses should fail – that might well be in the public's interests (an idea that Schumpeter [2013] refers to as "creative destruction," which aids market competition, innovation, and further entrepreneurialism). However, when education is accused of failing and forced to face 'creative destruction' by the market, the consequences represent national and collective failures: some individuals will be winners, but those who miss out and lose are also members of communities and nations. Their denunciation creates and exacerbates life's problems for them, and increasing social problems become problems for all of us. Similarly, the failure of 'uncompetitive' education institutions have knock-on effects for communities – witness of which is the public outcry when public education institutions close.

Hence, the means and discourses employed to assess education success or failure have inbuilt failure within themselves. Insufficient acknowledgment is paid to the effects of circumstance and context; their analyses herald blame and admonishment, while those pulling the policy levers escape and exempt themselves from public responsibility and scrutiny.

Neoliberalism and its effects are inimical to aims that ground education as a universal good, which are believed to be needed now as much as they ever were. Policy, therefore, is perceived to be based on flawed aims, the wrong assumptions, while seeking inappropriate outcomes, and producing 'wicked' consequences – all of which spawn negative leadership effects. Neoliberalism is antagonistic – an "enemy," as one educator put it – to education and its outcomes (see for example, Connell, 2013). Its negative impacts are not inconsequential and they make the role of education leaders more difficult. Examples of neoliberalism's negative impacts are too numerous to cite, but those most commonly referred to include:

- the effects of 'winning' and 'losing' on students, educators, education institutions and, ultimately, nation states
- intensifying external impositions, accountabilities, and audits that distract from teaching and learning
- increased labor intensification for education leaders with few perceived benefits for students, teaching, or learning
- increasing difficulty of leading and managing major change to meet externally imposed policy expectations and targets that are inimical to education and the prevailing beliefs of educators
- meeting the learning needs of diverse cohorts of students in a climate of diminishing resources
- testing regimes that shame and blame rather than support and enable
- low levels of respect, reward, or appreciation shown towards the education profession – from bad press to low pay
- the silencing of the profession with formal restrictions on freedom of speech and expression and attempts to curtail academic freedom
- difficulties retaining teachers who are leaving the profession due to disenchantment, low wages, and insecure, contractual employment
- failures in attracting education leaders resulting in problems of succession and retention
- governmental failures in releasing the findings of various consultative reviews.

Education remains a constant target for criticism and blame. Constant criticism continually undermines public confidence, incites inflammatory public discourse, and fuels and legitimates further 'reforms'. Meanwhile, politicians and policymakers evade responsibility for policy failures (see also Hlavacik, 2016). The resultant 'blame game' masks public policy failure while producing marked social and political outcomes (see Chapter 13).

One leader summed up the consequences thus: "they're sucking the joy out of it [education] – the work isn't as nourishing anymore." Another's assessment: "It's all about the numbers and data collections – we're being held to ransom. This isn't what education is about – it's off course." And another's: "education is going backwards."

The overriding mood amongst education leaders is that education has been corrupted and degraded. Many believe it is dangerously off course. The values and principles underpinning policy are believed to be incompatible with educators' moral compass and antithetical to what education should be about (see for example, Headteachers' Roundtable Doorstop Manifesto, 2017).

If greater productivity and improved student achievement are what political leaders and policymakers are looking for, the strong belief amongst education leaders is that current policy regimes deliver neither the means nor motivations to achieve these aims despite rhetoric to the contrary.

Market competition actually creates uncertainty and anxiety – the very opposite of the assurance and certainty governments are trying to achieve through high-stakes, performance-based accountabilities. Education leaders are unanimously opposed to such a stance, seeing education as a means of creating opportunities, not diminishing them; of changing society to be more inclusive, rather than exacerbating the gulf between the 'haves' and the 'have nots'.

Learning Suffers

Education is outwards focused, problem-oriented, and inquiry-based. It aims to be comprehensive, to cover all fields of knowledge and skill alongside common, interdisciplinary learnings such as literacy and numeracy, problem-solving, and essential social learnings such as being respectful, courteous, civil, law-abiding, and able to work in teams. Educators prescribe deep thinking and critical analysis, respectful debate, and discussion to explore topics as fully as possible, canvassing diverse perspectives and opinions. Students learn to work co-operatively and independently, to take initiative and learning risks, and pursue collective and individual avenues of inquiry. In addition, education institutions provide a range of co- and extracurricular offerings and a range of learning, social, and welfare support systems.

In neoliberal times, however, policy measures encourage very different motivations for learning. Competition is assumed to foster greater effort for improvements to yield greater individual returns. It is assumed that self-interests will be strongly attuned to what is valued and what is deemed to matter, but educators see the consequences as the market's tunnel vision.

The struggles confronting public education (at all levels) seem to be dimming hopes for its possibilities. Goals that educators have striven for over decades seem further away and elusive. Many claim that the 'publicness' of education is being redefined, is under threat and failing many citizens. It is difficult for education leaders to see how all this raises quality, induces authentic improvement, or improves returns on education investment. And this is ironic when education enrollment is compulsory for the young.

An entrenched preoccupation with 'performance' measurement is seen to be narrowing the focus and therefore dumbing education down (despite and perhaps also aided by growing credentialism), creating unwelcomed hierarchies of knowledge, and disrupting assumptions that everyone can succeed in learning. It undermines notions of 'individualism' and activities that can and do create improvements. And accountabilities can damage the reputations of individuals, institutions, and communities; undermine workplace satisfaction levels; incite employee stress; and destroy cooperation and collegiality. They change working and learning cultures, as the following comments from education leaders about standardized testing confirm:

> Testing is a waste of time and money and effort... [It] tells us nothing we don't already know.

> ...tests are very disruptive... They interrupt what we're doing and would rather be doing – they upset students. What are we doing this for? This might sound cynical, but it's not for our benefit or students' benefit.

There is substantial evidence that education practices can have a significant impact on student achievement outcomes, but incessant external change agendas and standardized testing regimes are not conducive to curriculum, pedagogical, or institutional renewal. And decades of education research (confirming that some students' backgrounds provide advantages in education while others are less fortunate) is ignored, which leads to concerns about equity in education – which are also concerns about policy integrity, morality, and ethicality, a topic to which this part of the book now turns.

References

Connell, R. (2013). The neoliberal cascade and education: An essay on the market agenda and its consequences. *Critical Studies in Education*, 54(2), 99–112.

Headteachers' Roundtable (2017). *Headteachers' Roundtable Doorstop Manifesto, General Election 2017*. London, UK: Schools Week on behalf of HTRT.

Hlavacik, M. (2016). *Assigning blame: The rhetoric of education reform*. Cambridge, MA: Harvard University Press.

Schumpeter, J. A. (2013). *Capitalism, socialism, and democracy*. New York, NY: Routledge.

13

WHAT HAPPENED TO EQUITY?

A clear concern amongst education leaders over the decades is the progressive and incremental diminution of equity and social justice policies and programs in education. Education leaders report equity goals as having progressively and silently slipped off the policy agenda without public debate, pronouncement, or agreement.

During the 1980s and 1990s, social justice, equal opportunities, equity, inclusion and diversity agendas, policies, programs, and action plans were promulgated by education systems across liberal democracies. While equity-oriented policies in education were never unproblematic and their targets were difficult to achieve,[1] these policies were, nevertheless, overt, they received broad support and endorsement, and there was an underlying understanding and expectation that education should and could make a difference in the lives of all students.

This stance changed dramatically during the 1990s, however, as current forms of globalization increasingly took root with broad-sweeping deregulation and states 'rolling back' their remit, their funding, and public commitments, and instigating market-neoliberal influenced policies and reforms. In the current day, active efforts towards equity in education are sometimes so marginal as to be practically defunct, with terms like 'social justice' rarely being used anymore in government policy documents (see for example, Starr, 1992; Zelizer, 2015).

Equity as Anathema in Market Liberalism

The abasement of equity as an education policy priority is hardly surprising, since the notions of social justice and equity are anathema to free market neoliberalism (Hayek, 1944, 1976, 1979a, 1979b). Policies underpinned by aims to create greater equity are incompatible with competitive individualism. There is also a free market neoliberal aversion towards redistributive economic policies as a means of trying to achieve greater social parity. These are considered as 'social engineering' which interrupts the price systems that coordinate market supply and demand.

Hayek (1979a, 1979b), for example, condemned governments' attempts to develop social justice legislation, arguing that government interference in social policy contravenes the social good derived from economic freedom with its intersecting forces of 'self-interest' and 'fellow feeling.' From Hayek's perspective, the term 'social justice' misconstrues the words 'justice' and 'injustice,' because they can only be applied to human action and conduct, and not to collective market actions. He argues:

> The term 'social justice' is today generally used as a synonym of what used to be called 'distributive justice'. The latter term perhaps gives a somewhat better idea of what is intended to be meant by it, and at the same time shows why it can have no application to the results of market order. There can be no distributive justice where no one contributes. Justice has meaning only as a rule of human conduct, and no conceivable rules of the conduct of individual persons supplying each other with goods and services in a market order would produce a distribution which could be meaningfully described as just or unjust.
>
> *(Hayek, 1979a, p. 4)*

In other words, because 'society' is the product of unplanned spontaneous order, no individual or group can be blamed for the range of variable outcomes amongst individuals. The game of catallaxy must be played fairly (with the law of the land ensuring this), but social realities within free market liberalism are a matter of effort, chance, and luck, not engineering. Individuals accept the conditions in which they find themselves, or will, by their own efforts, act to change their fortunes. Other individuals or the market cannot be blamed for poor results because the market remains 'neutral.' Nobody has behaved in an 'unjust' way, because in the market order "the overall outcome is completely unpredictable" (Butler, 1983, p. 88). Butler asserts:

> ...it would be a pointless exercise if losers could insist that the outcome was overturned every time. And how could the players play towards some specific results? There is no consistent strategy which they could adopt which would make the outcome certain in advance, and the more players in the game, the more impossible it would be to ensure the specific outcome.
>
> *(Butler, 1983, p. 101; cf. Hayek, 1979b, pp. 6–7)*

Social justice and equality of opportunity are thus an illusion "which would produce a nightmare if it were attempted" (Butler, 1983, p. 10). Hence, according to Hayek, social justice is:

...an intellectually unrespectable idea... I have come to feel strongly that the greatest service I can still render to my fellow men [*sic*] would be that I could make the speakers and writers among them thoroughly ashamed ever again to employ the term "social justice".

(*Hayek, as cited in Butler, 1983, p. 105*)

The free market, therefore, encapsulates its own self-evolving form of 'justice.' Relations between individuals and society are not ends-related but are means-related in terms of market purposes. Individuals have to trust the market as it resolves and reconciles the range of individual means. 'Justice' thereby changes from being a moral issue to the outcome of the unfettered market. As Friedman (1962, p. 195) argues, "One cannot be both egalitarian and a liberal."

Many commentators disagree. Stretton (1996), for example, argues that an ungoverned economy would result in 'anarchy,' and the belief that the market leads to greater efficiency is a 'fantasy.' And Pusey (1991, p. 19) poses his objections thus:

What counts as [economic] rationalisation and how do we know it's good for us? It is in the revealing answers to this question, or perhaps more frequently in the stratagems used to avoid it, that ideologies are dressed up as science, reform, public policy, development, structural adjustment, and modernisation.

Pusey (1991) endorses the opposite stance, believing a social democratic agenda would be fairer – it would focus on the economy, civil society, and the state, supporting a strong government, mixed economy, positive liberty – meaning individual freedoms within social restraints, instead of negative liberty or unfettered market individualism.

For education the OECD (2014, p. 193) defines 'equity' as "providing all students, regardless of their socio-economic status, with opportunities to benefit from education." This definition has self-established limits – it "does not imply that everyone will have the same outcomes from their education." 'Equity' is about "access to quality educational resources and opportunities to learn," which is a stance denoting 'social justice as fairness' (Rawls, 1972; see Starr, 1992) – it is not redistributive in intent and does not disrupt established social arrangements or power relations.

The small number of current policies proclaiming to address equity issues in education are limited and restricted in their scope – they address students' special learning needs or enable supplementary provisioning to assist with English language learning, for example. They are often funded on a short-term basis, are targeted to specific groups, or are distributed through competitive grant schemes with cumbersome formal application and reporting requirements.

The shift from a social democratic policy agenda in the 1970s and early 1980s to laissez-faire market liberalism has shored up a different set of policy terms associated with the OECD's equity conceptions: 'evaluation,' 'school improvement,' 'quality assurance,' 'accountability', 'compliance' – none of which are alleviating huge discrepancies in outcomes between advantaged and disadvantaged student groups. Discourses concerning competitive individualism and 'efficiency' and policy pursuits towards 'excellence' have overturned the previous social welfare consensus (see Starr, 2015).

In neoliberal terms, inequalities of various kinds are justified as the cost of sovereign liberty and choice, with individuals bearing responsibility for personal risk and life's outcomes. Followed through to its logical conclusion, it is possible to envision a continual diminution of publicly provided education and the public sector in general, and consequently of public provisioning and public assets. It is possible to see Margaret Thatcher's comments about society having become reality (see Chapter 2).

Neoliberalism's 'hands-off' approach to the common weal fails the equity test, especially in education. The game of catallaxy, driven by self-interest and competitive individualism, privileges short-term private interests and benefits over longer-term social interests, while conveniently denying the injustices of 'chance' (birthright, for example), in its wake. The invisible hand of the market operates through individual choices and efforts, and, because the market is presumed to be value-neutral, issues of context, circumstance, or probability are disregarded, yet for all players, the results are highly consequential. Further, education deals with children and young people who attend through compulsion, so education leaders accept that deliberate controls, interventions, and coordination to ensure access, diversity, and inclusion, and going some way to address social disadvantage are both reasonable and responsible policy and funding measures. The state benefits from its investment in education through an educated citizenry and the many benefits this brings to individuals, communities, and the nation.

In trickle-down economic theory, social benefits are supposed to be distributed in ways that enhance the lives of everyone – albeit to differing degrees and achieved in different ways (as indicated by the OECD's definition cited above). As such, education's traditional mission, and still pervasive expectation, demands accessibility and equity for all. But policy effects, such as closing or reducing funding to 'failing'/'unproductive' institutions and rewarding 'success stories' creates market 'winners' who reap even further rewards (to incentivize, motivate, and reward improvement and 'quality'), while the burden is shouldered by those most disadvantaged and least able to afford it (see for example, Trujillo & Renee, 2015). Those who have traditionally been disadvantaged in education are still disadvantaged and often more so. The main beneficiaries are those already advantaged who are also generally the highest educated. Market extemporization invisibly manipulates education policies overtly to sort, compare, and determine 'quality' – who is successful and who is unsuccessful. Hence, rather than playing its part in nation building, neoliberal education becomes instrumental in aiding and abetting greater social, economic, and political divisions along with the negative consequences so entailed.

Catallaxy's 'winners' revel in their successes. Those at the other end of the spectrum are made acutely aware of their needs and deficits and are shamed and penalized rather than supported and enabled. In pursuit of its principles, neoliberalism effectively trades off education aims promoting access and inclusion. The game of catallaxy is faultless, however, because it is spontaneous and unplanned with no pre-determined goals. Neoliberal's axioms absolve education systems and policymakers from responsibilities for outcomes – they become individual matters.

Equity in Education

The consequence of producing market "losers" (Butler, 1983, p. 101) is an acceptable outcome in neoliberalism, but this situation sits very uncomfortably with educators. Education leaders witness the overall consequences and lament what this means for individuals, communities, and nations. Public education institutions were established to provide for all – as the OECD asserts – but producing winners and losers is anathema to current (retentive) education sensibilities. Further, educators do not accept the notion that at the basis of 'failure' is a 'deficient individual.'

To education leaders this is the 'law of the jungle' (Harvey, 2007). In terms of real people and populations, the neoliberal free market fails any test concerning the common good. Leaders see first-hand how personal backgrounds and circumstances influence student participation, learning achievement, and other outcomes. They observe the unfairness of education policies that effectively discriminate against the poorest and least advantaged, even though they are purportedly designed by policymakers to produce the most propitious outcomes.

They say students with special needs are not well catered for in 'one-size-fits-all' policy pursuits, tightly targeted provisioning processes, and standardized instruments that compare, contrast, and rank learning outcomes. Disadvantage is further exacerbated by performative work cultures, the individuation of risk, and the hollowing out of social safety nets of all kinds.

Education leaders are disappointed that notions of education equity now serve discursive and symbolic purposes to legitimate, appease, and 'band-aid' over social problems rather than being substantive policy objectives with consequential social intentions. For example, one leader said:

> You don't hear about equity so much – I mean, you hear about it, but governments aren't splashing money around like they used to, to pay for it.... It's a pipe dream. It's not going to happen. There doesn't seem to be the will for anything to change.

An interesting finding from research across the decades has been the extent to which leaders blame themselves for the falling focus on equity. When asked how equity has become so diminished as to almost have disappeared as a major aspect of policy agendas without furore or fanfare, education leaders often looked to themselves, citing time constraints associated with work intensification. One said:

> People [educators/education leaders] may have noticed but they were too consumed with new realities to protest, so equity... expired.

And another:

> It was one less thing to have to worry about, one less meeting to attend... I can't remember how it happened, but it... vanished and we just kept on going.

Yet education leaders feel a great sense of dislocation and alienation when they talk about the loss of an overt policy stance on equity and social justice because they believe this is integral in 'making a difference' in students' lives, which they believe is (and what they thought was) one of education's major purposes, and which most maintain is an important aspect of their job. There is a strong sense that education policy should be undergirded by incontrovertible values about equity and there is a sense of amazement and disappointment that these have been downplayed or ignored, further disadvantaging those already disadvantaged and vice versa. For education leaders, equity is a tangible social issue – not something that can be reduced to and ticked off through a few 'targeted' measures directed at students in the direst circumstances.

Discourses concerning competitive individualism and 'efficiency' have overturned the previous social welfare consensus – viewed by educators as a triumph of those wielding 'core' power and influence.

Leaders' comments suggest the need (and preference) for central planning over the market order when it comes to social coordination – inherent are views that free market liberalism might provide suitable underpinning principles for trade and commerce, but it is inappropriate in the public sector in general and education in particular. Hence, despite free market concerns about individual sovereignty and freedom from coercive state powers, education leaders overwhelmingly dislike and distrust market-inspired policies that unravel aims to achieve some parity in and across education, and for the good of society. For education policy to abandon these ambitions is viewed as immoral. This is a clarion call for integrity, justice, and sheer common sense. It is an ethical issue, and, according to education leaders, education's greatest moral challenge.

Discussions about equity with leaders also concern levels of public (government) investment in education. Comparative resourcing levels are serious equity considerations concerning where and to whom resources go and how funds are spent, on top of the links between education outcomes and socio-economic status indicators. Unfortunately, these data are not publicly aired and promoted by politicians and policymakers – these are hidden and 'undiscussable' (Argyris, 1980) public accountabilities requiring more transparency and debate.

Alfred Deakin, Australia's second Prime Minister, argued:

> Instead of the State being regarded any longer as an object of hostility to the labourer, it should now become identified with an interest in his [sic] works, and in all workers, extending over them its sympathy and protection, and watching over their welfare and prosperity.
>
> (The Age, June 10, 1890, as cited in Pusey, 1991, p. 1)

Deakin's stance accords with the great majority of education leaders. Its quiddity supports education and the motivations of educators who want overt action for equity over lip-service.

In sum, the neoliberal treatment of equity in education actually intensifies disadvantage and inequitable outcomes rather than alleviating or reducing them, and education leaders agree that education is positioned to exacerbate social divides.

The Emergence of Anti-Equity Sentiments

However, there is one further worrying point to raise about leaders' comments on equity. Some recent observations make education leaders suspect that while equity policies are weaker and less genuine in intent than in the past and they would like to see them return, the worse may be yet to come. They cite emerging views about 'equity' that have disturbingly further divisive potential. Leaders explain:

> I'm noticing people getting antsy about equity... like it's... about political correctness and mainly for minorities, but it's not about them. It's not for them, it's against them – they're being left out... It [equity] comes at a cost – to me and my kind. Like, 'why should others get benefits... when I've worked hard all my life and get nothing?' That's what's coming through.

> There's resentment – immigration, jobs, rising costs, the housing crisis – things are tough and 'equity' is another threat – other people are getting a handout and making things even worse.

> People's lives are changing so fast they can't keep up... they're uncomfortable [and] prefer things the way they were... they don't like the changes they're seeing and they're blaming minorities for the disruption.

Equity is becoming an increasingly contentious issue. At the time of writing, debate is opening in Australia about the merits or otherwise of faith-based schools being exempted from anti-discrimination legislation on the basis of sexuality. And 'anti-equity' sentiments are appearing elsewhere (see for example, Abamu, 2018) – an apt segue into the next chapter's discussion on growing social fragmentation, intolerance, and distrust.

Note

1 Problems with equity policies were numerous. They were often: centrally developed, monitored, and controlled; under-theorized, ahistorical, and ill-defined; under-resourced and of short-term duration; rigidly targeted to increasingly specific groups making access difficult for many students in need; administered in technical, bureaucratic, inflexible ways; and usually vague on advice about achieving strategic priorities. Further, they privileged conservative economic interests and corporate management priorities and practices (see for example, Starr, 1992).

References

Abamu, J. (2018). Unpacking why some educators see the word 'equity' as a threat. *EdSurge*, March 27, 2018. Retrieved April 7, 2018 from www.edsurge.com/news/2018-03-27-unpacking-why-some-educators-see-the-word-equity-as-a-threat

Argyris, C. (1980). Making the undiscussable and its undiscussability discussable. *Public Administration Review*, 40(3), 205–213.

Butler, E. (1983). *Hayek: His contribution to the political and economic thought of our time*. London, England: Temple Smith.

Friedman, M. (1962). *Capitalism and freedom*. Chicago, IL: The University of Chicago Press.

Harvey, D. (2007). *A brief history of neoliberalism*. Oxford, England: Oxford University Press.

Hayek, F. A. (1944). *The road to serfdom*. London, England: Routledge & Kegan Paul.

Hayek, F. A. (1976). *Law, legislation and liberty, Volume 2: The mirage of social justice*. London, England: Routledge & Kegan Paul.

Hayek, F. A. (1979a). *Social justice, socialism and democracy: Three Australian lectures*. Turramurra, NSW: Centre for Independent Studies.

Hayek, F. A. (1979b). *A conversation with Friedrich A. von Hayek: Science and socialism*. Washington, DC: American Enterprise Institute for Public Policy.

Organization for Economic Cooperation and Development (OECD) (2014). *Education at a glance 2014: OECD indicators*. Paris, France: OECD.

Pusey, M. (1991). *Economic rationalism in Canberra: A nation-building state changes its mind*. Cambridge, England: Cambridge University Press.

Rawls, J. (1972). *A theory of justice*. Oxford, England: Oxford University Press.

Starr, K. (1992). *Running with the hares and hunting with the hounds: A critique of social justice strategies in South Australian state education* (Master's degree by research, unpublished thesis). University of South Australia, Adelaide, SA.

Starr, K. E. (2015). *Education game changers: Leadership and the consequence of policy paradox*. Lanham, MD: Rowman. & Littlefield.

Stretton, H. (1996). *Poor laws of 1834 and 1996, occasional paper*. Fitzroy, VIC: Brotherhood of St. Lawrence.

Trujillo, T., & Renee, M. (2015). Irrational exuberance for market-based reform: How federal turnaround policies thwart democratic schooling. *Teachers College Record*, 117(6), 1–34. Retrieved May 8, 2017 from www.tcrecord.org/Content.asp?ContentID=17880

Zelizer, J. E. (2015). How education policy went astray. *The Atlantic*, April 10, 2015. Retrieved April 1, 2017 from www.theatlantic.com/education/archive/2015/04/how-education-policy-went-astray/390210/

14

THE RISE OF ANTI-EDUCATIONALISM AND BAD FAITH

A Changing Social Psyche

Increasingly, education leaders have expressed growing concerns about anti-education, anti-intellectual, anti-authority, and anti-democratic sentiments infiltrating local, national, and global discourses. Embedded is distrust, derision, resentment, and a "global revolt against experts" (Hawking, 2018) – the political class and governments, intellectuals, traditional authority figures, educators and academics, scientists, journalists, elites, and professionals of any kind who are seen as a being out of touch with 'main street' interests, everyday realities, and those 'doing it tough.'

Divisive public opinion is gaining traction and legitimacy. Many are 'angry,' and feel disenfranchised and betrayed. Resented are major changes in the traditional social contract – loyalty to and from employers, gender relationships and roles, mono-racial and mono-cultural populations, protected economies and jobs for those who wanted them. Many want a return to this past (see Enfield, 2017; Faludi, 2000).

This anti-intellectual phenomenon is being more widely recognized and reported, often associated with localized forms of protest and militancy that are creating 'culture wars.' Increasingly, reports of new cultures of prejudice, intolerance, and fanaticism suggest this phenomenon is rising, violating and threatening civility, common respect, politeness, kindness, empathy and tolerance for diversity, and democracy itself. Misinformation, hoaxes, propaganda, fake websites that appear authentic, 'deep fakes' that can digitally make anybody look as if they said anything through convincing artificial intelligence (AI), and coordinated campaigns to promote certain causes and blame abound, while the easy switching on of aggressive defense mechanisms represent a return to a more primitive ego.

Current reality is increasingly augmented with convincing VR (virtual reality), smart machines, and clever AI. Big data and algorithms track individuals' lives, friends and associations, 'likes,' geographical location, choices, habits, predilections, and inclinations. They intrude with selections of goods, services, activities, views, and stories to appeal to our preferences, yet they disrespect and disallow individual privacy. Identity theft is lucrative, cyber-security appears impossible, while one fake tweet can bring down financial markets (see for example, White, 2018). The public is hampered by new and opportunistic forms of harassment and deceit, enabled by micro-targeting electronic communication tools providing anonymity to cloak bullying, threats, abuse, trickery, slander, and impersonation – let alone the activities of the 'dark web.' Amidst the "scams, shams and flimflams" (Reich, 2017), 'fake news,' 'alternative facts,' and conspiracy theories can get a following and a life, reported as 'populism,' 'information disorder,' the 'end of truth,' and the 'post-truth era.' It can be difficult to know who to trust, what is real and truthful, and what is not.

Noticeable are denials of verifiable facts, history or reality, and the discarding of usual rules of evidence and balanced media reporting, with broadcasting becoming 'narrowcasting.' Maligned or deceptive reporting, ill-researched and unsubstantiated stories, and sensationalized headlines prepared by non-specialists – referred to as 'phatic' or 'yellow' journalism – are presented as factual. There are fact-deniers, vicious ideological partisanship, and the public, in general, are warier, less trusting, and often don't know who or what to believe.

Traditional media outlets haven't helped, with journalists trying desperately to cope with 24/7 news cycles and competitive pressure to be first with 'breaking news.' Reporters have sometimes been too quick to respond using personal Twitter accounts for reports based on gossip that turn out to be wrong. Undermined are codes of ethics, thorough research, the double-checking of sources, and the issuing of apologies if information proves to be incorrect.[1]

Political slogans and oft-repeated mantras engineered to sidestep dissent and manipulate support are viewed as part of the problem, since the more the public hears a statement, the more likely it is that biased and simplistic views will stick – 'a lie told once remains a lie but a lie told a thousand times becomes the truth.' 'Facts' are unsubstantiated, justificatory statements are absent, and the language used often appropriates concepts and sentiments that contradict the stance being promoted (Starr, 1992).

In more recent times media polls and politicians appear to have vastly underestimated the anger, fear, doubt, bigotry, and cynicism of large sectors of the community who feel left out of conventional politics and left behind by decisions wielded in the name of neoliberal globalization. Galvanized by a sense that they can and will be heard, local, homespun and often unlikely agitators and protestors turn to one another (often through closed messaging forums) and have become a political force to be reckoned with. More commonplace now are unpredictable political electorates and election outcomes defying opinion polls.

Education leaders are increasingly concerned about obvious signs of social fragmentation that have increased over the past few decades, but especially over the past decade with the advent of social media. What were previously 'trends' and 'signs' of social disquiet have grown to be worryingly persistent and increasingly pervasive. What were initially noticed as the negative effects of policy and practice are now more clearly large scale and widespread – they are everywhere.

News reporting and social media are key in influencing political discourses around education policy (Baxter, 2015). Reports designed to attract reader interest in a crowded 24/7 media cycle assert particular opinions or raise certain issues, with the most obvious examples suggesting various education 'crises.' Negative public perceptions serve to legitimate further political interventions through changed education policies. Public opinion about education policy is channeled towards a very narrow, selective (and often deceitful) presentation of information to back a political position while foreclosing accurate public narratives or critique.

Leaders report noticing xenophobia and nationalism rooted in racism and mono-culturalism; various forms of harassment that are now increasingly psychologically violent; patriarchal, chauvinist and/or fundamentalist views rooted in sexism, misogyny, and multi-gender bigotry; and a pervasive rudeness and 'close-to-the-surface' anger and intolerance that attacks, vilifies and maligns, refuses to listen to alternative viewpoints, and poisons public debate. The moral high ground appears to be wherever each individual happens to stand.

The beliefs and behaviors that education's equity and social justice policies have tried to eradicate in the past are resurfacing (see Chapter 13). Social biases, injustices, and discriminations of the past are seen to have been renewed, revised, and reinvigorated in the global psyche – a phenomenon perceived as dangerous, divisive, and a wake-up call for education leaders and education authorities. Previously hard-won rights and accepted assumptions are more fragile and transient than many expected.

Along the same lines and sentiments, education leaders record their own knowledge and authority being more openly rejected or rebuked by individuals who are not educators. They say they have experienced encounters whereby the information or views they transmit are openly rejected, dismissed, or questioned. For example:

> I've been in this game for a long time now – I'm experienced and know education and this school very well... people think I'm good at what I do – I thought ... But lately I've been hounded down a few times by folk who'll want to argue with me – ignorant of the facts but they'll question me or openly disagree... no qualms. It flummoxes you. I think, 'How can you believe this? And what makes you think you can behave like this?'

There's only one view of the world... There's no convincing them otherwise – no point trying, they don't want to listen – they want to argue but don't have the facts...

Leaders report that these kinds of experiences are increasing in regularity and are representative of a more widespread phenomenon within the professions.

We are living in a world of 'radical' ignorance, according to Proctor (2008) – a new era or the 'age of agnotology' where never before has so much knowledge been so readily accessible and summarily ignored by so many. 'Agnotology' or culturally constructed ignorance derives from the Greek word 'agnosis' meaning ignorance or 'not knowing.'[2] Agnotology is adaptable – it can evade, delay, or repute information to undermine the facts or balanced debate.

Ignorance may not be the result of deliberate cultural or political exigencies (Proctor & Schiebinger, 2008). But special interest groups, corporations, and the political class aid agnotology through over-simplified messaging and one-sided propaganda (see Kenyon, 2016). Betancourt (2016) refers to 'agnotologic capitalism' since it relies on the manufacture and maintenance of 'ignorance' as a major feature of the contemporary political economy.

Agnotology is associated with the 'Dunning-Kruger effect' – individual biases that make everyone an expert in their own minds. The Dunning-Kruger effect is a sense of superior cognitive ability and competence (Dunning, Johnson, Ehrlinger, & Kruger, 2003; Kruger & Dunning, 1999). Kruger and Dunning (1999) suggest that we are products of our own ignorance and incompetence although we fail to recognize this within ourselves. People cannot comprehend their own lack of skill or the extent of their own inadequacies. They also fail to accurately gauge skill in others or their own skill deficiencies until *after* they are exposed to training for that skill. Worrying for education is Proctor's (2008) consternation that if educators don't understand the forces of ignorance, they will have little chance of surmounting this powerful 'anti'-force.

The corollary of agnotology is individuals of high levels of ability underestimating their competence while erroneously assuming that tasks that they find simple and straight-forward are similarly so for others (Kruger & Dunning, 1999; Dunning et al., 2003).

Education leaders see that a change has occurred in the general social psyche:

...common courtesy is lacking... people are getting more impatient and angry. Perhaps it's Twitter... people think they can say whatever and get away with it and don't care who's offended... More parents are rude and angry... and then you understand where their kids are coming from...

...bad behavior's on the rise – short tempers, disrespectful comments – staff too. People are happier to wear their opinions on their sleeves...

There's that sense of entitlement and absolute confidence – tin ears, like there's no other possible way of looking at things – they just don't want to know… Students aren't as polite as they used to be…

…we [education leaders] used to be held in some kind of esteem… I don't feel that so much now… I'm a public servant and that's where I'm pigeonholed… I feel much more insignificant in the scheme of things. I'm not a voice of authority.

…one minute you're having a normal conversation and all of a sudden things can turn very nasty… We [education leaders] can't afford to behave like that. Emotions are kept in check… but some people behave badly and don't seem to care.

Contradictions and paradoxes abound. Individuals acting in their self-interests find and form mass movements; 'mobocracy' can run roughshod over democracy; democratic governments who create legislation can behave illegally or disingenuously (see, for example, Adams, 2018).

Education leaders say, for example:

…hard-nosed social policy is pretty ruthless and unforgiving and that sense of 'I couldn't care less', 'what have I got to lose?' is rubbing off – everywhere. 'Why should we give a damn about anyone else?' – that sort of sentiment.

And social and political leaders are not helping:

Do we really want students to think the media are 'the enemy of the people'? No, but that's what our political leaders want us to think. Do we really want them to condemn the bastions of society? No, but so many have let us down badly…

Fake news and fallacious beliefs have "true and real effects" (Sharpe, 2017). Public debate is corrupted, some voices are silenced, and views about education and educators can become jaundiced, but the damaging consequences of this practice go free and there are few apologies for incorrect information or interpretations. Education, educators, and education leaders are increasingly targets for derision or blame. The views of educators or their professional associations are often absent in published debates, so many reports are unverified and unfounded. In many jurisdictions, education leaders (in the schooling sector, for example) are not permitted to speak to the media on issues beyond their institution – they are silenced.

Distrust of Governments

Education leaders lament a political obsession with simple messages and slogans designed to 'sum up' complex problems to capture the public's mood, which dumbs down public discourses. Governments appoint their own selected key people in top roles who can be relied upon to support political intentions and avoid 'inconvenient truths' through denial and sidestepping questioning.

Governments can be trusted, like individuals, to act in their own self-interests and provide their authoritative version or 'take' on a matter. Internally, political parties' machinations can make for as much turmoil as they receive from outside. Governments and policymakers expect and demand the truth from education leaders and education institutions, but they can be deceptive in their own operations. One leader sums this up thus:

> There's a lot of distrust... but I look at myself and it's hard to know who to trust. You might think you know, but you only really know who you can trust when it comes to the test. I mean, would you trust the department (education department)? You only have to make one decision that someone doesn't like...!?

Paradoxically, this undermines the neoliberal value of transparency to aid the rational, well-informed decision-making amongst sovereign individuals in the marketplace. Larger sections of populations are questioning whether what political leaders say can be believed and are demonstrating frustration with governments, and with democracy itself (see for example, Steinglass, 2017).

Australia, for example, is a perfect case in point, having had seven prime ministers in less than 11 years with not one since 2007 serving out a full first term in office before being brought down by their own political party room.[3] Self-obsessed politicians are perceived as 'empathy deficient,' unable to put themselves in others' shoes, or work for the common good (which was presumed once to have been their work) (see Bazalgette, 2017). The result is, according to Barack Obama that "...in the meantime, our problems are left to fester" (Obama, 2006).

Numerous reports of political discontent are heard around the world. Politics is a ruthless, unsettling, and unsettled business. Nasty internal politics entailing bullying, rudeness, revenge, and bad behavior, and endless feuding do not augur well for social tolerance, civil etiquette, and cultural life in society in general. With little or no consensus or will to strike a compromise, leadership, direction, and confidence is lacking. When the future is uncertain, direction and leadership are proving to be wanting. Populations are dismayed.

Changes in leaders and governments make for constant policy churn. In uncertain times, and with unpredictable politics, education then takes on another purpose. It is a great distractor from political turbulence and instability – it is public focused and in everyone's interests. Even more than usual, political 'promises' for education try to appear certain and assured, appealing to the masses who are presumed to want what spin doctors determine they need: improvement, higher standards, further evaluation, with a gamut of drummed-up education 'crises' justifying new policy responses. Education leaders know a lot of this is more fake news, serving political self-interests but not the interests of educators or students. They also know that these sentiments will undermine 'fellow-feeling' and are imbued with the ingredients of negative cultural change which they see to be education's undoing.

The Effects on Education

Education leaders fear the consequences of all these kinds of worrying 'anti-education' trends. One pondered:

> What about the wonder, the curiosity, the awe of discovery, the doubts and questions – the intrinsic 'stuff' of education?

But in an uncertain world only certainty appears to be acceptable, even if based on flimsy or incorrect facts or assumptions and even if unethical and immoral.

Education is a continual quest for knowledge and skills – it builds capability and wisdom. Education is about considering many world views and perspectives. It respects diversity and diverse views as long as they stem from factual information. In debating and considering various standpoints, individuals come to determine their own positions and values. Education is a quest for finding out and learning more, but it is undermined by prejudice and bias and deliberate attempts to skew the facts, hide information, or to silence and shut down debate.

Arguments are won on their strengths rather than by trying to silence dissent. Educators want students to think for themselves, to think critically and deeply, to interrogate the 'facts,' and to examine all sides of an argument to arrive at their own considered judgments and opinions. Educators would hope that an educated person comes to understand how much they don't know and will listen to the views of others in order to learn and construct their own thoughts. Otherwise, rationality, logic, and evidence for effective public discourse are at risk.

For educators, persistent and pervasive anti-intellectual, anti-educational forces undermine their aims for their students and their learning, and for their vision of a fair and civil, democratic society.

Enfield (2017) contends that the use of labels such as 'fake-news,' 'post-truth,' and 'alternative facts' require critical analysis and underpinning points of reference. Enfield's points are highly relevant and applicable in education (paraphrased thus):

- It is important to discern fact from opinion and find out the facts behind opinion before believing a statement is truthful
- Statements are products of their time and context

- Statements are socially constructed and are, therefore, politically and culturally laden – speakers choose certain words, and use a particular language within its historical traditions. They emphasize specific aspects and elide others – hence, the way accounts are framed suits certain self-interests
- Beliefs obstruct the truth because individuals generally exhibit strong confidence in their beliefs. Beliefs are rooted in identity and history and are not easily discounted. Furthermore, human memory is fallible, accounts can change over time, and emotions can affect memory and reasoning
- False information may be fully believed by the speaker – there may not be an intention to mislead whereas a lie is intended to mislead. False information can also be used as a form of narcissistic, psychological bullying – 'gaslighting' for example, where truth distortion and denial is designed to make individuals doubtful and unsure of their own sense of judgment
- Narrative story-telling can have more appeal than straight-forward factual information. A good story can persuade a wider audience even if it is fanciful. Facts don't speak for themselves, but a good yarn does
- Once disseminated, false information can be used as a basis for other propositions which can corrupt reasoning, decisions, and actions – even official policymaking. Statements are usually uttered with the goal of having others believe them, so in asserting and standing by a statement, individuals inherently endorse its consequences
- Political power can have fuller potential if the 'politics' behind an intention are avoided, hence the reasoning or rationale behind policy decisions may be evaded. Certain facts can be ignored or rendered untrue. Backing up disruptive intentions can be a host of consequences rendered by state instrumentalities, from violence, incarceration, suppression to fearful threats – but they don't make a statement any more truthful or acceptable, or any less fateful.

Listeners must be wary and critical of what they hear.

Education Can Be Its Own Worst Enemy

Education leaders cite instances, however, when educators, education institutions, and students can also be accused of dumbing down or compromising fundamental aspects of what lies at the heart of 'good' education and ethical practice.

In universities, for example, there are concerns about intolerance against a range of perspectives being aired for discussion and debate. Critics are concerned that freedom of speech (included in the first amendment of the U.S. Constitution) cannot be assured – for example, when certain guest speakers or social commentators are banned or when social media mediates and condemns certain activities or events and shuts them down. Strident views asserting inclusivity, for example, can be simultaneously and paradoxically exclusionary and undemocratic when some persons or views are excluded (see for example, Furedi, 2018; Howard, 2018). In such circumstances, individuals can be comprehensively defamed with little or no recourse, even if social media aspersions are false (which is then narrowcasting). Reasoned arguments or conjectures can't then be contemplated, debated, weighed up, contested, or refuted. This is anti-educational.

Eacott (2017) notices a trend in academia by which opinions circulate amongst like-minded academics and various popular works are cited "by politicians and associations as though [they were] irrefutable fact" while counter-narratives are condemned rather than refuted through logical explanation and debate: a matter of treating "those with whom we disagree with benign neglect and apathy more than intellectual engagement" (2018, p. 1), making inquiry "prone to parallel monologues" (*Ibid.*, p. 6).

In recent years there are claims that educators 'mollycoddle' and 'pander' too much to students – being over-zealously concerned about individuals' sensibilities. New considerations are 'microaggressions' (words or debates that might be experienced as forms of aggression) or the need for 'trigger warnings' within courses (to alert students to topics, discussions, texts, and actions/behaviors that may cause discomfort, distress, anxiety, or offense [see for example, BBC, 2018 and Palmer, 2017 which includes a list of topics that trigger 'warnings']). The students' union of the University of Manchester, for example, has banned clapping due to the discomfort it may cause students with autism, sensory issues, or deafness, and instead has endorsed the British Sign Language (BSL) custom of 'jazz hands' – a silent waving of both hands (BBC, 2018). While defended in terms of 'rightful concerns about individuals' feelings and responses,' and 'encouraging an 'environment of respect,' critics complain that these actions are 'ridiculous,' 'absurd,' a failure to prepare students for the 'real world,' with Lukianhoff and Haidt (2015) referring to the 'wilting flowers' of the 'snowflake' generation. Others claim that such actions embody the potential for biased censorship and the curtailing of free speech, which undermine the essence of education (Furedi, 2018; Howard, 2018; Schlosser, 2015).

Universities condemn all forms of cheating amongst students and staff (plagiarism, assignment outsourcing, falsification), yet are accused of cheating themselves by 'dumbing down' higher education in a bid to gain market share, and therefore greater funding. At the time of writing, for instance, in Victoria, Australia, universities will be under government investigation for admitting students into teaching degrees who have extremely low or failing tertiary entrance scores (Argoon, 2018; see also Anderson, 2016). This practice has been criticized as an affront to the education profession and every education institution, insulting to the students undertaking teaching degrees, the future students they may potentially teach, and disrespectful of the entire community. This is a case of education eating itself, but some universities go to these lengths in order to survive in the face of tough neoliberal competition against others (Anderson, 2016).

How can this commentary and these perceptions be analyzed? The roots of this 'phenomenon' are not spoken about or canvassed by education leaders in neoliberal terms. But their commentaries and ponderings strike back to neoliberalism's axioms. Without being referred to in such terms, there are clear concerns about growing social fragmentation, a regression to basic human instincts around both tribalism and individualism, competition and adversaries, fear of difference – 'us' and 'them,' 'everyman for himself' [sic] – winners and losers. What matters concerns one's 'turf' and positioning. Groups that have considered themselves 'unheard' now have the tools and are making themselves heard and are making sure others listen.

There's a growing alarm, cynicism, and doubt. What happens to and within markets when distrust is pervasive? The market is assumed to operate optimally when it is free and unfettered, but how can markets function if individual market players lose trust in each other (and their market behaviors), and are losing faith in influential market players such as governments? Is this not loss of faith and trust in the market itself?

The final theme canvassed in this part of the book encapsulates a range of topics and issues from education leaders about leadership and their role in neoliberal times.

Notes

1   As a result, Wardle (as cited in Compton, 2018) calls for the need for 'slow journalism.'
2   Proctor (2008) cites his colleague, linguist Iain Boal, as coining this neologism in 1992 because a name was needed for this noticeable and widespread phenomenon.
3   Even before the latest spill in August 2018, Australia's capital city – Canberra – was being referred to as the 'coup capital of the democratic world' where "bloodletting has become so brutal that party rooms have come to resemble abattoirs" (BBC, 2015). (Prior to the latest leadership spill, the country had had five Prime Ministers in six years.) In a harsh and aggressive internet era, acrimonious momentum is maintained by opinion polls and constant media speculation. The general public is appalled and disillusioned while commentaries designed to reassure and provide a sense of normalcy are distrusted when they are proven to be lies.

References

Adams, S. (2018). Student loans watchdog's resignation threatens borrowers. *Forbes*, August 28, 2018. Retrieved August 31, 2018 from www.forbes.com/sites/susanadams/2018/08/28/student-loan-watchdogs-resignation-threatens-borrowers/#483f98da1427

Anderson, S. (2016). *Entry scores for teaching courses in Victoria increased to ATAR of 70 by Andrews Government*. Australian Broadcasting Corporation, News, Melbourne, VIC, November 23, 2016.

Argoon, A. (2018). School of dunces. *The Herald Sun*, August 12, 2018, p. 1.

Baxter, J. (2015). *School governance: Policy, politics, and practices*. Bristol, England: Polity Press.

Bazalgette, Sir P. (2017). *The empathy instinct: How to create a more civil society*. London, England: Hodder & Stoughton.

BBC (2015). Australia: Cup capital or the democratic world. *BBC News*, September 14, 2014. Retrieved August 31, 2018 from www.bbc.com/news/world-australia-34249214

BBC (2018). University of Manchester students' union bans clapping. *BBC News*, October 2, 2018. Retrieved October 10, 2018 from www.bbc.com/news/uk-england-ma nchester-45717841

Betancourt, M. (2016). *The critique of digital capitalism: An analysis of the digital economy of digital culture and technology.* Brooklyn, NY: Punctum Books.

Compton, L. (2018). 'Fake news' era of media disinformation will take 50 years to unravel, expert warns. *ABC News*, September 11, 2018. Retrieved September 11, 2018 from www.abc.net.au/news/2018-09-10/fake-news-era-legacy-hobart-media-literacy-confer ence/10223510

Dunning, D., Johnson, K., Ehrlinger, J., & Kruger, J. (2003). Why people fail to recognize their own incompetence. *Current Directions in Psychological Science*, 21(3), 83–87.

Eacott, S. (2017). School leadership and the cult of the guru: The neo-Taylorism of Hattie. *School Leadership and Management*, 37, 413–426. http://dx.doi.org/10.1080/ 13632434.2017.1327428

Enfield, N. (2017). Navigating the post-truth debate: Some key co-ordinates. *The Conversation*, May 15, 2017. Retrieved May 26, 2017 from https://theconversation.com/na vigating-the-post-truth-debate-some-key-co-ordinates-77000

Faludi, S. (2000). *Stiffed: The betrayal of the American Man.* New York, NY: HarperCollins.

Furedi, F. (2018). Free speech on campus. *Big Ideas*, ABC Radio National, October 8, 2018. Retrieved October 10, 2018 from www.abc.net.au/radionational/programs/bigi deas/free-speech-on-campus/10342460

Hawking, S. (2018). *Brief answers to the big questions.* London, England: John Murray.

Howard, J. (2018). John Howard on threats to free speech and robust debate. *Big Ideas*, ABC Radio National, October 8, 2018. Retrieved October 10, 2018 from www.abc. net.au/radionational/programs/bigideas/john-howard-on-threats-to-free-speech-and-ro bust-debate/10342226

Kenyon, G. (2016). The man who studies the spread of ignorance. *BBC Future*, January 6, 2016. Retrieved May 26, 2017 from www.bbc.com/future/story/20160105-the-ma n-who-studies-the-spread-of-ignorance

Kruger, J., & Dunning, D. (1999). Unskilled and unaware of it: How difficulties in recognizing one's own incompetence leads to inflated self-assessments. *Journal of Personality and Social Psychology*, 77(6), 1121–1134.

Lukianhoff, G., & Haidt, J. (2015). The coddling of the American mind. *The Atlantic*, September 2015 issue. Retrieved October 10, 2018 from www.theatlantic.com/maga zine/archive/2015/09/the-coddling-of-the-american-mind/399356/

Obama, B. (2006). *Address to Northwestern graduates at 2006 Commencement*, June 19, 2006. Retrieved August 31, 2018 from www.northwestern.edu/newscenter/stories/2006/06/ barack.html

Palmer, T. (2017). Monash University trigger warning policy fires up free speech debate. *ABC News*, March 29, 2017. Retrieved October 10, 2018 from www.abc.net.au/news/ 2017-03-28/monash-university-adopts-trigger-warning-policy/8390264

Proctor, R. (2008). Agnotology: A missing term to describe the cultural phenomenon of ignorance. In R. Proctor & L. Schiebinger (Eds.), *Agnotology: The making and unmaking of ignorance* (1st ed., pp 1–36). Stanford, CA: Stanford University Press.

Proctor, R., & Schiebinger, L. (Eds.) (2008). *Agnotology: The making and unmaking of ignorance* (1st ed.). Stanford, CA: Stanford University Press.

Reich, R. (2017). *Economics in Wonderland: A cartoon guide to a political world gone mad and mean.* Seattle, WA: Fantagraphics Books, Inc.

Schlosser, E. (2015). I'm a liberal professor, and my liberal students terrify me. *Vox.com*, June 3, 2015. Retrieved October 10, 2018 from www.vox.com/2015/6/3/8706323/college-professor-afraid

Sharpe, M. (2017). *Is the politics of lying the slippery slope to post-truth society? Media release.* Retrieved April 1, 2017 from www.deakin.edu.au/about-deakin/media-releases/articles/is-the-politics-of-lying-the-slippery-slope-to-a-post-truth-society

Starr, K. (1992). *Running with the hares and hunting with the hounds: A critique of social justice strategies in South Australian education* (Master's degree by research, unpublished thesis). University of South Australia, Adelaide, SA.

Steinglass, M. (2017). Democracy is not functioning well enough without a common demos to make it work. *The Economist*, July 14, 2017.

White, G. (2018). Falling short – fake news and financial markets. *BBC File on 4*, July 1, 2018. Retrieved August 1, 2018 from www.bbc.co.uk/programmes/b0b7fj3g

15

EDUCATION LEADERSHIP IN NEOLIBERAL TIMES

'Leadership' is in focus. A Google search or a wander through an airport bookshop will attest to leadership being a hot topic. 'Leadership' in education is valorized as a major plank by which nations hope to achieve international economic competitiveness, greater labor force productivity, and high international education rankings, alongside delivering education outcomes and policy expectations for an educated, self-sufficient citizenry.

Neoliberal leadership is in a liminal state – over the decades it has changed and is changing to something very different. To achieve new policy purposes and imperatives, governments are investing in leadership development and support programs – they are keen to have education's key agents 'lead' (in the very traditional sense of the word – see Starr, 2009a, 2014) and inspire 'followers,' to achieve desired improvements and outcomes. Leadership professionalism, leadership 'standards,' performance appraisal, leadership tracking and monitoring systems, and programs to identify and nurture leadership 'talent' have been developed – all designed to further leverage leadership potential, performance, and productivity. Leaders clearly see that over the decades, leadership and their work is constantly re-shaped and transformed to suit changing times.

Leadership Revered

Neoliberal changes to policy have had profound effects on education, education institutions, education leadership, leadership practice, and leaders' lives. They are strategic and political and have proliferated the education landscape with official, legal mandatory requirements encompassing new values, underlying principles, and forms of power. They work in ways that spawn new leadership behaviors, new norms of professional practice, and neoliberal subjectivity – the self-managing, self-regulating, constantly adjusting and learning, responsive, and performative neo-liberal individual, who is compliant, malleable, and 'auditable' (Shore & Wright, 2000).

Over the past three decades there have been significant changes in education leadership: more women hold leadership positions; employment is generally contracted, short-term, and contingent; constant policy change and churn is normal; employee retention is often short-lived and not lifelong; autonomy requires leaders to work within strict accountabilities and risk management structures; digitized labor enables 24/7 connectivity; leadership work is intensified, and has expanded in scope and complexity. As neoliberal, marketized, 'small government' policy regimes replaced social democratic agendas, leaders have acquired additional responsibilities delegated to them through the downsizing of education bureau-cracies. And they respond to government-appointed agents who conduct work once undertaken by government officials.

Education and its leaders have been pushed into new ways of thinking and speaking about leadership practice. This is an important point, because how we speak and think about education leadership influences how we enact it and how we respond to it, which has subsequent consequences for education itself.

Interviews reveal evidence of adaptive practices to accommodate and adjust to neoliberal policy agendas with many examples, including increasing the 'market spend' on advertising; institutions 'individualizing' their curriculum offerings or pedagogical practices to announce their 'point-of-difference' or unique mission; education workforces being 'downsized' and 'casualized' to be 'efficient' and 'flex-ible'; favorable comparative student test rankings, external exam results, or positive satisfaction surveys being used for marketing and promotion purposes to attract fur-ther enrollments and enhance reputations; the creation of new programs or activities to provide choice and convenience (from out-of-hours child care to peer-mentoring and support programs) – alongside hundreds of other examples. It is clear that edu-cation leaders have accommodated and adjusted to policy changes emphasizing individualism, choice, competition, and efficiency – they are 'agile,' 'competitive,' and 'nimble' as governments and policymakers want them to be.

Neoliberal policy agendas have also fundamentally changed speech, thinking, and activities within and about education. While conducting the numerous interviews that formed the basis of this book, words, terms, and ideas were recorded that would not have been documented two or three decades earlier. A new range of business-related acronyms are now fully entrenched and com-monplace: KPIs, SIPs, RFQs, EAR, EOI, ROI, and the list goes on. Leaders' comments demonstrate their take-up, understandings, and activities associated with neoliberalism. For example:

- "we take a commercial approach to enrollments but are still relationship-based"
- "it means managing and prioritizing the client-facing elements of the school but getting the back-facing elements to support our corporate identity"
- "our key strategic priority is to increase enrollments"

- "analytics customize student services"
- "striving to be 'best in class'"
- "managing the dynamics of competition"
- "making tough decisions about efficiency"
- being more "customer-centric"
- having to "fully understand our funding and revenue models"
- "we source our international students through a brokering service"
- "problems are opportunities for strategic partnerships"
- "the review found a distinct cultural disalignment [sic] between our practice and our mission statement"
- "business continuity and planning for unexpected downtime and data privacy are new things to worry about."

Some of the work leaders and the experiences they cited were also steeped in neoliberalism. One leader expressed surprise at a governing councillor's focus:

> Someone asked, 'So what was the ROI?'... straight after my education report. I couldn't believe it. You're on a school board and you throw a question that bypasses education altogether and home in on return on investment? What sort of answer do they expect? This is a school.

Others described activities to 'customize' education and institutional services to enhance competitiveness and meet individuals' needs:

> We customize learning right down to the tablet, phablet, laptop, or desktop – students have a menu to choose from – user experiences can be differentiated for individual preferences.

> The website's custom-designed – everything's interlinked and responsive so information and solutions are seamless – they can get advice or further information or we can call them back. They don't need to keep inputting the same information – it's all user-friendly and totally customized...

The language and terminology used is often infused with neo-speak, underpinned by neoliberal principles, and this appears more noticeable the higher the level of education. Clearly, the work of education leadership is changing.

There is no denying that some education leaders excel in a neoliberal policy environment, especially those who lead institutions that are able to compete on the basis of notable student performance outcomes. Those in this fortunate situation achieve personal recognition and satisfaction, while their institutions gain high positioning on league tables, and propitious status in the eyes of the community. In 'winning' situations, leaders can use neoliberal discourses to their intended effect – individualizing their institutions and creating a market niche for enrollments and/or curriculum offerings, focusing on raising achievement levels, advertising improvements, and marketing their brand to elevate reputation as well as results – all of which also bring personal and institutional advantages and benefits. In these circumstances leaders are optimistic, their 'personal brand' is enhanced and protected, their employment and that of their staff is secure, rewards are great, reputations are enhanced, and future prospects are promising. The institutions they lead are fortified by the market ensuring high enrolment demand, securing future funding and stakeholder satisfaction. There is no doubt that this situation lauds leaders like never before, and who wouldn't revel in it? This is not to imply that education leadership is a 'cakewalk' in any context – it is not. This is to say that as 'success' and 'quality' are currently measured, and as previous chapters in this book reveal, some contexts are more easily 'successful' than others.

As Braun (1995, p. 8) reminds us, "competition looks much more desirable from the vantage point of the winner than from that of the loser."

Leadership Restrained

All manner of audit, compliance, and accountability mechanisms have been introduced at all levels of education, so that authorities can maintain control over education institutions and obtain the information required to watch and monitor. In this context, on top of oversight responsibilities for education programs and students' learning, leaders assume accountability for global budgets, facilities maintenance and development, marketing, promotional work and public relations, people and culture ('human resource management'), workplace safety and a gamut of other legislative requirements, and the list goes on.

Some leaders resent feeling that so much of their work is under 'surveillance,' that so much is measured. They perceive the ways in which performance is judged and calibrated as signaling a lack of trust. And there are concerns about judgments being made by people who do not perform education leadership work and the technical instruments by which leadership performance is calibrated. There is a strong sense that measures only cover so much – and not the full extent of leaders' work nor what leaders consider to be the most important aspects of their roles (which will be different in every context – see Chapter 11). But a significant impression is that:

> …it all comes down to the numbers, there in black and white… no explanatory prose so no excuses – the whole thing – it's all passed off all too easily and that's wrong.

And another:

> If everything's going fine, we're fine. If it's not, there'll be ways to make us clean up our act…

Performativity keeps people on the 'straight and narrow,' on a 'short leash.' Hence subjectivity is a key site of political resistance and subversion in education leadership (Ball, 2016) – discussed later in this chapter. Leaders have agency at the institutional level and within their professional associations, but this is hampered by neoliberal constraints and a long list of diversionary requirements that demand compliance, take time, and steal focus from education, innovation, and creativity.

Education leaders refer to current (neoliberal) policy regimes variously as 'technical,' 'authoritarian,' 'directive,' 'inflexible,' 'hierarchical,' 'risk adverse' – in sum, very constraining and managerial in approach and designed to keep education institutions under watch and education leaders on track. They are instrumental in preserving and strengthening core power structures and keeping the agency of individuals and individual institutions peripheral and respondent to centralized power regimes. Two decades ago I summed up the new positioning of education leaders in education institutions, for example, as 'perfunctory middle management' (Starr, 1999). The intended result is leadership compliance with invisible policy disciplinary power – as a result of leadership pragmatism and fear of reprisal (discussed later) – which is effective while hiding from view much of what leaders do, think, or believe (discussed later in this chapter).

To cope with the increased workload and significant turnabout in leadership foci, many leaders report having to delegate day-to-day curriculum and student-related responsibilities to deputies and assistant leaders –further removing them from students. In a nutshell, assistant and deputy leaders have had many new responsibilities delegated to them through reforms that maneuver leaders' work towards the business, compliance, and strategic aspects of education management. Usually the bigger the institution, the more formal leaders are removed from education's 'core' functions because their time is so consumed. This has constituted an intensification of workloads at all leadership levels and makes for quite separate leadership functions to ensure the smooth running of education institutions.

Some education leaders feel too small in the scheme of things to be able to contest or complain – their agency is constrained. Intensified work schedules often make leadership work feel atomistic and isolating.

Compliance instruments are effective in keeping institutional leaders in tow, on task, and attentive to regulations, while short-term employment contracts keep them compliant. Education leaders and their work is governed and overseen, and to remain in favor, cooperation, compliance, and obedience are expected. However, leaders see few if any tangible outcomes for themselves, the institutions they lead, or for students or teachers, for the time-consuming invisible labor incurred on behalf of governments or instrumentalities to which they are answerable and accountable.

There are many aspects and consequences associated with these concerns, including the side-lining of educational matters to the urgency and timelines attached to externally imposed accountabilities and managerial tasks, feelings of leadership isolation, rising stress levels, and unrealistic expectations rooted in an overriding frustration of policy inappropriateness and inimicality.

Beyond personal risk, neoliberalism incurs considerable consequences for education leaders. A failure to build relationships over silos, the constant rush amidst the interruptions and 'busyness' of leadership life, exacerbated by untold impositions on time and energy that are extraneous to learning and teaching means the big picture can often get out of focus. Despite official strategic plans and mighty political pronouncements, constant policy churn makes the big picture hazy. Education policy and leadership is prone to be too focused on the 'now' to consider thorny issues just over the horizon.

But in a competitive education marketplace personal risks are also significant, with education leaders being as expendable as any other CEO. The whim of governments or perceptions of boards or 'clients/customers' can deride best efforts and achievements, so naturally, leadership also entails the self-protecting mechanisms on offer, with publicly available comparative data being an obvious example.

Who Are the Real Leaders?

Leaders are instrumental in strategy and decision-making. Interview data reveal, however, concerns about where education leadership comes from – who are the leaders in education, the strategists and decision-makers who make critical determinations about policy, judgments about funding levels and resource allocations, and who casts verdicts on education purposes, aims, and outcomes? Many areas of discontentment within interview commentaries boil down to these apprehensions, not only about where education is heading, but who is leading it down unwelcomed paths. The answer from education leaders is that politicians and policymakers are the real leaders of education.

Policymakers consistently fail to canvass educators' views and input or consider independent empirical research evidence. One or two chosen representative leaders on a high-level inquiry or committee is not practitioner participation, and credible, peer-reviewed research in education is largely ignored and could have bigger impact. The very strong view amongst education leaders across national borders is that there is too little debate, discussion, or consultation with the profession in major education policy decision-making. Further, there is little or no collaboration or participation of institutional leaders with policymakers – and who are the policymakers? What are their backgrounds and beliefs? Leaders are charged with 'implementing' policy decisions, but they are not involved in making or developing them at the central level, and they feel de-professionalized as a result. Wright (2001) adds:

> Leadership as the moral and value underpinning for the direction of education institutions is being removed from those who work there. It is now very substantially located at the political level where it is not available for contestation, modification or adjustment to local variations.

> *(Wright, 2001, p. 280)*

Interviews with education leaders reveal a pervasive concern that the most important elements of education – its purposes and therefore direction, policy, education's place and role in society – are determined by individuals and groups who are not educators, who do not work in the education sector, and who have never worked with students, yet whose decisions have huge and ultimate impact on practice and outcomes. With little acknowledgment of academic research, government advice and advocacy has come from a new and increasingly powerful source of policy reformers: 'on-side' political advisors, consultants, think tanks (often with well-networked and resourced backers), pollsters, and auditors – who are widely believed to shape decisions that are ideologically motivated and often based on ignorance of actual education practices. The overriding perception is that education policy and, therefore, its practices, have been appropriated by the political class and their apparatchiks – referred to as the 'consulteaucracy.'

Politicians and policymakers are perceived as too insulated, out of touch with everyday realities and lacking insight, with the result that mandated policies fail to acknowledge education's growing complexity and diversity and take little or no account of the unpredictable quotidian of education institutions. Neoliberal policy maneuvers are also generally goal (outcome) focused rather than process (input) oriented, and hence policy enactment is – as one respondent put it – "obviously designed by people who have never done the job." In other words and paraphrasing former U.S. Defense Secretary Ronald Rumsfeld (2002), the overriding concern is that policy decision-makers "don't know what they don't know." Hence, according to education leaders, public pronouncements about education often lack the practical, contextual knowledge to substantiate claims about problems or ideas for reform, although they shape public perception. One said: "It all seems so easy – just do this... They've got no idea – on the ground nothing's that simple."

Another point often raised in interviews concerns the evidence on which policy decisions are made. While exhorting the need for an 'evidence' base, education policy often emerges out-of-the-blue through populist and politicized obsessions. While education institutions must produce myriad evidence as to their operations, policy evidence is often weak, flimsy, or based on non-existent or insufficient data (such as point-in-time standardized test results). Commentary explaining underlying the political and economistic rationale of policy is often foregone. At other times what passes as 'evidence' would not meet any test of adequacy in education, such as those based on populist ideas that serve political rather than educational needs and trumped up as responses to various 'crises.'

Too often education policy is party-political, with new policies announced to remedy 'failing' education systems. Education then becomes a prime target for negative media attention which paints simplistic pictures of complexity and delivering contentious criticism against educators for declining education standards. It appears that education is constantly on trial and consistently fails to deliver positive attention and appreciation.

Education leaders tell different stories from those pushed by politicians and media commentators, so there is widespread unease that much public information is a damaging fiction (see Chapter 13). A perception amongst leaders is that education has been subjected to much blame and derision to hide systemic problems, political mistakes, or to serve populist political ends.

Spanning left and right of politics, neoliberalism has also produced paradoxical or contradictory policy pursuits, making leadership practice even more challenging (Denzau & Roy, 2004; Starr, 2015). For example, 'efficiencies' or cost savings or cutbacks are pursued alongside policies designed to extract greater productivity and performance outcomes – or doing more with less. When efficiencies cut into staffing budgets, for example, the tasks previously undertaken by those made redundant fall to those who remain, taking time away from the greater productivity being sought.

Policy change is believed to occur too often, with new policy being introduced before another has fully taken effect, with the regular change of governments or political leaders exacerbating policy's short shelf life. Despite the presumed empowerment of sovereign individualism, there is unease that education appears more reactive than proactive in a neoliberal policy environment (see also Kay & Goldspink, 2016).

The end game is:

- market values infiltrating education policy and practice
- incremental governmental retreats from public education
- the shift of responsibility, problem-solving and risk management from government/systemic instrumentalities to individual leaders, autonomous institutions and their governing bodies
- new expectations that are unrelated to teaching, learning, and scholarship
- populist-inspired education policy pursuits
- acceptance of inequitable education outcomes.

In a dynamic and uncertain world, policymakers seek and strive for certainty. Market-inspired policies purport to be locally empowering but they tighten the screws on education leaders, ramp up state controls for compliance, and shore up centralized core power and regulatory control through invigorated systems of governance, compliance, and performance auditing.

Free trade proponents and agents don't like their own interests being subjected to market effects, for example, the rise of commercial in-confidence contracts which elide transparency, the failure to consult widely enough or at all, and the lack of any feedback loop to both appraise policy and policymakers. Hence, although politicians and policymakers put education to market, they fail to apply underlying market neoliberal principles to their own operations. Leaders cited a huge range of failures on this front:

- a lack of transparent and democratic decision-making processes
- a lack of community involvement or consultation
- a failure to canvass a full range of viewpoints
- a failure to provide adequate policy 'evidence' about the need for new policy or policy revisions (research-proven/'evidence-based')
- a failure to provide adequate rationale for action
- an imperviousness to criticisms or suggestions
- standardized, one-size-fits-all policy measures that ignore diversification despite market mantras espousing 'individualism,' 'autonomy,' 'point-of-difference,' and 'individuation'
- the strait-jacketing of education's creative and transformative capabilities
- one-way, top-down accountability protecting politicians and policymakers from mistakes and deficiencies
- a narrowed conception of education's purposes
- an undermining of education's social transformation capabilities
- the reproduction and exacerbation of existing social inequalities
- inefficient resource distributions, and often, increased costs
- increased resource distributions going to those who may least need them
- short-termism over a long-term outlook
- constant rapid policy turnover
- too little consideration of policy effects.

Education dreams run into and collide with realities. Policy aims and expectations confront the actualities of everyday existence, and create obstacles for teaching, learning, and education leadership.

It would seem that if the aim is for education improvements, then the most fitting starting points for amelioration would sit with educators and education leaders. The notion of listening to people who work in the field who are familiar with problems and who may have ideas about improvement has been a long-held wisdom in industry, yet practitioner insights in education are ignored. Excluding the critical perspectives and ideas of educators, who will be most impacted by policy decisions, means that policymakers fail to gather multiple viewpoints, including the wisdom of leaders. Policy, therefore, is deficient before it leaves the starting blocks.

Leadership Disengagement

Not so long ago education leadership positions were sought-after and desirable posts, with high competition for appointments. Now, however, education leadership is increasingly viewed as an unappealing rather than privileged position, which is causing widespread leadership disengagement (see Starr, 2009a).

Attracting leaders is one problem; retaining them is another. The work of leaders is no longer attractive enough for many existing leaders to want to continue in the role, while for others it is not attractive enough to apply for the position in the first place.

The reasons for poor attraction and retention rates in education leadership are many and complex, but the prime reason appears to be that leadership is viewed as increasingly burdensome and complex (d'Arbon, Duignan, Duncan, & Goodwin, 2001; Millikan, 2002; Myers, 2006) and more time and task intensive, leaving too little private time (Lacey, 2002a; 2002b). Many eschew possibilities of career advancement past middle management positions in education institutions, since leadership is perceived to come at too high a cost to personal and family life (Leech, 2006; Milburn, 2006).

Prospective leadership applicants cite various other disincentives: institutional location; institutional size (very small or very large institutions are not as attractive to many); institutional reputation; an incumbent leader who is presumed to be re-applying for the job at the expiration of a contract; and rigorous, impersonal application and interview processes (ASPA, 1999; Barty, Thomson, Blackmore, & Sachs, 2004). There are perceptions about 'biased' selection panels and education boards/councils who have a preferred applicant (Barty et al., 2004). There are also concerns about 'cloning,' which favors similar types of people for leadership appointments; others presume leadership potential is outweighed by experience (Gronn, 2003).

Remuneration levels are considered to be too low for the level of responsibility assumed (Thomson et al., 2003; Cervini, 2003), and there is a view that it is safer to stay with permanent, tenured employment in a lower-paid position than risk trading these favorable conditions for a limited-term contract, with longer hours, fewer holidays, and no guarantee of continuity.

Some aspirants have expressed disaffection with policy regimes, which are inimical to their own values or social democratic principles. Along the same lines, there is concern that too much of leaders' time is spent implementing state-mandated reforms (Cervini, 2003; Starr, 2000;). Policy pressures for accountability, resource reduction and a general malaise in the morale of the education workforce are also deterrents to promotion (Cervini, 2003; Starr, 2000).

Media reports don't help the leadership disengagement problem. They "accentuate long hours including weekends and at night, high stress, pressure, dealing with conflicting demands and being pulled from one activity to another at frenetic pace" (Thomson et al., 2003, p. 5). Highlighting the supply issue only serves to reinforce negative perceptions about leadership, thereby abetting the problem (*Ibid*, p. 8). Front-page media attention given to increasing stress levels and instances of suicide amongst leaders exacerbate already negative perceptions (Myers, 2006; Thomson et al., 2003; Tomazin & Waldon, 2004).

New appointees to education leadership are often shocked to find what their new job actually entails, such that Sarason (1982) questions the suitability of a background in teaching as preparation for education leadership. Some leaders state that even deputy, vice, and assistant leadership positions are no longer adequate training grounds for higher leadership roles (Starr, 2006).

A long list of short- and longer-term succession planning measures have been enacted across nations to address the leadership supply problem in education.

Government funds are available to develop the professional learning of aspirants in the hope that they will seek promotion into leadership positions. Current
leaders are being encouraged to delay their retirement and those who have retired
are being encouraged to return in short-term locum positions. Aggressive advertising, training, and recruitment campaigns have been launched to attract aspirants
to difficult-to-staff locations. Executive search companies are employed to seek
out and appoint leaders. Mentors have been assigned to encourage and develop
new 'talent.' Work shadowing, peer partnering, and orientation programs have
been developed. Along the same lines, financial support and time have been
provided for some aspirants to participate in higher degree courses. Education
departments are pressing for stronger links between leaders' work and university
leadership preparation programs; and supervised and structured internships are
being developed that include field experience. Education leaders and aspirants are
being educated into the business and governance aspects of education. Stronger
relationships between networks of education institutions are being fostered, and
authorities are taking greater responsibility for the support, induction, and professional development of leaders and leadership aspirants. Programs designed to
encourage and support women in educational leadership have been established.
To counter concerns about the higher incidence of stress amongst leaders (DET,
2004), there are programs fostering health and work–life balance. Additional
benefits are being negotiated, such as sabbaticals, personal trainers, executive
coaches, and improved conditions, especially in 'unattractive' localities. These
developments are logical and have been well received by leaders. However, some
leaders interviewed believe that these initiatives have arrived too late, since a
leadership shortfall has been looming for many years now:

> You can't criticise departments for stepping up support and inducements.
> They should just have done it earlier and should've seen this problem
> coming a long time before they did. I wish these incentive and supports were
> there when I started.

And a further criticism from the leaders interviewed relates to concerns about a
lack of time and money:

> If you really want to attract people to be leaders, how about offering more
> money? The job isn't attractive because you spend much more time and
> have a lot more stress for little extra pay. People can see the hours you put
> in. They know you have the major problems to deal with, and they look at
> the salary and ask 'why bother?'

Leaders seek greater status, recognition, and levels of remuneration to adequately
reflect the expectations and responsibilities of the role. They say consideration
should also be given to what constitutes a reasonable working week for

employees and to institute family-friendly working hours. Leaders often feel that their own children suffer due to their commitments to other people's children.

With leadership disengagement currently receiving high public visibility, it is not surprising that researchers are arguing it is time for the leadership to be reconfigured/re-thought/reformed (see for example, Lacey, 2002b; Thomson et al., 2003). Most of the leaders interviewed did not imagine that the traditional models of leadership would change significantly. However, if the current leadership crisis continues, leaders can envisage scenarios such as job sharing, co-leadership positions, or more examples of the UK model of executive leaders overseeing several education institutions (see for example, Starr, 2009b).

In line with some emerging premises of government policy, any changes should occur alongside a shift away from traditional trait theory models of leadership to a full endorsement of distributive leadership with all the corollary consequences for educators in education institutions. If a distributive model of leadership is desired for education institutions – and leaders agree unanimously that it is – and if teachers and educational leaders are to share power and decision-making for improvement activities, then responsibility for institutional improvement and student learning outcomes must rest with all education employees. As such, these responsibilities should be reflected in job and person specifications, performance appraisal policies (for teams and individuals), and employment contracts. Currently this is not the case – these policy-related artifacts embody a very narrow, traditional, singular 'heroic' conception of leadership and hierarchical responsibilities (see Starr, 2014). Hence, leaders are concerned that position descriptions, appraisal mechanisms, and professional development programs fail to capture the reality of the job but feel even more aggrieved about bearing the onus for institution-wide results which rest entirely with them. Power, professionalism, and responsibility shared across an institution would reflect a truer commitment to shared leadership and give credence to emphases on leadership teams and leadership at all levels. Ultimately, a shared, distributed conception of leadership speaks to democracy and a redistribution of power and responsibility.

Exacerbating the problem of leadership disengagement is a shortage of teachers in many countries, and this situation will worsen, with too few trainees entering the profession and approximately 50 percent of qualified teachers leaving within the first five years of appointment due to work overload and a lack of support (see for example, Riley, 2018; Singhai, 2017). There are calls, therefore, for greater diversity amongst teachers and education leaders, with Australia's *Top of the Class* report into teacher training (Hartsuyker, 2007, p. 37, citing Skilbeck & Connell) arguing that education employees do not reflect the diversity in the population – instead, teaching is "a lower middle class Anglo-Celtic position." Increasing the diversity of education employees would assist in alleviating shortages. The report blames low retention rates in teaching on a lack of support in the early years and recommends a workload reduction of 20% for graduates in their first year of teaching, alongside mentoring, ongoing professional learning, and a longer-term induction program.

Much research, including *The Privilege and the Price* (DET, 2004), suggests that leaders mostly 'love' their jobs 'but' – there many aspects they would like to change, as revealed in the discussion above. If acted upon, the commentary and suggestions from incumbents could influence the future experiences of education leaders in beneficial ways, including alleviating problems associated with attracting and retaining leaders.

Clearly, many concerns of leaders are not reflected in government policy. If leadership disengagement is a problem to be solved, then a good starting point would be listening to, and addressing, the concerns and suggestions raised by leaders themselves. Governments attempting to solve the new crisis of leadership disengagement should consider strategies that address the concerns of current leaders. In addition, re-definitions of the leadership could be canvassed, based on realistic expectations of collective agency in the pursuit of continual improvement.

Leaders 'Shaping' Policy

Every educator knows and sees the fruits of his/her labors in the development and accomplishments of students and colleagues (discussed further below). To get on with the job and enjoy their role, education leaders, while feeling constrained, also describe the ways and means by which they 'make policy work,' 'make policy do-able,' bypass, work around, 'tweek,' or 'outmaneuver' policy.

The mediating relationship between education leaders and policy processes produces a range of responses: compliance (in the case of agreement or when they judge the effects of resistance would extract too high a cost – mandatory accountabilities often come with strings attached, making outright non-compliance untenable); resistance if they consider it necessary and expedient; adjustment or modification to make policy more contextually edifying, if possible. Overt resistance to policy directives may incur turning a blind eye or being vocal about personal opposition, but covert resistance is more likely. There are also issues of timing – policy work may be put off and delayed for any number of reasons.

Resistance is not always about outright opposition to change (see Starr, 2011). For example, it occurs when education leaders 'reinterpret,' 'translate,' or 'adjust' policy intentions – through pragmatic understandings about how to best enact policy, or through inherent disagreements about aspects of policy (and alterations make it 'palatable').

These activities are often private or unarticulated but they occur in the busy context of constant interruptions and the fast-paced change of focus and events. Leadership roles are complex and huge in scope. It would be nigh impossible to 'implement' policy and other bureaucratic directives as they might originally be intended. Too many leadership considerations are completely contextual and circumstantial, let alone considerations about the 'true' interpretations of policy discourses and their intended effects. It is naïve to think that policy texts will not incur a variety of interpretations by those charged with enacting them – and policy conformity can't be mandated while sovereign agency and heroic leadership are revered (see Starr, 2014). Hence, policy 'in action' (Ball, 1994) can differ and detour markedly from original intentions and usually does. As one leader said:

> We know what works and what won't. They have to trust that – we can prove what we do works.

However, some policy decisions are considered very difficult, dangerous, or impossible to change – for example, the pervasive use of standardized testing to measure, rank, and compare students.

Subversion has many negative connotations – destabilization, non-compliance, interference, and resistance, and can be used for unethical or improper purposes. But subversion can entail distractions for the good (even if only in the eyes of the resistor). These include 'bending the rules' for what a leader considers to be for the best for others – which is in focus here. Hence, leaders open up possibilities through subversive activities.

Ball (2016) refers to subtle forms of resistance as 'refusal,' acknowledging the agential power of leaders and, Rose (1999, p. 279) suggests the improbability of power as 'domination.' However, education leaders are employees, they depend on their jobs for their livelihoods, they bear huge responsibilities, so it is understandable that they are accountable for their actions and the work they do on behalf of education communities. But leaders are pragmatic, which includes subversion if needs be to protect what they believe is educationally right or politically expedient, and they are not afraid of exercising their power to 'make policy work' – they are agential in using institutional and positional power to steer policy intentions along agreeable or tolerable lines.

Education leaders see it as morally correct, time-saving, and part of their leadership role to intervene and mediate to avoid potentially negative policy effects. Negative policy effects include anything perceived to be counter-productive to education or student equity, anything with the potential to create animosity from teachers, or anything involving too much time or energy to be worthy of efforts. Policy enactment rests on interpretation and contestation in battles (often hidden), for 'truths' and justice – albeit these too are open to individual analysis and questioning. At the basis of subversion are issues such as remaining true to strategy, philosophy, or values; the protection of students, staff, or the community; and pragmatic judgments about the current contextual climate (see Ball & Olmedo, 2013). It is about the welfare of students, educational beliefs, and the wisdom of contextual knowledge and experience – knowing what is 'right,' best, possible, and acceptable.

Sedition involves the courage of convictions and, in the case of education leaders, rests on their positional power. Education leaders pursue pragmatic means by which to enact policy by translating, modifying, or adapting intentions in efforts to ensure educational appropriateness and the least disruption so that policy more easily cuts muster with local stakeholders, especially teaching staff. Subtle or passive forms of resistance enable policy to correspond with prevailing education values and implicit ethics regarding students, learning, teaching, leadership practice, business management, and institutional governance. Policy may be subtly resisted and re-buffed as means of personal "struggle against mundane, quotidian neoliberalizations, that creates the possibility of thinking about education and ourselves differently" (Ball & Olmedo, 2013, p. 85).

Diversionary practices enable new mandatory policies or policy revisions to gain the acceptance of educators more easily (which may not mean gaining agreement indicating that without such intervention, compliance would be difficult or impossible). They also clear leaders' consciences − leaders can attest to official overseers that they and their institutions are policy compliant, but they are also abiding by what they know is right and just.

The "political game" (Ryan, 2010, p. 360) of education leadership requires policy decisions − obvious or personal − to promote, contest, or ignore policy (Wang, 2018). Such decisions are best conducted circumspectly, diplomatically, and covertly (MacBeath, 2007; Wang, 2018). Leaders are supremely busy and prefer pragmatism and political expedience over overt belligerence or antagonism.

Subversion amongst education leaders is very rarely overt. Leaders could not be labeled as openly confrontational, treasonous, disobedient, or insubordinate − their actions are much more likely to involve ideas being challenged, asking or encouraging uncomfortable questions or discussion, or subtle but polite rejection. Opposition is dangerous so the safest forms of resistance are covert or collective. Certainly, leaders express their need to be respectful and courteous no matter what actions they take.

Whatever course a leader takes is contingent on numerous specificities of context − time, place, culture, the political and economic milieu, agential relationships including hierarchical agendas, and leaders' own values and beliefs about education.

Subversion and resistance are discussed in terms of common sense and denote deep understandings about the capacities and tolerances of context, people, and culture.

Leaders do not destabilize or incite sedition, and do not describe their subversive acts as being disloyal, dishonest, or deceitful − they see such activities as an important and necessary part of the job.

Hence, leader resistance is not a black and white issue − it is not a matter of 'conform or resist'. From the frank admittances of leaders, this is a gray area of education leadership, but leaders see decisions to comply or resist as critical aspects of leadership. Resistance and compliance take many forms and are underpinned by a variety of motivations, but they are political and strategic acts.

Education leaders do not label such activities as 'subversive'. They describe their policy 'intervention' and 'translation' activities as essential. Policy 'translation' is simply what it takes to get the job done and they use a range of idioms and analogies to describe how they operate and the thinking behind it. Leaders said they "play the game" and "just get on with it" to "stay in the race", "keep up", "try and get ahead", and "get the nuisance tasks out of the way", so they can concentrate on education. Policy enactment is about "tinkering around the edges to make things easier, and everyone's for an easier life" (school principal) – especially when it comes to externally imposed policy of extrinsic value to the institution that does not accord with internal priorities. Such is the power of education leadership within institutional autonomy. This is about leaders upholding some very clear principles promoting equity, inclusivity, social justice, and fairness. These principles are mostly about caring for people. In this sense, education leaders buffer students and education colleagues from a full onslaught of neoliberal intentions.

Reporting on principals' protests about education budget cutbacks in the UK, for example, Lightfoot (2018) rightly argues that education leaders speaking out is rare and dangerous:

> Direct action does not come easily to these school leaders, who are nervous about putting their heads above the parapet. They worry the Department of Education will brand them as political activists or the media will accuse them of taking the day off for a jolly.

And, adding to this fear, England's Department for Education has warned teachers against expressing political views, stating that "all staff have a responsibility to ensure that they act appropriately in terms of their behavior, the views they express (in particular political views) and the use of school resources at all times, and should not use school resources for party political purposes" (Adams, 2018; see also, Marsh & Adams, 2017). One headteacher speaking on behalf of the *Worth Less?* campaign[1] responds:

> If... the DfE wishes headteachers to be gagged as they simply tell the truth about the financial and teacher supply crisis that our schools are facing then this is unacceptable... *Worth Less?* always uses independent evidence [including DfE data] to support the legitimate concerns it raises with parents and the public. Our claims are never disputed, but frequently ignored.
>
> *(White, as cited in Adams, 2018)*

This example shows not only that it's dangerous to speak out – and education authorities make every effort to dissuade or prevent dissent – but it demonstrates that collectively (and reluctantly) education leaders can and do protest when the stakes are high. They are not puppets.

There is also evidence that leaders' subversion can actively work against performative aims – they may report, for example, certain activities or outcomes in their best light, or they may exaggerate outcomes. Other policy expectations can be more easily ignored or side-stepped. Hence, performativity may produce "opacity rather than transparency" (Ball, 2003, p. 215) through intentional fabrications.

Elmore (2003, p. 189) speaks to these matters as issues of policy accountability, arguing that "...education institutions construct their own conceptions of accountability – to whom they are accountable, for what, and how." And further:

> ...all education institutions, consciously or unconsciously, have well-worked-out ideas of accountability, and... they respond to new accountability policies by adjusting their existing ideas of accountability to the external influences introduced by the new policies. Accountability policies... work on the margins of existing organizational norms, structures, and processes in education institutions. (*Ibid.*)

As mentioned earlier, there are few if any formal opportunities to voice objections or submit ideas or suggestions to policymakers before policy pronouncements are made. Without being party to policy development there is little option but to do what can be done realistically and sensibly on site to appease authorities without upsetting the institutional applecart, for example:

> A new policy statement comes out. Staff won't read it because they don't see the relevance most of the time. They're too busy and would get their backs up if we gave every policy the fulsome [*sic*] attention they [authorities] expect...

> ...yet another new policy. The eyes roll, people get that 'oh, no!' look on their faces. They just want to get on with it – seen it all before – they know what they're doing. It's just another timewaster and they don't have the time.

> ...co-opt the loudest objectors when something fairly major needs to happen – get them onside, on an *ad hoc* committee to take ideas to the whole staff. If you can get them onside, there's more chance of stopping a riot.

Others were candid about a personal rationale behind policy adaptation:

> If I don't agree with directives, I can't expect others to. Sometimes it's possible to put things on a shelf for a while – and sometimes they stay there. Other times we talk about it and decide what we're going to do, but in effect, nothing much will change.

There are also 'smoke and mirrors' stories in every leaders' closet – times when rapid repairs or amendments or turnarounds had to be made to avoid trouble.

One school leader told of an unannounced 'work safe' visit [government inspection of occupational health and safety in the school]. While an assistant principal took the safety officer on a 'strategic' tour around the campus, the principal and her personal assistant were busy finding and copying a work safe policy from another school before the inspection turned to internal policies and procedures. In this instance, a very strict and overt measure was put in place by government to ensure policy compliance, but it was still possible to pass muster through a quick smokescreen operation to hide what was really going on behind the scenes. (The leader was new to the school, but any policy slippage from her predecessor would not have saved the school [and no doubt – inadvertently – herself] from what she foresaw as "a heap of unwanted trouble.")

This story, and many others like it, are yet another reason why policy and procedural changes are so regular. Policy mechanisms are constantly 'strengthened' to counter on-site manipulations, yet it's impossible that policy is ever water-tight and impervious to agential alteration or manipulation of some kind.

Another interesting observation is the confidence leaders build up over time, with those with long experience being more inclined to follow their instincts and pursue their own course of action.

The pervasive sense concerns a kind of façadism – what's going on up front and overtly does not always resemble what's going on behind the scenes. Education leaders should be a solid source of information about how education organizations operate, yet their accounts differ from the discourses and pronouncements of policymakers, education authorities, and governments.

Education leaders perceive themselves as facilitators, which includes protecting students and teachers from extraneous interferences as far as they can. Leadership includes the stewardship of education values concerning its common good and egalitarian remit in social democracies. Education leaders view the important aspect of their role as being to manage in a way that enables teachers to keep their eye on the main game.

These values and beliefs appear so imbued and entrenched in education cultures as to be impossible to dislodge. Their expression is found everywhere, yet they are under severe duress under neoliberal policy regimes (see Chapter 12). Whether they voice such a position or not, education leaders position themselves as guardians of the promise and potential of education, its freedoms and endless possibilities for good, and as protectors of the integrity of knowledge advancement and discovery, the development and engagement of people, and as stewards of education institutions as vitally important community and cultural assets.

Leaders' commentaries and stories demonstrate that their self-interests extend beyond the self – beyond the individual leader. Almost universally, they are more likely to be 'selfless.' Returning to Adam Smith (see Chapter 2), leaders are more interested in 'fellow feeling' than 'self-interest,' but neoliberal education policy does not encourage this stance. These stories also give more than a hint of distrust between systemic and institutional leaders. It appears there is not a 'two sides to the same coin' sense of leadership operating, but rather two sides that are often in contention with each other, with each playing against the other to assert their needs and goals.

Adjustment to constant change is normalized, but education leaders also have to deal with change resistance from others (see Starr, 2011). Initially change heralds stress, insecurity, unpredictability, and confusion. Hence, major change involves both the logical and the psychological (Bolman & Deal, 1991; Evans, 1996). As Evans (1996, p. 35) points out:

> Even when the elements to be changed are heartily disliked by a majority of staff and are the object of chronic complaints, the change itself commonly provokes more upset and distress than anyone anticipated.

Change involves conflict and friction, as varying individuals and groups attempt to secure their interests and position to influence the course of events.

Change, therefore, has a dual personality, according to Evans (1996), with its creators and advocates often seeing a different side to the story than those charged with 'implementing' change. Change creators are enthusiastic and optimistic about their reforms and the positive effects that the change will bring, but 'implementers' are likely to have different views and question whether any change is required at all. In other words, it is human nature to see the change required of others in a positive light and change which others ask of us in a negative light, even when those who create the change initiative express understandings about how difficult making changes making can be. "We readily make the case for innovation – on the part of someone else. For ourselves we are likely to resist it stoutly" (Evans, 1996, p. 38). For Evans, the critical thing is that since resistance and ambivalence are actually natural human reactions to change, they need to be respected and accepted by those who are responsible for change management.

The major issue in education is that change of any magnitude occurs amidst many other changes – imposed and created. It usually strikes people as "one damned thing after another" (Baker, Curtis, & Berenson, 1991, p. 13). Leaders believe it's best to focus on what is possible to benefit the people for whom they are responsible – a matter taken up in the final chapter.

Note

1   The *Worth Less?* campaign rallies for fair funding and adequate investment in all UK schools, improved teacher supply and retention, and greater assistance for disadvantaged students. The campaign has involved research, rallies, petitions, disseminating information to parents, and issuing press releases.

References

Adams, R. (2018). DfE warns teachers against expressing 'political views'. *The Guardian*, September 6, 2018. Retrieved October 15, 2018 from www.theguardian.com/education/2018/sep/05/education-department-teachers-express-political-views-headteachers-unions

ASPA: Australian Secondary Principals' Association (1999). *School leaders: Shortage and suit-ability in Australian public schools*. Retrieved August 1, 2006 from www.aspa.asn.au/Poli cies/Pollead.htm

Baker, P., Curtis, D., & Berenson, W. (1991). *Collaborative opportunities to build better schools*. Chicago, IL: Association for Curriculum and Development.

Ball, S. (1994). *Education reform: A critical and post-structural approach*. Buckingham, UK: Open University Press.

Ball, S. J. (2003). The teacher's soul and the terrors of performativity. *Journal of Education Policy*, 18(2), 215–228.

Ball, S. J. (2016). Subjectivity as a site of struggle: Refusing neoliberalism? *British Journal of Sociology of Education*, 37(8), 1129–1146.

Ball, S. J., & Olmedo, A. (2013). Care of the self, resistance and subjectivity under neoli beral governmentalities.*Critical Studies in Education*, 54(1), 85–96.

Barty, K., Thomson, P., Blackmore, J., & Sachs, J. (2004). Unpacking the issues: Researching the shortage of school principals in two states of Australia. *The Australian Educational Researcher*, 32(3), 1–18.

Bolman, L. G., & Deal, T. E. (1991). *Reframing organizations: Artistry, choice, and leadership*. San Francisco, CA: Jossey-Bass.

Braun, E. (1995). *Futile progress: Technology's empty promise*. Abingdon, England: Earthscan.

Cervini, E. (2003). Shortage of school principals looming. *The Age*, August 17, 2003. Retrieved August 17, 2008 from www.theage.com.au/articles/2003/08/16/ 1060936102586.html

d'Arbon, T., Duignan, P., Duncan, D. J., & Goodwin, K. (2001). *Planning for future lea-dership of Catholic schools in NSW*. Paper presented at the BERA Annual Conference, Leeds, UK, September 13–15, 2001.

Denzau, A., & Roy, R. (2004). *Fiscal policy convergence from Reagan to Blair: The Left veers Right*. London, England: Routledge.

Department of Education and Training (DET), Victoria (2004). *The privilege and the price*. Melbourne: Victorian Government Printer. Retrieved August 1, 2006 from www. deect.vic.gov.edu.au

Elmore, R. (2003). Accountability and capacity. In M. Carnoy, R. Elmore, & L. S. Siskin (Eds.), *The new accountability: high schools and high-stakes testing* (pp. 188–202). New York, NY: Routledge,.

Evans, R. (1996). *The human side of school change: Reform, resistance, and the real-life problems of innovation*. San Francisco, CA: Jossey-Bass Publishers.

Gronn, P. (2003). *The new work of educational leaders: Changing leadership practice in an era of school reform*. London, England: SAGE/Paul Chapman.

Hartsuyker, L. (2007). *Top of the class: Report on the inquiry into teachers education*. House of Representatives Standing Committee on Education and Vocational Training. Canberra, ACT: House of Representatives Publishing Unit, Australian Parliament.

Kay, R., & Goldspink, C. (2016). *Public sector innovation: Why is it different?*Sydney, NSW: Australian Institute of Company Directors. Retrieved September 3, 2017 from http://aicd. companydirectors.com.au/~/media/cd2/resources/advocacy/governance-leadership-cen tre/pdf/05493-1-pol-glc-public-sector-innovation-research-paper-a4-may16_web.ashx

Lacey, K. (2002a). Avoiding the principalship. *Principal Matters*, November 2002, 25–29.

Lacey, K. (2002b). *Understanding principal class leadership aspirations: Policy and planning implications*. Melbourne, VIC: Department of Education & Training, Victoria.

Leech, R. (2006). Through the glass ceiling. *Teacher*, 170, June 10–11, 2006, 6–11.

Lightfoot, L. (2018). Headteachers to petition Downing Street: "There's nothing left to cut". *The Guardian*, September 25, 2018. Retrieved October 15, 2018 from www. theguardian.com/education/2018/sep/25/headteachers-p etition-downing-street-budget-cuts

MacBeath, J. (2007). Leadership as a subversive activity. *Journal of Educational Administration*, 45(3), 242–264.

Marsh, S., & Adams, R. (2017). Headteachers warn parents: There is not enough money to fund schools. *The Guardian*, September 28, 2018. Retrieved October 15, 2018 from www.theguardian.com/education/2017/sep/27/headteachers-tell-parents-you-are-sti ll-in-a-postcode-lottery

Milburn, C. (2006). Principal goes to court over onerous hours. *The Age*, April 10, 1.

Millikan, R. (2002). *Governance and administration of schools: The importance of stability, continuity and high quality board and school leadership*. Melbourne, VIC: IARTV, Occasional Paper No. 77, October 2002.

Myers, T. (2006.) Principals under pressure. *Teacher*, June 2006, 12–16.

Riley, P. (2018). *The Australian Principal occupational health, safety and wellbeing survey data*. Fitzroy, VIC: Institute for Positive Psychology & Education, Faculty of Education & Arts, Australian Catholic Education.

Rose, N. (1999). *Powers of freedom: Reframing political thought*. Cambridge, England: The Press Syndicate of the University of Cambridge.

Ryan, J. (2010). Promoting social justice in education institutions: Leaders' political strategies. *International Journal of Leadership in Education*, 13(4), 357–376.

Sarason, S. (1982). *The culture of schools and the problem of change* (2nd ed.) Boston, MA: Allyn & Bacon.

Shore, C., & Wright, S. (2000). Coercive accountability: The rise of audit culture in higher education. In M. Strathern (Ed.), *Audit cultures: Anthropological studies in accountability, ethics and the academy* (pp. 57–89). London, England: Routledge.

Singhai, P. (2017). Why up to half of all Australian teachers are quitting within five years. *The Sydney Morning Herald*, June 7, 2017. Retrieved April 1, 2018 from www.smh.com. au/education/why-up-to-half-of-all-australian-teachers-are-quitting-within-five-yea rs-20170605-gwks31.html

Starr, K. (1999). *That roar which lies on the other side of silence: An analysis of women principals' responses to structural reform in South Australian education* (Doctoral dissertation, University of South Australia, Adelaide, SA). Retrieved from http://search.ror.unisa.edu.au/media/researcharchive/open/9915955288701831/53111935600001831

Starr, K. (2006) Leadership disengagement. *Directions in Education*, 15(19), 2.

Starr, K. (2009a). Confronting leadership challenges: Major imperatives for change in Australian education. In L. Ehrich & N. Cranston (Eds.), *Australian educational leadership today* (pp. 21–38). Bowen Hills, Australia: Australian Academic Press.

Starr, K. (2009b). Job-sharing in the Principalship: Too hard or a dream come true? *Redress: Journal of the Association of Women Educators*, 18(2), 21–24.

Starr, K. (2011). Leaders and the politics of resistance to change. *Educational Management Administration & Leadership*, 39(6), 646–660.

Starr, K. (2014). Interrogating conceptions of leadership: school principals, policy and paradox. *School Leadership and Management*, 34(3), 224–236.

Starr, K. (2015). *Education game changers: Leadership and the consequence of policy paradox*. Lanham, MD: Rowman & Littlefield.

Thomson, P., Blackmore, J., Sachs, J., & Tregenza, K. (2003). High stake principalship: Sleepless nights, heart attacks and sudden death. *Australian Journal of Education*, 47(2), 118–132.

Tomazin, F., & Waldon, S. (2004). Stress making principals ill: Study. *The Age*, October 22, 2004, p. 1

Wang, F. (2018). Subversive leadership and power tactics. *Journal of Educational Administration*, 56(4), 398–413. https://doi.org/10.1108/JEA-07-2017-0081

Wright, N. (2001). Leadership, 'Bastard leadership' and managerialism. *Educational Management Administration & Leadership*, 29(3), 275–290.

CONCLUDING REMARKS

Exposing Education's 'Dirty Little Secret': The Emperor Has No Clothes

Neoliberalism has been world-changing, in every respect. Education leaders have witnessed the changes and their effects and argue that neoliberal change has not been for the better. Education has been turned on its head – aims, purposes, values, practices, assessment and evaluation, and curriculum outcomes have turned 180° in little more than three decades. Neoliberalism's instrumental, economistic, '*quod erat demonstrandum*' view of the world dominates, while education no longer serves all individuals equitably and, in many places, doesn't even try to. Education gets bad press from politicians with the power to endow or condemn, and many blatantly oppose systemic, publicly provided education (which happens to educate the majority of citizens). In short, neoliberalism is "deeply corrosive of education" (Connell, 2013, p. 107).

It would be easy to pass this whole story off as the triumph of the political right over the political left – it is not. Governments of all major political persuasions have pursued and supported increasingly market-oriented neoliberal policies and practices in education and other areas of social policy. Leftist, presumably 'progressive' governments and thinkers have often been swayed along the same lines as conservative thinkers – some say, "the left has veered right" (Roy & Denzau, 2004; see also Wennström, 2015). Governments, however, must bear responsibility for the problems neoliberalism has created, as they have outsourced their twentieth-century remit, responsibilities, and advice sources progressively to the commercial/private, for-profit sector.

And further, this is not to say that the free market might not be good for trade, commerce, and industry. It's simply to say, it should stay out of the way of social policy, including education.

In their 'busyness' many education leaders do not equate policy measures with pervasive neoliberalism. They are so busy with the daily busy and demanding practicalities of their role, that they have little time to think or read academic or professional literature. But leaders have observed change over time, and their descriptions and concerns speak strongly to neoliberal tenets; the overriding perception is that 'things are getting worse.'

Education leaders believe education is 'off course,' heading in the wrong direction, misguided, and producing the very opposite results to those it seeks – higher standards, 'quality.' 'Quality,' as currently construed and measured, concerns only a small segment of what education is actually about. Yet this small slice of education's fundamentals takes precedence, focus, energy, and effort away from the much larger portion left behind. Neoliberal policies and the practices they spawn inherently endorse a myopic interpretation, not a broadminded, satiated, and complete view of what education is, entails, and can achieve. Being 'off course,' education is not being permitted to achieve its optimal results because leaders and educators are too distracted (the 'free market' incurs no such freedom in education, despite the mantra of 'small government'). Ironically, education could achieve more if educators and leaders were not waylaid by the strictures of externally devised accountabilities and measurements that waste a huge amount of time and money and don't reveal anything educators didn't already know. Neoliberal policies in education are in and of themselves, inefficient, unproductive, and ineffective.

Education policy is moving away from equity and social justice ambitions because these are anathema to neoliberalism. Human dignity and freedoms can't get traction when submitted to the vicissitudes of competitive individualism. Neither individuals nor individual institutions can be assured of outcomes, but they are forced to compete, some win, some lose, but either way, it's no one's fault. Outcomes are individualized, along with the risks, efforts, and activities these may entail. Are citizens a means to an end, or an end in themselves? One leader says:

> It's like 'Who cares? We're all in this together' right? But that doesn't mean what it used to. You take your chances, I take my chances, like we all have to – that's what it means. It means you're actually on your own.

Collective, democratic decision-making is being undermined by bad faith narratives and pervasive anti-educational/anti-professional/anti-traditional authority narratives. And polarized populations and their equally polarized governments exacerbate such phenomena in the contest for power, voice, legitimacy, resources, and the dominance of narratives, ideologies, and ideas. None of this augurs well for education. Such trends strike at what it means to be 'educated.'

Education leadership has changed – some say irrevocably. Institutional leaders have power in micro contexts but are so subsumed in intensified leadership work and labyrinthine accountabilities, that they do not have the time or much where-withal to extend leadership capability beyond the institution. Hence while being effective agents of social change at the local level, their agency does not extend far enough. And rewarding as a local, institutional focus is, working for people and pursuing local purposes, it delimits leadership potential for the wider good.

The real leaders are politicians, policymakers, and the consultants who advise them. This leadership may be good or bad, depending on its inherent notions about education and society, and its processes of inclusion and exclusion, but it is severely criticized by institutional leaders when it doesn't consult, and when it has the arrogance to denounce, which is often the case. Despised are those who have never worked as education leaders, educators, or had responsibility for students who arrogantly assume they know better. Subsequently, education leadership is a lot about 'intercepting' policy, to make it palatable, suitable, and workable. Education leaders feel they have been forced into exercising what they know to be right in education by working against policy and practices they know to be wrong – in order to protect students, parents, education institutions, and the values they hold dear. So if education leaders feel they have to be subversive or 'resistant' to some degree, what has education 'leadership' become? One leader's view sums it up thus:

> Oh look, it's broken really – in its current form. Your best work you can do [*sic*] can sometimes be hidden because it might be risky... But you know what you're doing and why you're doing it and in your heart of hearts, you know it's the right thing to do. It'll work – it's what we're here for.

Education leaders possess a strong sense of stewardship and have more inclinations towards 'fellow feeling' than they do 'self-interest.' But sadly, many do not wish to pursue this occupation any longer, and around 50 percent of teachers leave the profession within their first five years because they feel overwhelmed, stressed, and unsupported.

Over three decades of research reveals this is an 'emperor has no clothes' story.

Tides always turn but is the 'rising tide' that 'lifts all boats' ebbing? Everywhere there is evidence of fracture, social dislocation, slippages in market theory, increasing difficulties in politics and governing, deepening discontents and global problems, but will there be turnaround change? One leader's view:

> It's time we exposed education's dirty little secret – education's being tampered with by the wrong people for the wrong reasons – they're making it worse.

Education leadership is an occupation considered trustworthy and ethical, but is ethicality breached when being party to something many within the profession consider to be 'off course' and wrong?

Neoliberal practice has been effective in individualizing education leadership and education institutions. Any individual crusade against the tide is dangerous. But the time is ripe for action through professional associations and other collective means for education leaders to have a voice, make a statement, and have an impact. This would herald a new form of education leadership entrepreneurialism whereby education leaders are more active shareholders and stakeholders in education and its improvement – as they would define it.

Leadership in education needs to change focus – to take responsibility for a broader education purview, including using empirical research. For the good of education, the public must be educated so they see and know what is important to protect and enhance in education and why. Educators must also educate politicians so misguided policies that detract can be de-railed before they take root and effect. And education leaders must intervene to steer discourses about education so they are used for education, not to manipulate or denigrate, or to legitimate populist policies. This includes educating the media. Through expanding its educative remit, the profession that educates all professions may be accorded the credit and respect it deserves.

Education is too important to be hostage to the game of catallaxy.

References

Connell, R. (2013). The neoliberal cascade and education: An essay on the market agenda and its consequences. *Critical Studies in Education*, 54(2), 99–112.

Roy, F., & Denzau, A. T. (2004). *Fiscal policy convergence from Regan to Blair: The Left veers right*. New York, NY: Routledge.

Wennström, J. (2015). *A left/right convergence on the New Public Management? The unintended power of diverse ideas*. Research Institute of Industrial Economics, IFN Working Paper No. 1087, 2015. Retrieved August 4, 2018 from https://doi.org/10.1080/08913811.2016.1234158

INDEX

Page numbers followed by 'n' refer to notes.